CONTENTS

HOW TO USE THIS BOOK

This book is divided into two distinct sections: AS and A2.

Chapters 1 to 5 are AS-style sections covering both the rise and decline of Spain as a European superpower in the period 1474–1700. The text might best be described as a descriptive analysis, which gives the student in-depth information and some clear analysis of the main features of the period.

Each chapter has a broad over-riding key question, which both helps to focus the material for the student and to show how answers to questions should be structured. The text of each chapter is divided into manageable and logical sections to help the student digest the material more easily. If time allows it is very useful to read through a whole chapter quite quickly in order to get an overview of the ideas and information. Notes can then be taken more easily and precisely on a second reading of the chapter. The questions at the end of each chapter will challenge the student to use the information and ideas that have been presented, to analyse, prioritise and explain important aspects of the subject.

The A2 section of the book looks in more depth and detail at important aspects of the topic as required by the three exam boards at A2 level and could be used as the basis of a piece of coursework as required, for example, by Edexcel in its Unit 5 looking at change and continuity in one European country over a 100-year period.

At the end of each of the AS and A2 sections, there is an assessment section. These assessments are based squarely and deliberately on the requirements of the new AS and A2 specifications provided by the three awarding bodies – Edexcel, AQA and OCR. There are exam-style source and essay questions followed by detailed guidance on how such questions should be answered, as well as sample answers. In the A2 assessment section, there are a number of primary sources (pages 280–2 and 285–7) which can be used to deepen understanding of both AS and A2 sections.

This book is meant for those exploring this topic for the first time. While it is designed with AS and A2 examinations very much in mind, it is also hoped that it will be interesting and thought-provoking for the general reader and student alike. The story of Spain in this period provides fascinating insights into the rise and decline of a great power and it is hoped that readers will make use of the bibliography at the end of the book to enhance their understanding of this exciting, dynamic and colourful topic.

AS SECTION: THE RISE AND FALL OF SPAIN, 1474–1700

INTRODUCTION

The story of Spain's rise and apparent fall as a great power in Europe in such a relatively short time span has long fascinated historians. In 1450, the unified country of Spain did not exist. By 1550, it was clearly the most powerful nation in Europe.

- Spain was at the heart of an empire, which stretched from Bohemia and Hungary in the east, to Italy in the south, the Low Countries in the north and South America in the west.
- It was the great opponent of the Reformation within Europe and the Ottoman Turks outside Europe.

However, by 1650 Spain was apparently in decline. Government was in the hands of unpopular ministers, and the country faced revolts at home and defeat abroad. France was now the dominant power in Europe, and the gold and silver from the South American empire was drying up.

By 1700 Spain, once so powerful, was associated with feeble monarchs, a corrupt government and an empty treasury.

The Spanish people paid the price of maintaining an empire in the form of social and economic hardship. Spain seemed to have returned to the dark days of the mid-fifteenth century. This book hopes to explain the reasons for the rapid rise and decline of Spain.

THE FOUNDATIONS OF THE RISE OF SPAIN: FERDINAND AND ISABELLA

In the Middle Ages the Iberian peninsula, which we now

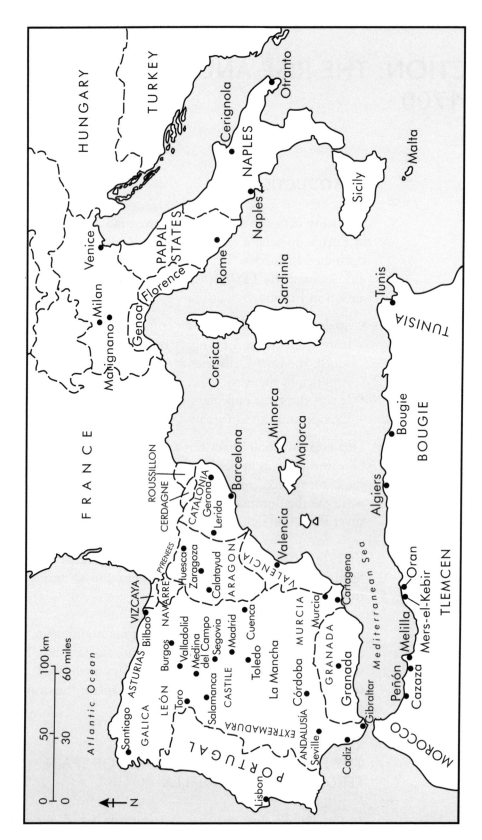

The regions of Spain and the countries around it during the reigns of Ferdinand and Isabella, 1474–1516.

know as Spain and Portugal, was made up of a collection of five major states, which were often at war with one another.

- The largest states, Castile and Aragon, suffered prolonged periods of civil unrest with ineffectual rulers pitted against hugely powerful noblemen, regions and cities effectively outside royal control and a Catholic Church, staffed by noblemen and answerable to itself or the Pope in Rome. One of the best-run states, Granada, was not even Christian; it was the remnant of the great Moorish (Muslim) kingdom that had once covered most of the peninsula. From this rather unpromising collection of kingdoms emerged modern Spain.
- The process of the union of Spain began when Castile and Aragon were united by the marriage in 1469 of Isabella of Castile (1451–1504) and Ferdinand of Aragon (1452–1516). They ruled their two kingdoms jointly from 1479 until Isabella's death in 1504, putting an end to the hostility of old and, once united, proceeded to conquer and Christianise the kingdom of Granada. By this means, among others, Ferdinand and Isabella were able to tame the nobility and towns, and take control of the Catholic Church. With the power of the monarchy enhanced and Spain united around Castile, the new Spain was in a position to influence affairs beyond its borders.
- Through the efforts of a few daring and greedy men, Spain conquered and acquired, almost by accident, a huge empire in South America, which would bring in the gold and silver to fund Spain's great power status. Equally by chance (via accidents of births and deaths), the marriage of Ferdinand and Isabella's daughter, Joanna to Philip, the son of the **Habsburg** Emperor of Germany, produced a Spanish ruler who was also ruler of Germany and **the Netherlands**. Thus were laid the foundations of Spain's greatness.

KEY DYNASTY

The Habsburgs (also spelt Hapsburgs) Originally from Austria, their power grew mainly through marriage rather than fighting. It was through the marriage of Philip of Habsburg with Joanna of Spain that their son, the Emperor Charles V (King Charles I of Spain) became ruler of the Holy Roman empire, the Netherlands and Spain.

KEY PLACE

The Netherlands A series of thirteen contiguous independent provinces between France and Germany ruled over by the dukes of Burgundy. The Habsburgs inherited these territories when the Emperor Maximilian von Habsburg married Mary of Burgundy, only child (and thus heir) of Charles the Bold, Duke of Burgundy.

SPAIN AS A GREAT POWER: THE REIGNS OF CHARLES I AND PHILIP II

From 1516 to 1598, Spain experienced the triumphs and tribulations of its status as a great power. Tribulations came in the form of having a foreign ruler, Charles I (**Charles Habsburg**), who ruled from 1516 until his abdication in 1556.

- Charles was a Burgundian born in modern-day Belgium. He was often absent from Spain and pursued interests of his own, which did not coincide with Spanish interests.
- In addition, Spain increasingly became the paymaster of Charles' personal imperial ambitions. As Charles' reign progressed, so future revenues were mortgaged away leaving the Spanish Crown close to bankruptcy.

On the other hand, Charles' reign also saw triumphs for Spain and a growing awareness that it was now a world power.

- The Spanish empire in the so-called New World was expanding and proving extremely lucrative.
- France, Spain's great rival, was defeated in numerous battles, which left Spain ruling the entire Italian peninsula.
- Apart from two serious revolts at the start of Charles' reign, Spanish administration and government became stronger and more centralised in this period, and Spain was more peaceful and more united than ever before.

The reign of Charles' son and successor, Philip II, who ruled from 1556 to 1598, is often seen as Spain's Golden Age.

- Spain was ruled by a Spaniard – one who lived in Spain and governed from his splendid new monastery palace of El Escorial.
- As France descended into a long period of religious civil wars, its power was eclipsed by that of Spain.
- Religiously and politically united, Spain embarked on a series of great conflicts, which established the country's claims to greatness. The Turks were decisively defeated in a naval battle at **Lepanto** in 1571. Great **armadas** were sent against England and huge amounts of money sent to the Catholic League in France in an attempt to stem the tide of the **Protestant Reformation**. Portugal was added to Philip's domains.
- Meanwhile the great treasure fleets brought to Spain yet more wealth from its empire in the Americas.

Yet alongside the power and the glory, the spirit of the

Charles Habsburg (1500–58) Son of Philip and Joanna, he was officially Charles I of Spain but he is also known as Charles V, as this was his title as Holy Roman Emperor in Germany. Personally unprepossessing, shy, ugly and still only sixteen years old, he lacked the charm and guile needed to win over his new Spanish subjects. Charles had been educated in Flanders and when he arrived in Spain he was surrounded by a large Flemish following. These followers looked on the Spaniards with contempt. In 1556 he abdicated as King of Spain in favour of his son, Philip.

KEY EVENT

Lepanto Great naval battle of 1571 where the Spanish and Papal fleet defeated the Ottoman fleet off the coast of Greece.

KEY TERMS

Armada is the Spanish term for a fleet of warships. The word comes from the Spanish *armata*, meaning 'to arm'.

Protestant Reformation After 1517 some European rulers and churchmen broke away from the Catholic Church, in protest at the power of the Pope and the supposed corruption of the Church. They formed new Protestant Churches.

HEINEMANN ADVANCED HISTORY

Conquistador The name given to those who, literally, conquered the New World. These *conquistadors* included Christopher Columbus, Hernando Cortés and Francisco Pizarro.

Dutch provinces Those northern provinces of the Netherlands where Dutch, as opposed to French or Flemish, was spoken. Later, when they became independent of Spain, they were known as the United Provinces.

Catalonia was and still is a Spanish province in the north-east of Spain, bordering on France. Catalonia was part of the kingdom of Aragon.

Regional separatism The tendency for some regions or areas of a country to enjoy or want to enjoy independence from the power of the central government.

Thirty Years War A series of battles and campaigns, mainly in Germany in the period 1618–48. Many countries outside Germany, including Spain, France, Sweden and Denmark, were involved in the conflict.

Dutch Revolt A rebellion by Dutch provinces against Spanish rule. Starting in 1556, it lasted officially until 1648.

conquistador and the Catholic missionary came defeat and debt. Like others that have aspired to the title of superpower, Spain over-reached itself and thought that it was invincible.

- The cost of warfare was spiralling out of control in Philip's reign and Spain went bankrupt on several occasions.
- Spain also faced a protracted and bloody revolt in the Netherlands, which resulted in half the territory being lost to the rebels.
- At home Philip faced internal revolt, and many of his people experienced social dislocation and economic ruin.

SPAIN IN DECLINE: THE REIGNS OF PHILIP III, PHILIP IV AND CHARLES II

The reigns of Philip III (1598–1621), Philip IV (1621–65) and Charles II (1665–1700) confirmed that Spanish power in Europe was on the wane. Unable to extricate itself from conflicts in Europe, Spain continued to shoulder the great burdens of empire but with little chance of recovering its position as Europe's foremost power.

- By 1659, Portugal had broken free of Spanish control and the **Dutch provinces** had been officially lost.
- A great revolt broke out in **Catalonia** lasting from 1640 to 1652, reminding Spain's rulers of the long-term difficulties with **regional separatism** in what was still a far from unified peninsula.
- By 1659 in Europe, France was once more in the ascendant and Spain had been crippled by its long-term involvement in the **Thirty Years War** and the **Dutch Revolt**.
- While Philip IV had some good qualities, Philip III ruled via unpopular favourites and Charles II was mentally unstable. (Charles was, it was claimed, the product of too much inbreeding among the Habsburgs.) Court life continued behind a charade of empty ritual.
- As the revenues from the New World began to dry up, the long-term weaknesses of the Spanish economy became apparent for all to see. Spain's days as a great power were over.

CHAPTER 1

1474–1516: In what ways and to what extent did Ferdinand and Isabella lay the foundations for Spain's achievement of great power status in Europe?

KEY POINTS

Ferdinand and Isabella succeeded in laying the foundations for Spain's future greatness. They ruled over both Castile and Aragon, which had not been done before, and they conquered the Muslim kingdom of Granada. They also took back from France the kingdom of Navarre, and the regions of Cerdagne and Roussillon.

Throughout their reign they increased the power of the Crown in Castile by increasing Crown revenue and curbing the power of the nobility and the independence of the towns. Restoring law and order and taking greater control over the powerful Catholic Church further increased the Crown's power.

They also followed an expansive foreign policy, which saw conquests in South America, North Africa and Italy.

FERDINAND AND ISABELLA RULE CASTILE AND ARAGON

The kingdoms of Spain

In 1469, when Isabella (half-sister of Henry IV of Castile) married Ferdinand (son of John II of Aragon – see family tree on page 13), it seemed very unlikely that Spain would become the greatest power in Europe and, arguably, the world within the next 100 years. Politically, Spain did not exist. Instead the Iberian peninsula was made up of a series of smaller kingdoms that were internally divided and that often fought among themselves. Rather like Italy in the same period, Spain in the late-fifteenth century was no more than a geographical expression, linked to the two ancient Roman provinces of Hispania. The main kingdoms

KEY PEOPLE

Ferdinand was King of Aragon from 1479 until 1516. He married Isabella of Castile in 1469.

Isabella was the daughter of John II, King of Castile and León. She was born in 1451 in Madrigal de las Altas Torras. In 1469 she married Ferdinand II of Aragon and in 1474 became Queen of Castile. Isabella was a patron of scholars, learning Latin and educating her children well, including Catherine of Aragon who became Henry VIII of England's first wife.

were Portugal, Castile, Aragon, Navarre and Granada (see map on page 2).

Portugal. This was probably the most powerful and united kingdom. Its strengths were its long Atlantic coastline and growing commercial interests in Africa and the East.

Castile. This was the largest kingdom and although the monarch was, in theory, very powerful, incompetent rulers like John II (1406–54) and Henry IV (1454–74) had allowed that power to be undermined by a land-rich aristocracy and a militant and powerful Catholic Church.

The kingdom of Aragon. This was, in fact, a federation of three separate kingdoms: Aragon (which was poor and landlocked), Catalonia (which wanted its independence) and Valencia. These three states were ruled by one monarch (called the King of Aragon), but in each his powers were slightly different depending on local laws and customs. In these states the power of the monarchy was severely restricted by provincial *Cortes* (parliaments) and constitutions, which said that the king could only rule as long as he behaved himself. Thus the power of the monarchy in Aragon was always more restricted and circumscribed compared to the theoretical power of the Crown in Castile.

Navarre. Located in the north, Navarre was an independent kingdom usually under French protection.

Granada. Located in the south, Granada was a **Muslim** kingdom, the last of the great Moorish or Arabic kingdoms, which had covered most of the peninsula several centuries earlier.

Therefore throughout the fifteenth century, politically at least, the Spanish peninsula was weak and divided.

Political instability in Castile and Aragon before 1479

In addition to the problems associated with the existence of multiple kingdoms in the Spanish peninsula, both Castile and Aragon suffered serious civil wars in the second half of the fifteenth century.

KEY TERMS

Cortes The regional parliaments in Spain representing the main towns and the aristocracy. There was one for Castile and one each for Aragon, Catalonia and Valencia. The last three (in the kingdom of Aragon) could be called together in a *Cortes Generales*.

Muslim A follower of Islam. Someone who follows the doctrines of the Prophet Mohammad as revealed in the Qur'an.

period 1462–72, John II of Aragon faced a
s revolt in Catalonia in general and Barcelona (the
of Catalonia) in particular.

... .462, he lost the provinces of Cerdagne and
Roussillon, and was forced to agree that he would not
enter the province of Catalonia without the express
permission of the **Catalans**. Later, the Catalans
renounced their allegiance to John and appealed to
France to provide them with a new ruler.

Meanwhile, in Castile, matters were if anything worse. At
the so-called Farce of Avila in 1465, a group of rebel
nobles, led by the Archbishop of Toledo, renounced their
allegiance to Henry IV. Not content with this, they
denounced his daughter, Joanna 'la Beltraneja', as the
bastard offspring of the Queen and a leading courtier, and
therefore declared that the true king of Castile was Henry's
half-brother Prince Alfonso, Isabella's elder brother (see
family tree on page 13). Just for good measure they
executed an effigy of Henry as a symbol of their protest.

Matters calmed down a little when Prince Alfonso died
suddenly in 1468 and Henry was persuaded to recognise
Isabella rather than Joanna as his heir. But more problems
ensued when Henry IV later changed his mind about who
should succeed him. His death in 1474 led to a protracted
civil war in Castile between Joanna and Isabella. The sides
were quite evenly matched.

- Isabella had help from Aragon via her husband
  Ferdinand.
- Joanna received backing from King Alfonso V of
  Portugal.

Risings occurred in many parts of Castile in favour of one
claimant or the other. There was one major battle at Toro
in 1476, after which the Portuguese forces retreated,
leaving Isabella triumphant. Nonetheless, it was another
three years before Isabella's hold on the throne was secure.
Portugal renounced its support for Joanna and the
unfortunate lady of doubtful parentage became a nun! Of
course, the claim that she was not the daughter of Henry
IV cannot be proved, so it may be that Isabella's accession

was in fact an act of usurpation and that the unlawful party took the throne from the rightful queen.

Social and economic problems

Political instability was not the only serious problem facing Castile and Aragon in the second half of the fifteenth century. Socially and economically both had serious weaknesses, which would make it hard for them to sustain great power status.

Agriculture. Arable farming was primitive and much of the soil was dry, rocky and unproductive. In the great central plateau of the peninsula, there was a serious shortage of water in the long and hot summers. In Castile, however, sheep farming was booming. It is estimated that Castile had around 20 million sheep at this time producing huge quantities of wool for export. Although this was a prosperous part of the economy, it meant that the *Mesta* (the sheep owners' guild) had powerful privileges, which allowed sheep to trample through peasant fields.

KEY TERM

Early Modern Europe
Refers to Europe in the period *c.* 1500–*c.* 1700.

Social structure. Neither kingdom seemed to have a social system designed to produce the internal peace and stability needed to sustain imperial ambitions. Castile and Aragon were both very unequal societies, even by the standards of **Early Modern Europe.** Some 95 per cent of the people were peasants, most of whom did not own the land on which they worked. Their lives were hard, and there seemed little chance of reform or improvement. At the other end of the scale were the great noblemen, or grandees, who owned vast tracts of land. In Castile, some 2 per cent of the people owned 95 per cent of the land. There was little by way of middle classes except in the coastal towns where merchants and other professional people were located. Meanwhile many of the towns were at war with the local nobility and trying to assert their own independence. They also resented interference from the Crown and also from the Church, which was one of the greatest landowners in Spain.

The Catholic Church

The Catholic Church was another potential problem facing Ferdinand and Isabella. The Church was a great landowner, which owed allegiance to the Pope in Rome, who controlled **ecclesiastical** appointments.

- As the Church had been involved in the protracted *Reconquista* (reconquest) of Spain from the hands of the Muslim conquerors, it was a seriously military institution.
- Three great religious Orders of knights (Santiago, Calatrava and Alcantara) had been established in Castile during the medieval period, and two (Montesa and St John) had been formed in Aragon. These Orders of Chivalry were extremely powerful and could raise large numbers of troops, some of whom fought against Isabella in the war with Joanna.
- The bishops too had military muscle, which might not always be used to back the Crown. The Archbishop of Toledo maintained an army of some 1000 men, while the Archbishop of Santiago could raise some 3000 troops as occasion demanded.
- Most leading churchmen were not quiet scholars and pastors but aristocrats with independent ideas and power bases. Keeping such men happy (or at least quiescent) would take considerable political skill.

The nobility

These great churchmen and the military religious Orders were not the only threat to royal power. Far more numerous and potentially more threatening were the Spanish nobility. The Spanish **grandees** were proud, greedy and serious fighters. They were exempt from taxation, had their own castles and were committed to the ideals of the Christian *hidalgo*.

Half a century after the accession of Ferdinand and Isabella, the Duke of Infantado, a member of the great Mendoza family, was lord of 90 villages and 90,000 *vassals*. After Isabella's death in 1504, the Duke of Medina Sidonia offered Philip of Burgundy 2000 cavalry and 50,000 *ducats* to keep her husband Ferdinand out of Castile! Faced with an untamed and independent nobility, the prospects for the Spanish monarchy to assert itself on the international stage did not seem promising.

Castile and Aragon united

Despite the apparent difficulties, the combination of

KEY TERMS

Ecclesiastical From the Greek word '*ecclesia*', meaning to do with the Church.

Reconquista (reconquest) A very important concept for the ruling classes, especially in Castile. The Moorish conquest of Spain between the eighth and tenth centuries was gradually pushed back by Spanish Christian armies in a series of crusade-like ventures. The most famous leader of the *Reconquista* was El Cid. He reconquered Valencia in 1094. It was not until the fall of Granada in 1492 that the Moors were finally defeated.

KEY PEOPLE

Grandees Spanish noblemen of the highest rank.

Hidalgo Men of honour who would fight for Church and family.

Castile and Aragon would prove to be a very powerful one. When Ferdinand succeeded his father in 1479, he and his wife brought about a political and dynastic union combining the two kingdoms for the duration of their marriage.

By the marriage contract, it was clear that neither had a claim to the other's kingdom. However, their unity of purpose and the good relations between the two meant that, together, they had a good chance of increasing the power of the monarchy in Castile to new heights. A change in circumstances after 1479 also helped to bring about an improvement in the power and success of the monarchy.

- After 1479, Isabella, unlike her half-brother Henry IV, faced no noble revolts because there was no great cause or issue, such as a disputed succession, which could act as a focus for aristocratic and ecclesiastical grievances. This contrasted with the period between 1464 and 1479 in which disagreement about the succession had focused the discontent of the nobility and Church, and led to civil war.
- Although Joanna 'la Beltraneja' came out of her nunnery on occasions and indeed lived on until 1530, still styling herself as Queen of Castile, she was never able to mount a serious challenge to Isabella's power.
- In the kingdom of Aragon, the Catalonian Revolt was over by 1472 and there was little chance of further regional revolts after that date. As in Castile, revolt needed a focus. In 1462, it was provided by the harsh treatment of the heir Carlos at the hands of his father and Carlos' sudden and suspicious death. By 1472, Barcelona had been crushed and Ferdinand's claim as heir to the Aragonese throne was undisputed. In addition, Ferdinand's absence in Castile, assisting his wife, may have helped to pacify his realms. Although he was involved in serious government reforms in Castile, he respected the *fueros* (traditional constitutional rights) of his Aragonese subjects and was able to protect the kingdom from the assaults of France.

Overall, the combination of the two kingdoms was rather more powerful than the sum of the separate parts.

KEY TERM

Fueros The traditional rights and customs in the three kingdoms that made up the Crown of Aragon. On his accession, the king had to swear to protect them and could be brought into line if he did not.

- They no longer needed to fear each other as they had in the past, and internal opposition was cowed and defensive.
- Furthermore, together the two monarchs could now embark on rather more ambitious policies, which would unite their peoples in a spirit of common endeavour.

It is clear that the personal qualities of the two sovereigns helped their cause immensely. Isabella was proud and pious, while Ferdinand was wily, pragmatic and seriously astute.

Perhaps because of the long struggle to take power, Ferdinand and Isabella were aware of the potential for self-destruction and were determined to increase the power of the monarchy in Castile. While Henry IV had been too self-indulgent and untrustworthy, Isabella and Ferdinand devoted themselves energetically to the business of government, as seen in their frequent journeys across Castile to administer government and to be seen administering government.

The table below shows how the combined kingdoms of Castile and Aragon could now dominate the Iberian peninsula and become a great power in Europe.

	Area (000s sq kms)	% total area of Iberian peninsula	% total population
Castile	320	55	65
Aragon	100	17	12
Total	420	72	77
Granada	58	10	8
Portugal	90	15	13
Navarre	12	2	2

(Source: adapted from J.H. Elliott, *Imperial Spain 1469–1716*, 1970.)

THE CONQUEST OF GRANADA, 1482–92

Reasons for conquest

The greatest triumph of Ferdinand and Isabella was their

The Trastamara dynasty (dates are dates of reigns).

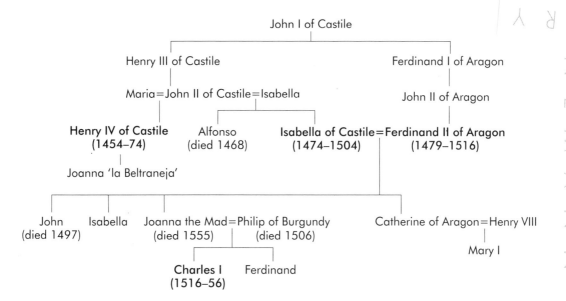

ten-year conquest of the Moorish kingdom of Granada. With hindsight it is easy to see this as a natural part of a policy of expansion during their reigns, which would later include control of the kingdom of Naples in Italy and the conquest of Mexico (or New Spain) in Central America. In fact, there were good reasons for leaving Granada alone.

- At the start of the reign, relations between Castile and Granada were cordial, and the ruler of Granada paid an annual tribute (tax) to the ruler of Castile.
- Previous attempts to conquer Granada had ended in failure and a sustained campaign would be very expensive, especially in view of the mountainous terrain and the well-fortified Moorish towns.
- In addition, war against the Moors in Granada might stir up trouble among their fellow Muslims in the kingdom of Aragon. After all, 30 per cent of the population of Valencia were Muslims, as were 20 per cent of the population of Aragon.
- An attack on Granada by Castile might also bring in fellow Arabs from North Africa.

So it is not surprising that the great war of *Reconquista* began not as an act of policy by Ferdinand and Isabella, but as the reaction of a great Castilian nobleman to the apture, by the Moors, of the Castilian town of Zahara, just across the border from Granada, in December 1481.

Early in 1482, a Castilian force led by the Marquis of Cadiz took the Moorish fortress of Alhama, deep inside the kingdom of Granada. Ferdinand and Isabella received the news in Medina del Campo, then decided they would have to commit themselves to the war or run the risk of losing the newly conquered town.

Although the reconquest of Granada began rather unexpectedly, Ferdinand and Isabella became entirely committed to the task. Isabella's piety, combined with Ferdinand's cautious but tenacious military leadership, eventually brought success.

Reasons for success

There were a number of reasons why the armies of Ferdinand and Isabella were so successful in their fight against the Moors.

Divisions among the Moors. Ferdinand and Isabella's success in recapturing the kingdom of Granada was helped by divisions within the Moorish ruling family.

- The ruling Emir's son, Boabdil, rebelled against his father and offered his services to Ferdinand.
- The Emir was then dethroned in 1485 by his own brother al-Zagal.
- In turn, al-Zagal was ousted by Boabdil two years later.

Not surprisingly, this lack of strong leadership helped to ensure that the Moors in Granada received no help from Moors elsewhere in Spain or in North Africa.

Support for Ferdinand and Isabella. By contrast, the Spanish war effort was strengthened by the financial and military resources that Ferdinand and Isabella could call upon from across Spain and beyond. Crucial to its success was that important members of the nobility joined the great crusade. What had been started by the Marquis of Cadiz was carried on by the likes of the Duke of Medina Sidonia, the Count of Cabra (who captured Boabdil), the Duke of Infantado and many others. In 1481, Ferdinand had declared that his aim was 'to expel from all Spain the enemies of the Catholic faith and dedicate Spain to the service of God'.

So for the great military noblemen, the *Reconquista* represented their highest duty, combining as it did the chivalric response to a crusade against the **Infidel** and the patriotic duty to conquer Spain's enemies. At the same time the nobles could see themselves as re-embodiments of the legendary figure El Cid, who had fought with great valour against the Moors hundreds of years earlier. As if that wasn't enough, the *Reconquista* would also present them with opportunities to enlarge their already extensive lands.

The development of artillery. In addition to the efforts of the nobility, the Spanish army was greatly assisted by the development of heavy artillery during the war. By the end of the campaigns, Ferdinand had approximately 200 heavy cannon, which proved invaluable during the long periods of siege warfare. The Muslims, by contrast, had no such weapons.

The contribution of the Church. The war effort against the Moors was also helped materially by the wealthy Spanish Church. In the first year of the war (1482), Pope Sixtus IV was persuaded to grant a *cruzada* (a special tax), to help defray expenses. The *cruzada* was granted annually until 1485 when the new Pope, Innocent VIII, granted it for the duration of the war. At the same time, the conquest was attended by great outpourings of Christian zeal. Ferdinand and Isabella went on a much-publicised pilgrimage to seek divine help at the shrine of Spain's patron saint, **St James of Compostella**. From 1488, knights engaged in the war usually wore **crusader crosses** on their uniforms and the Pope presented Ferdinand with a huge silver cross, which was carried at the head of his troops.

Taxation. At the same time, Ferdinand and Isabella raised huge sums of money by levying harsher taxes on the Jews. This racial minority contributed some 58 million *maravedis* of special taxes during the war. In addition, enormous loans, as opposed to taxes, were raised from

KEY TERMS

Infidel In the eyes of Christians and the Christian Church, 'infidel' means those who follow a religious creed other than Christianity – in this case the followers of Islam. By contrast, 'paganism' refers to people who have no religion or who believe, like the Greeks and Romans, in a number of gods rather than one God.

Cruzada A tax on Indulgences granted by the Church. Indulgences were a means of forgiving sins and could be purchased by the faithful.

Crusader cross When going on Crusade (originally a religious war to recapture Jerusalem from the Muslims), Christian soldiers would 'take the cross' and wear a red cross on their clothes.

Maravedi A Castilian coin, usually used when reckoning up accounts. The three main Castilian coins were the *blanca* (worth half a *maravedi*), the *real* (worth 34 *maravedis*) and the *ducat* (worth 375 *maravedis*). All the Spanish kingdoms had different coinage.

KEY PERSON

St James of Compostella The patron saint of Spain. His shrine at Compostella in northern Spain is still a centre of pilgrimage for Catholics.

more powerful interest groups such as the aristocracy and the *Mesta*. The Duke of Medina Sidonia alone contributed 17 million *maravedis* and the *Mesta* 27 million. These loans could not be paid off by the Crown with any speed, so they were often converted into government bonds, known as *juros*, which paid the creditor a healthy return of 10 per cent each year.

Santa Hermandad. Another source of both money and men was the so-called *Santa Hermandad*. The *Hermandades* were originally peacekeeping forces attached to particular towns. Isabella had created a *Junta General* (great council) of the *Santa Hermandad* in 1476 and demanded that every town with more than 50 inhabitants should set up its own section of the brotherhood. Then, during the long-drawn-out struggle against Granada, she called on them to supply money and troops, which they did with some enthusiasm. In 1483, the Junta voted 8000 infantry to help the cause and this had risen to 10,000 by 1490, which was a quarter of all Ferdinand's forces. The Junta also raised money from the towns to the tune of some 22 million *maravedis* a year in the late 1480s and reaching 32 million *maravedis* a year by the end of the campaigns.

Results of the conquest

The war to capture Granada became a national epic and did much to enhance the prestige of the monarchs. Although it was hard fought on both sides, the combination of Spanish strengths and Muslim weaknesses ensured final victory for the Christians and Granada became part of Castile.

The defeat of the Moors did much to strengthen the monarchy. Contemporary Christian chroniclers hailed the capture of Granada as a wonderful triumph against the old enemy. In 1494, Pope **Alexander VI**, himself a Spaniard, granted Ferdinand and Isabella the special title *Los Reyes Católicos* (the Catholic Kings), and it is clear that the conquest did much to enhance the power and prestige of the joint monarchy.

The whole enterprise kept the nobility occupied and loyal to the Crown, while the powerful Spanish Church also added its strength to the great cause, thus backing royal power. So the two most powerful groups beneath the Crown, which had helped to undermine royal power in the past, were now brought firmly into line over a long period of time and all shared common goals. In addition, the *Reconquista* was genuinely popular with most Spaniards, who saw the triumph as heralding a God-given golden age for Spain.

Added to this, the recapture of Granada helped to make Spain a great power in Europe. At the time, both France and England, like Spain, were also emerging from long periods of civil unrest and monarchical weakness, while the Holy Roman Empire and the states of the Italian peninsula were weak and disunited. So a united and triumphant Spain could immediately take its place as a great power, all the more so as the crusade against the Moors was not just a Spanish struggle against internal enemies but part of an ongoing, international and Christian struggle against Islam. In 1452, for example, the Ottoman Turks had captured the city of Constantinople thus posing a serious threat to the security of Christian Europe as a whole.

While other powers hesitated, Spain after 1482 now had a claim to be the leader of Christian Europe against the Infidel. Indeed, after the capture of Granada, Isabella carried out plans to take the fight to the Arabs of North Africa, just across the narrow straits from **Andalusia**.

In 1505, 10,000 Spanish troops, organised, financed and led by Cardinal Cisneros, attacked this region, and four years later with some 15,000 troops, he captured the city of **Oran**. With Granada firmly under control, Ferdinand and Isabella could now also look beyond the shores of Africa. They could dream of a Spanish empire stretching from America and Italy. It was the conquest of Granada that gave real impetus to the idea of **Spanish imperialism**.

Results of 1492 for the Moors

The results of the conquest for the Moors of Granada were rather less exciting. At first they were treated quite well. Their laws, customs, lands, dress and religion were to be respected and they were allowed to keep their own officials.

KEY PLACES

Andalusia The name given to the southern part of Spain. It includes Cadiz, Seville and Granada. It is thus the region of Spain closest to Africa.

Oran is a port on the Mediterranean coast of what is now Algeria (see map on page 2).

KEY CONCEPT

Spanish imperialism
Conveys the idea that Spain hoped to rule territories outside the Spanish peninsula. Imperial powers such as Spain believe that their civilisation can enhance the well-being of less developed societies. In this period, imperial powers talked mainly in terms of the benefits of spreading Christianity to barbarous and pagan peoples outside Europe.

Boabdil was given a small kingdom in the **Alpujarras Mountains**, and the two men put in charge of the province by Isabella acted with moderation and discretion. Inigo Lopez de Mendoza, second Count of Tendilla, was given charge of secular government. Meanwhile, Isabella's confessor, **Hernando de Talavera**, was made the first Archbishop of Granada.

These men followed the traditional peaceful policies known as *convivencia*, which had often distinguished relations between the different races and religions in medieval Spain. Talavera showed a considerable respect for Arabic achievements and was genuinely interested in Arabic studies. He admired acts of practical charity carried out by the Moor community and thought that the Castilians had much to learn from them.

However, the story of the *Reconquista* has a darker side of intolerance and brutality, and it was these qualities that came to dominate Christian Spanish society in the coming decades. Even during the war there had been acts of savagery.

- The entire Moorish population of Malaga (some 15,000 people) was enslaved after its capture in 1487.
- Some 100,000 Moors are thought to have been killed during the war.
- A further 200,000 may have fled.

Despite government efforts to stop it, Castilian nobles gained enormously at the expense of the Moors. The war left enormous social and economic problems in a kingdom that was once better governed and more prosperous than the rest of Spain. Landless Spanish peasants, perhaps some 40,000 of them, flocked to Granada in search of land and spoils. All in all, even as Boabdil's wondrous Alhambra Palace in the city of Granada was being handed over to Ferdinand and Isabella, the war had caused chaos and devastation for the native population.

The Inquisition

Even more threatening to the Moorish community than the political reconquest of Spain were the efforts to

Alpujarras Mountains
Mountain range in Granada.

Hernando de Talavera (1428–1507) Isabella's confessor and first Archbishop of Granada. A humanist scholar, his policy towards the conversion of the Moors to Christianity was one of gentle persuasion and education. 'We must adopt their works of charity, and they our Faith,' he once said.

Convivencia This meant 'living together' and denoted the ideal of all three Spanish faiths – Christian, Muslim and Jewish – living peacefully together. *Convivencia* was at the opposite extreme to the ideals of some of those who engaged in *Reconquista*.

KEY PERSON

Francisco Jiménez de Cisneros (1436–1517)
One of Isabella's favourite churchmen. He was Primate of the Spanish Church, serving as Archbishop of Toledo (1495–1517). One of the ablest statesmen of his time, he was heavily involved in Isabella's attempts to reform the Church. He acted as Regent of Castile after the death of Isabella (1504) and Regent of Spain after Ferdinand's death (1516). His attitude to the Moors was rather harsher than that of Archbishop Talavera. He is usually referred to as Cisneros.

KEY TERMS

Moriscos The official term used by the government to denote Moors who had converted to Christianity. The Inquisition often persecuted the *Moriscos*, fearing they had secretly re-converted to Islam.

Genocide Where a nation or people are deliberately exterminated.

conquer the Moors spiritually. **Francisco Jiménez de Cisneros** was unhappy with the liberal policies of Tendilla and Talavera. In 1499, while Ferdinand and Isabella were visiting Granada, he persuaded Isabella to end the old policy of *convivencia*. A devout Catholic, Isabella allowed Cisneros to have his own way.

- Immediately he introduced mass baptisms and forcible conversions on the hapless Moors.
- When this led to serious revolts, he claimed that this showed that religious non-conformity was the same as treason.

By 1501, Isabella had ordered that all the Moors in Granada must convert to Christianity or emigrate. In 1502, she announced that all unconverted Moors must be expelled.

- Throughout the process, she maintained the fiction that no Moors had been forced to convert, since they had the option of leaving the realm!
- In order to be entirely consistent, she then announced that all Moors living in the rest of Castile (Granada had been annexed to Castile) must now convert to Christianity or flee.

Despite the fact that many Moors did convert to Christianity and were all officially Christian, the *Moriscos* (as they were known) were still subjected to discrimination. Isabella in particular remained suspicious of them for no good reason.

- In 1501, she held a huge public bonfire of Arabic books in Granada and attacks were made on other aspects of Arabic culture.
- By 1526, this process was formalised when the authorities in Granada outlawed Moorish dress, jewellery and the ritual slaughter of animals.

As usual a policy of intolerance, once set in motion, became more extreme as the years went by and ended close to **genocide**. It is to Ferdinand's credit that he did not pursue his wife's policies towards the Muslims in the kingdom of Aragon.

FERDINAND AND ISABELLA GAIN MORE SPANISH TERRITORY

Cerdagne and Roussillon

The conquest of Granada was just one aspect of the growing power of Spain during the reigns of Ferdinand and Isabella. Granada was annexed by Castile but a year later it was Aragon's turn to expand.

Cerdagne and Roussillon (known to the Spanish as Cerdaña and Rosellón) were Catalan provinces in the Pyrenees (see map on page 2). Louis XI of France, who had occupied them in 1462, formally annexed them in 1463 and reoccupied them with extra forces in 1475.

During the Aragonese Civil War and the long wars against Granada, Ferdinand could do little to get them back. However, when the next king of France, Charles VIII, invaded the independent duchy of **Brittany** in 1488, Ferdinand made an alliance with Henry VII of England via the Treaty of Medina del Campo in 1489. By this treaty it was agreed that:

- England would keep France out of Brittany
- Ferdinand would regain control of Cerdagne and Roussillon.

Ferdinand duly marched into the two counties but his expedition was a failure. Luckily for him, Charles VIII had turned his attention to the rather ambitious scheme of invading Italy with the aim of conquering Naples and launching a prospective crusade in the **Holy Land**. Therefore, he agreed to give back the two provinces to Spain in return for an alliance and in the hope that this would stop the Spanish intervening against him in Italy.

In 1493, Charles signed the Treaty of Barcelona handing over the two provinces peacefully to the Crown of Aragon. Coming so soon after the Granada triumph, this peaceful acquisition of territory was seen as another sign of Spain's new power and influence in the world.

KEY PLACES

Brittany French province in the north-west of the country. Independent duchy until taken over by Charles VIII in 1488.

Holy Land Part of the Middle East centred on the city of Jerusalem and seen as the historic centre of Christianity. At this time it was part of the Muslim Empire of the Ottoman Turks.

The kingdom of Navarre

Castile and Aragon's domination of the Iberian peninsula was furthered in 1515, when the southern part of the kingdom of Navarre was incorporated into Castile. Once again this was done peacefully without the need for expensive military conquest.

- Navarre had been ruled by John II of Aragon until his death in 1479. It was then passed to Catherine de Foix and her French husband Jean d'Albret.
- After Isabella's death in 1504, Ferdinand married Germaine de Foix, thus giving himself a claim to the kingdom.

In 1512, Ferdinand led an invasion and then agreed to partition Navarre with the French. But the French, under Louis XII, were (once again) too busy in Italy to fight for the area and so Spain was (once again) enlarged. Sensibly, Ferdinand made no attempt to change the laws and customs of the kingdom, which ensured that the region remained peaceful.

The acquisition of Granada, Cerdagne, Roussillon and Navarre thus created a unified and powerful Spanish nation, which seemed an unlikely outcome when Ferdinand and Isabella married in 1469. By the time of Ferdinand's death in 1516, Spain could look forward to enjoying the benefits of great power status.

INCREASING THE POWER OF THE CROWN IN CASTILE

The Crown in Castile, unlike that in Aragon, always had the potential to enhance its power since it was not held back by a constitution that defined its powers or by institutions that could act as a brake on a monarch's commands.

The Aragonese constitution. By looking at the constitution of Aragon, the freedom of action of the Crown in Castile becomes clear.

- In Aragon, each of the three kingdoms had its own *Cortes* (assembly), which represented the nobility, clergy and towns. These *Cortes* met regularly and had to give their approval for the raising of taxes and passing new laws. In addition, they had the power to voice grievances, and expected the king to listen as they discussed matters of concern to him and the kingdom. The three *Cortes* could meet together as *Cortes Generales*, which further underlined the power of these institutions.
- In the kingdom of Aragon there was also an official known as the *Justiciar*, who could question royal commands. His task was to ensure that neither the Crown nor the nobility was infringing the laws. Although a royal appointment, the office had become hereditary in one noble family, so the Crown could not control him.
- Although Catalonia had no *Justiciar*, it did have a standing committee of three *Diputats* and three *Oidors*. These men, representing the three estates of the *Cortes*, had originally been financial officers who oversaw the collection of taxes voted by the *Cortes*. However, they had developed into watchdogs of the rights or 'liberties' of the people represented in the *Cortes*. In time this idea had also spread from Catalonia to Valencia and Aragon.

So the king was clearly subject to the *fueros* (constitutional rights) of the kingdom and he was expected to observe existing customs. Overall, the limitations on Crown power in Aragon were re-emphasised by the **Aragonese oath of loyalty** to their sovereign.

The Castilian constitution. By contrast, this contractual relationship between ruler and ruled did not exist in Castile. Here the *Cortes* was relatively powerless. Isabella made use of it in the early part of her reign as a means of gathering support but then dispensed with it. She was not obliged to call them, they were not necessary for the passing of new laws, and they had little interest in grants of taxation as the nobles and clergy were exempt. Between 1480 and 1498 no *Cortes* was called in Castile.

Increased royal control of the towns
Royal control of the *Hermandades* was one way in which

the Crown played a more intrusive role in the affairs of the towns, since they were paid for by urban taxation. However, there were other ways in which Isabella took greater control over the towns. At the *Cortes* of Toledo (1480), she insisted that all major Castilian towns should accept a royally appointed official called the *corregidor*. He was to:

- oversee justice and public order
- arbitrate between different factions in town government.

Such officials had existed since medieval times in certain towns in Castile but now Isabella decided to widen the practice. The process was a gradual one.

- By 1494, 54 towns had them.
- By 1515, they had been appointed only to a further 32 towns.

Isabella's aim of appointing one to every town in Castile was never fulfilled and part of the increase that there was came from new appointments to towns in Granada, after the conquest.

Generally, the *corregidores* were outsiders but they were paid for by the town where they worked. Appointed usually for just two years, they did not give Isabella control of the towns but they did help to keep the peace. Often they arbitrated in disputes between city councils and local noblemen. Nonetheless, the *corregidores* often caused more problems than they solved. Towns and cities in Castile had a long history of near-full independence from royal control. Many towns resented the presence of the *corregidor*.

- Murcia asked for its *corregidor* to be withdrawn in 1481.
- Segovia, Burgos and Jerez all refused to accept theirs in 1483.

From the start, the *corregidor*'s freedom of action was limited by his short tenure of office and the fact that the town had the right to publish a report on his activities at the end of his two-year term. Contemporaries also noticed that the system was less effective after Isabella's death in 1504, when there was conflict between Ferdinand and his daughter Joanna over the government of Castile. Many *corregidores* were forced to flee during the great **Comuneros Revolt** of 1520. Furthermore, the *corregidor* experiment was limited to Castile. Aragon completely refused to accept them and, wisely enough, Ferdinand did not press the matter.

Apart from the *corregidores*, the Crown did appoint a limited number of other town officials but this did little to enhance Crown authority. In certain towns, the Crown had the right to appoint some of the *regidores* (town councillors), but this often resulted in:

- town councils becoming too large and unwieldy
- the office of *regidor* becoming hereditary in particular families.

Likewise the Crown appointed some of the *alcaldes* (town magistrates), but that did not mean their judgements were overseen or influenced by the Crown. Many towns in Castile, the so-called *villas de senorio*, were controlled directly by a nobleman or by the Church. Here, the royal writ simply did not run. Perhaps the most effective means of royal control was exercised when Isabella personally intervened in disputes in the towns, as she did in Carceres in 1477 and Salamanca in 1493. But the temporary and personal nature of these interventions highlights again the limitations of Crown authority over the towns. Royal control over some towns in Castile did increase but not by much. Elsewhere royal control over the towns remained limited.

Strengthening the Royal Council

As with the towns, so with the Royal Council, royal authority did not increase by very much as a result of reforms during the reigns of *Los Reyes Católicos* (the Catholic Kings). The *Consejo Real* (Royal Council) of Castile was divided into five *ad hoc* departments or chambers, which advised on a range of issues.

- The first chamber dealt with foreign affairs.

Comuneros Revolt In 1520 a group of cities led by Toledo organised a Holy League against the government with the aim of protecting their traditional rights. The Holy League was defeated in battle at Villalar in 1521 and its leaders executed.

- The second acted as a supreme court of justice.
- The third oversaw royal finances.
- The fourth oversaw the *Santa Hermandad*.
- The fifth dealt with the affairs of the Crown of Aragon.

The last two chambers were new, but the significance of reform here was that it was a natural and limited response to the Granada war and Ferdinand's long absences from the Crown of Aragon. It did not represent serious reorganisation of the Royal Council. Most of the Royal Councillors continued to be trained *letrados* (lawyers) rather than the great men of the kingdom. The nobles were not wholly excluded but were allowed to advise the sovereigns, particularly over the Granada war and foreign policy.

Under Ferdinand and Isabella, the Royal Council was still very small and had little by way of a bureaucracy to carry out its commands. The sovereigns, like their predecessors, continued to impose their will directly and in person rather than by delegating authority to officials. In Aragon it could be argued that royal authority, via the Royal Council, was diminished because of Ferdinand's long absences. In his 37-year rule, he spent four years in Aragon, three years in Catalonia and a mere six months in Valencia. The Council of Aragon attended on Ferdinand in Castile and the kingdom was ruled at one remove by a series of **viceroys**.

New and more bureaucratic Councils would emerge at the centre of government later on, but only when:

- the monarch, Charles I (who ruled 1516–56), was absent from Spain for prolonged periods of time
- Madrid came to be seen as the capital of the Spanish state.

Throughout the reigns of Ferdinand and Isabella, Castile still had no capital city. The Royal Council attended on the monarchs as they continually moved around their growing kingdoms. One small group of officials – the royal secretaries – did become more important at this time. With more business being transacted by the two monarchs, secretaries like Hernando de Zafra and Luis de Santángel became increasingly significant in royal administration.

Letrados Usually university graduates in law who formed the backbone of the upper levels of Church and state bureaucracy.

Viceroy Individual appointed to rule in place of the sovereign during the sovereign's absence.

In truth, the rule of Ferdinand and Isabella was still a medieval and personal monarchy, not a modern and bureaucratic one. Central government in general and the Royal Council in particular became more effective under Ferdinand and Isabella because the Catholic Kings devoted themselves so wholeheartedly to the business of government, not because there was a wholesale reform of administrative methods.

Strengthening royal justice

The pacification of Castile and Aragon depended on the restoration of law and order. Isabella dispensed much royal justice personally from the *Alcaza* (fortress) in Madrid. Nonetheless, she recognised the need for more *Audiencias* (royal courts of justice). In 1489, an *Audiencia* was permanently established in Valladolid, consisting of a president and eight *letrados* appointed annually. Another court was set up for southern Castile initially in Ciudad Real (1494) and then in Granada (1505). Lesser courts were also newly established in Seville and Santiago. Such measures met with the **approval of a number of contemporaries**.

Increasing royal income

As always in medieval society, power was directly related to income. The Catholic Kings were successful in raising royal income quite considerably in this period.

- Between 1481 and 1510, ordinary (permanent) annual income from taxes more than doubled from 150 to 320 million *maravedis*. Some 90 per cent of this income came from the *alcabala* (sales tax), from which the Church and nobility were exempt.
- At the same time extraordinary revenues, such as the *cruzada* granted by the papacy and those sums collected by the *Hermandades*, also doubled from 52 million *maravedis* in 1483 to 112 million in 1504.

These were impressive increases in revenue, which were achieved not just by introducing new taxes but by ensuring that the existing ones were collected more efficiently. An enquiry into royal finances early on in Isabella's reign recommended that a central record of taxes should be kept

KEY THEME

Approval of contemporaries Fernandez de Oviedo, a contemporary chronicler, joined the chorus of approval for the improved enforcement of law and order when he claimed that Isabella's reign was 'a golden time and a time of justice'.

and that *arrendadores* (tax farmers), who collected a very large part of royal revenues, should have their accounts audited every two years.

Although income was increased, financial success should not be exaggerated.

- The tax system remained regressive, with the wealthy paying far less, proportionately, than those at the other end of the social spectrum. This shows again that Ferdinand and Isabella were not powerful enough to attempt to raise new taxes from the great landowners, nor did they consider wide-ranging reforms.
- In addition, the use of tax farmers as opposed to royal tax collectors allowed for corruption and fraud on a large scale.
- Finally, though income rose, so too did expenditure.

There were a number of specific problems that further complicated the financial position of the monarchy.

- Financing the Granada campaigns, war in Italy (see pages 34–5) and increased diplomatic activity with other European powers was very expensive, and the Crown had to resort to loans from the nobility and *Mesta* to make ends meet.
- Even worse was the issuing of *juros* (government bonds) to royal creditors, where the Crown agreed to pay an exorbitant 10 per cent in interest. In 1504, these payments alone cost the royal treasury 112 million *maravedis*. This figure had reached 131 million by 1516. Thus around one-third of ordinary income was being used to service royal debt.

Nonetheless, royal finances were in a reasonably healthy state by the time of Ferdinand's death. Granada had been reconquered and there was more than enough income to run the government during peacetime. Unfortunately, later Spanish sovereigns, trapped and beguiled by Spain's new imperial status, went to war far too often. The result was a series of humiliating bankruptcies.

Increased royal control of the Church in Spain

The Church in Spain was very wealthy. It was a great landowner, had huge military resources, was led by aristocrats and owed allegiance to a **foreign ruler in Rome**.

One of the great achievements of Ferdinand and Isabella was that they gained more effective control over the Church in Spain and thus turned a potentially powerful opponent into a trusted and loyal ally.

- The Church's potential for independent action and even rebellion had been brought home to Isabella when Don Alfonso Carrillo, the Archbishop of Toledo (Primate of the Castilian Church), took up arms against her at the Battle of Toro in 1476. At the end of the War of Succession in Castile, Isabella forced Carrillo to agree that all Church fortresses should be placed in the hands of royal officials.
- In 1478, under pressure from Ferdinand and Isabella, the Ecclesiastical Council in Seville agreed that the appointment of all higher clergy should be in royal hands. This would hopefully ensure their future loyalty to the Crown. Although the Pope did not agree to this officially, Isabella got her candidate chosen as the new Bishop of Cuenca in a test case in 1479. In practice, this meant that in future the monarch would choose new bishops and the choice would be ratified by the Pope.
- The principle of royal control was furthered in 1486 when Pope Innocent VIII granted Ferdinand and Isabella complete control over the Church in those areas of Granada that they had conquered.
- In 1493, the Catholic Kings were given papal approval for a monopoly on **evangelism** in the New World. This was followed up by a grant of universal 'Patronato' over the Church in South America from Julius II in 1508.

One reason for papal concessions was that the Popes wanted Spanish help in fighting papal enemies (usually the French) in Italy (see pages 34–5). Papal control over the Spanish Church was also eroded when Ferdinand and Isabella refused to allow **appeals in legal cases** to be taken to Rome. After 1488, all Church cases could be finally decided in Valladolid.

Control over Church revenues

Royal control over the Church was further enhanced by gaining ecclesiastical revenues for the Crown. The *cruzada*

List of Popes during the reigns of Ferdinand and Isabella

(apart from Alexander VI, who was Spanish, the Popes were all Italian)

1471–84	**Sixtus IV**
1484–92	**Innocent VIII**
1492–1503	**Alexander VI** (Roderigo Borgia)
Sep–Oct 1503	**Pius III**
1503–13	**Julius II**
1513–21	**Leo X**

KEY CONCEPT

Evangelism Refers to the spreading of religious ideas, in this case Catholic doctrine among non-Christian peoples of South America.

KEY TERM

Appeals in legal cases In theory, the Pope was the supreme judge in legal cases arising from spiritual causes anywhere in Christendom. It was thus important for Ferdinand and Isabella to undermine this aspect of papal authority. Henry VIII in England denied Catherine of Aragon's right to appeal to the Pope when Henry wished to divorce her.

HEINEMANN ADVANCED HISTORY

KEY TERMS

Indulgences These were granted to individuals by the Catholic Church as a means of forgiving sins. When Martin Luther began his attack on the Catholic Church in 1517 (which led to the Protestant Reformation), he challenged the way in which Indulgences were being sold for cash.

Tithe payments Payments made by all Spaniards to support the clergy. Technically, these payments represented 10 per cent of income. But often payments were made 'in kind' (that is, in agricultural produce) rather than in cash.

Erastian Church Refers to a national church, which is controlled by the secular ruler (king or prince) rather than by the Pope. As early as the thirteenth century, Marsiglio of Padua had written an influential book, *Defensor Pacis* ('The Defender of the Peace'), arguing that princes not Popes should control the Church.

KEY PERSON

Christopher Columbus (1451–1506) Born in Genoa in Italy, the son of a weaver. He persuaded Ferdinand and Isabella to sponsor an expedition to prove that the world was round and to find a new route to the Indies. In 1492, he set sail on an expedition that was to come across a number of Caribbean Islands.

tax (a fixed contribution on **Indulgences** bought by the faithful) was first granted to help fund the conquest of Granada. However, Ferdinand managed to persuade the papacy to continue to grant the *cruzada* tax long after Granada had been reconquered. Alexander VI, himself a Spaniard, granted it after 1492 and Julius II granted it indefinitely in 1508, supposedly to help the spread of Christianity in the New World.

Further financial assistance came from the Church in 1494 (Alexander VI again!), when the Crown's ability to take one-third of all **tithe payments** (the so-called *tercias reales* or royal third) was granted to Spanish monarchs forever. In the same year, the Spanish Pope signalled his approval of Ferdinand and Isabella by granting them the official title *Los Reyes Católicos* (the Catholic Kings).

Isabella and Reconquista

Ferdinand and Isabella thus established an increasingly **Erastian Church** in Spain, one that was increasingly controlled by and loyal to the secular rulers. Isabella in particular won the loyalty of the Church through her genuine religious zeal and the range of policies which she undertook in the name of the Catholic faith.

- The reconquest of Granada was a good start and was followed by two major expeditions to North Africa in 1505 and 1509. Admittedly, these were after Isabella's premature death but were inspired by her last will, which demanded 'the conquest of Africa and war against the Moors'.
- After five years' hesitation, it was Isabella who agreed to help **Christopher Columbus'** expedition in 1492. The desire to discover new lands was partly inspired by financial and economic considerations, but for Isabella it was primarily a new *Reconquista*, which, instead of converting Moors, would spread Christianity among pagans in new lands. Columbus himself claimed that the New World of the Caribbean and South America was 'the new heaven and earth foretold by our Lord in the Apocalypse'.

Reform of the Church

Isabella also took seriously the idea that the Church in Spain and, more particularly, the clerics who held Church office, were in need of reform. She and Archbishop Cisneros obtained a Papal Bull in 1493 allowing them to investigate the Monastic Orders in Spain. A number of **Visitors** were sent in but had little impact. More significant was the suppression of all the Conventual Franciscan Houses in Spain. These were already under attack from the so-called Observant wing of that Order and Archbishop Cisneros, himself an Observant Franciscan (as well as Isabella's confessor), was particularly busy in this area.

The attack on the Jews

Ferdinand and Isabella's religious policies also involved an attack on the Jews of Spain. Anti-Semitism was widespread in Spain at this time but the main attack was directed at the *Conversos*. If they did revert to Judaism, then such *Conversos* were guilty of **heresy**. The instrument of persecution was the Spanish Inquisition. This was set up with papal approval in 1478 at the start of their joint reign in both Castile and Aragon. Another Papal Bull (in 1482) established a further seven Inquisitors, including the infamous **Thomas de Torquemada** who became Inquisitor General in both Castile and Aragon. As with the Moors in Granada, persecution soon became widespread and violent. Furthermore, the victims of persecution were soon to be *all* Jews, not just those who had converted to Christianity.

- Jews were made to live in designated ghettos in many Spanish cities and forced to wear badges to distinguish them from 'real' Spaniards.
- *Conversos* found guilty of heresy a second time often faced being burnt or roasted alive in an *auto de fé* (act of faith). In 1500, some 130 died this awful death in Córdoba in just one day.
- In 1492, the Jews were given four months to convert. After this, all remaining Jews (possibly as many as 200,000) were expelled from Spain.

So the religious zeal of Ferdinand and especially Isabella

Visitors Church officials charged with the task of inspecting churches and their officials.

Conversos Those Jews who had converted to Christianity but who were suspected of secretly following their old Jewish ways.

Auto de fé A religious ceremony (usually public) at which persons accused of heresy were sentenced by the Inquisition. Technically, the burning of heretics was not part of the *auto de fé*.

Heresy When individuals or groups hold ideas that go against the fundamental ideas (or doctrines) of the Catholic Church. Such people are called heretics and the standard punishment for such people, in this period, was being burnt alive at the stake. (See also page 79, which explains heresy in the context of the Dutch Revolt.)

Thomas de Torquemada (1420–98) A Dominican prior of Santa Cruz in Segovia. Confessor to Isabella after 1474, he was appointed first Inquisitor General in Castile in 1483. By 1487 he was Grand Inquisitor, or Inquisitor General for the whole of Spain. During his term of office, it is thought that some 2000 people were burned at the stake by the Spanish Inquisition.

made Spain an intolerant society. Old ideas of *convivencia* gave way to new ones emphasising *limpieza de sangre* (purity of blood). This purity of Spanish Christian blood could only be brought about by rejecting other racial and religious groups in Spain – most notably the Jews and the Moors. Although this policy made Spain less tolerant than before, it did ensure that the Catholic Church in Spain supported the Crown. Isabella and Ferdinand were indeed the most Catholic of Kings.

FOREIGN POLICY AND THE ACQUISITION OF EMPIRE, 1469–1516

Spain's highly successful foreign policy and the acquisition of lands outside the Iberian peninsula during the reigns of Ferdinand and Isabella confirmed its rise to great power status in Europe. Well before the reign of Charles I (1516–56), Spain possessed an extensive overseas empire.

- To the west, there was the New World of the Caribbean, Central and South America.
- To the south were a few ports along the North African coast.
- To the east was Sicily, Sardinia and southern Italy.

The New World
In the Treaty of Alcacovas in 1479, Portugal renounced its rights to the Canary Islands off the Moroccan coast. Thereafter the three main islands – Grand Canary, Palma and Tenerife – were conquered by Castile and would prove to be useful stepping stones on the way to the New World. The Portuguese concession of these islands also heralded a period of friendship between the two Iberian powers.

- In 1490, Ferdinand and Isabella married their eldest daughter, Isabel, to Manoel, the heir to the Portuguese throne (who died the following year).
- In 1497, Isabel married his cousin, another Manoel, the new King of Portugal.
- Left as a widower, Manoel married his sister-in-law Maria, then Maria's niece, Eleanor.

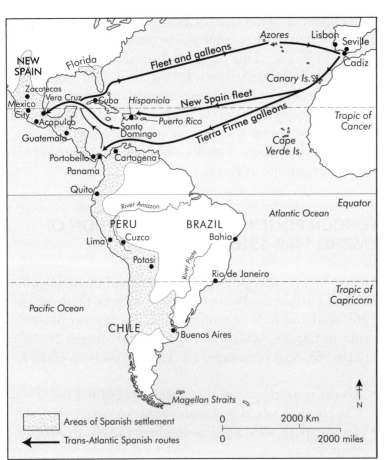

Spain's empire in the Americas in the sixteenth and seventeenth centuries.

Having established good relations with Portugal and a foothold in the Atlantic, the Catholic Kings began to look further afield to expand Spanish power. Originally rejected by Ferdinand and Isabella, and by the Portuguese, Christopher Columbus finally won the reluctant backing of the Catholic Kings in 1492 for his voyage westwards to find a new route to China and the Indies. With just three ships and a crew of 90, he set sail from Palos near Cadiz. They stopped off in the Canaries, sailed west and finally reached land in the Bahamas in the West Indies.

When Columbus returned triumphant in 1493, Ferdinand and Isabella got the Pope to draw up a special Bull *Inter Caetera*, which gave them title to all the lands that might be discovered. The Portuguese complained vigorously at the vague wording of the Bull, which seemed to threaten their interests. So, by the Treaty of Tordesillas (1494), they persuaded Spain to draw the line of demarcation between the two empires further west, which later allowed Portugal to claim Brazil.

By the time of Ferdinand's death in 1516, Spanish possessions in the New World remained limited. By 1500, Spain occupied the Island of Hispaniola (now called Haiti) with about 1000 white settlers. In 1508, Puerto Rico was conquered, with **Cuba** being added to Spain's growing empire in 1511.

Exploration and settlement on the American mainland was slow-moving as the conditions and landscape proved hostile and unwelcoming. By 1509, there were a couple of small settlements in Central America. By 1513, one *conquistador* had managed to reach the **Pacific coast**.

Though of limited value at this time, Spain had acquired the foundations of a great and wealthy empire.

Cuba was conquered by Diego Velásquez who went on to found the settlement of San Cristóbal de la Habana, which is now the capital of the island, Havana.

Pacific coast The first Spaniard to set eyes on the Pacific was Vasco Nuñez de Balboa who was governor of the Spanish colony east of Panama.

North Africa and the war against Islam

The logical extension of the conquest of Granada completed in 1492 was to carry the religious war of Christians against Islam across the straits to North Africa. Other commitments meant that this project was delayed but it received fresh impetus when Isabella died in 1504. Her dying wish was that Africa should be conquered for Christianity and the wish was carried out, to a limited extent, by her confessor Cardinal Jiménez de Cisneros. Spanish forces proceeded to capture the ports of Mers-el-Kebir (1505), the Penon de Velez (1508), Oran (1509), Bougie, Tripoli and Algiers (1510–11). While Ferdinand ignored Cisneros' pleas to extend the African conquests inland, the captured ports helped to improve trade with Spain's other Mediterranean possessions and confirmed Spain as the dominant power in the western Mediterranean. At the same time Ferdinand contributed to other campaigns against Islam.

- In 1481, he provided 70 Castilian ships to a league of powers that expelled the Turks from the Neapolitan port of Otranto.
- Some 20 years later, he helped the Venetians to expel the Turks from the fortress of St George in Cephalonia off Greece.

These campaigns would be pre-echoes of later co-operative ventures by worried Christian powers against Ottoman expansion in the Mediterranean.

Italy and France

Spain's claims to be seen as the greatest power in Europe, chief ally of the Pope and major foe of the Infidel, came to fruition with its acquisition of the kingdom of Naples in 1504. This was further strengthened by an alliance with the papacy and increasing influence throughout the Italian peninsula.

Ferdinand's policy towards other European powers revolved around the traditional Aragonese hostility towards its more powerful neighbour, France. Armed with the military and diplomatic muscle of a united Spain, together with the novelty of resident ambassadors in a number of key European cities, Ferdinand's diplomacy and wars bore rich fruit for Spain.

- Charles VIII of France played the first move in the drama when he invaded the Italian peninsula in 1494 and conquered the southern kingdom of Naples the next year.
- Ferdinand himself had a good claim to Naples as it was ruled by his cousin and he was determined to oust the French. Disguising his ambition to annex Naples to Aragon, he used his diplomatic skills to organise a **Holy League** in 1493 against France, claiming that the papacy was in danger.
- By summer 1496, the French had decided to beat a hasty retreat, and Ferdinand decided to pursue his hostility to France and his claim to the kingdom of Naples. He was already allied to England via the Treaty of Medina del Campo (1489), which had seen the betrothal of his daughter Catherine to Arthur Tudor, Prince of Wales.
- In the wake of the French intervention Ferdinand now made a double alliance with the Holy Roman Emperor, Maximilian von Habsburg, who ruled over Germany and the Low Countries. Maximilian's daughter Margaret married Ferdinand's son John and, for good measure, Maximilian's son and heir, Philip the Fair, married

KEY THEME

Holy League The league included the Emperor Maximilian, the Pope (who was Spanish) and other Italian states, all of whom had reason to fear France. The Spanish general Gonzalo Fernandez de Córdoba, who landed in Naples from Sicily, spearheaded the military wing of the Holy League.

Ferdinand's daughter Joanna. This alliance was based on fear of French expansion and the claims of the two parties to different parts of Italy. Maximilian claimed Milan in the north as an imperial fief, while Ferdinand now pursued his claims to Naples in the south.

- In 1500, France and Spain agreed in the Treaty of Granada to divide Naples between them. However, Ferdinand soon found occasion to renew the fighting and the Spanish commander Gonzalo de Córdoba obliged by driving the French out of Naples after battles at Cerignola and Garigliano (both in 1503). By the Treaty of Blois of 1505, Louis XII gave his rights to Naples to his niece, Germaine de Foix, whom Ferdinand married that same year. This left Ferdinand with a powerful Mediterranean empire comprising not only Naples but also the islands of Sicily and Sardinia, which he had already inherited.

Further success against France

After the death of Isabella in 1504, Ferdinand was no longer ruler of Castile and feared Castilian aggression against Aragon. This led to a brief reversal of his anti-French foreign policy when he married Germaine de Foix. But this diplomatic transformation did not last long.

When Ferdinand reasserted his **position in Castile** and the French conquered Milan, he constructed another Holy League in 1511 hostile to France. In 1512, he drove the French out of Navarre. In 1513, German and Spanish troops drove Louis XII out of Milan. Although the French returned to Milan in 1515, Ferdinand's diplomatic skills and constant fears of French expansion would help to ensure that, in the long term, Italy would be Spanish not French. So by 1516 Spain's foreign policy had been very successful in establishing it as a great, possibly the greatest, power in Europe. 'The crown of Spain,' claimed Ferdinand in 1514, 'has not for over seven hundred years been as great or resplendent as she now is.' The truth of this assessment cannot be denied, and it is a measure of Ferdinand and Isabella's work that it was so.

KEY THEME

Ferdinand's position in Castile When Isabella died in 1504, the heir to her Castilian throne was Ferdinand and Isabella's daughter, Joanna. Immediately Ferdinand had the *Cortes* agree that Ferdinand should carry on the government on his daughter's behalf. However, Joanna was married to Philip, Archduke of Austria, and in 1506 they tried to claim the throne. In 1506, Philip and Ferdinand agreed at the Treaty of Villafranca that Philip should be regent. The same year, Philip died and Joanna was declared insane. Ferdinand was therefore able to regain full control of Castile.

DID FERDINAND AND ISABELLA CREATE A UNITED SPAIN?

The Catholic Kings certainly did a great deal towards the creation of a more united Spain during their lifetimes, though that unity often hung by a thread in the years between the death of Isabella in 1504 and the death of her husband in 1516. What they did was to unite politically and religiously the Iberian kingdoms (except Portugal) and hand them on to a single (if foreign) ruler thereafter. Thus they transformed the warring and unstable kingdoms, which they inherited, into imperial Spain, the great power of sixteenth- and seventeenth-century Europe.

Aspects of political disunity

Of course, there were serious limitations to the degree of unification that could be achieved in the circumstances prevailing at that time.

The monarchy. The monarchy in Castile was rather more powerful than that in Aragon. Long centuries of feudalism in Aragon had forged a contractual monarchy where the power of the Crown was circumscribed by the privileges and powers of aristocracy and towns, safeguarded by the *Cortes* and *Justiciar*. In Castile, the absence of such feudal structures allowed the Crown greater flexibility and freedom in dealing with its most powerful subjects.

Government. No attempt was made to create a common centralised Spanish government. There is no evidence that Ferdinand and Isabella ever contemplated such a thing. Indeed, medieval monarchs had a strong sense of the need to preserve and conserve the proper workings of their societies as handed to them by God. They saw their kingdoms as a sacred trust and had only a limited appreciation of ideas of political or bureaucratic reform or unification.

Separation. Throughout their joint reign Ferdinand and Isabella never used the term 'Spain' but continued to refer to their separate kingdoms.

- All the kingdoms had different *fueros* (right, or laws) and these were respected.
- The Catholic Kings had inherited and passed on kingdoms that were politically autonomous and

independent of each other. Even the three kingdoms that made up Aragon retained their separate institutions of government.

- The continuing separation of the kingdoms can be clearly seen in the acquisition of territory in this period. The New World, Granada and Navarre were all annexed to Castile and trade with the New World was a Castilian monopoly, operating through the Castilian port of Seville. Meanwhile, the provinces of Cerdagne and Roussillon and the kingdom of Naples were taken over and controlled by Aragon, since these areas had, in the past, belonged to Aragon not Castile.

- Castile and Aragon came close to resuming their ancient hostility by having separate rulers after the death of Isabella in 1504. With no surviving sons, Isabella named Joanna and Joanna's eldest son Charles as her heirs. Therefore, when Joanna and her husband, Philip of Burgundy, returned to Castile in 1506, Ferdinand lost his position as Regent of Castile and retired to Naples.

- At the same time Ferdinand took a new wife, which would mean that any son of that marriage would have inherited Aragon but not Castile. Fortunately for Spain there was no such son.

Ferdinand's heirs. Though restored to the position of governor of Castile after Philip's unexpected death and Joanna's descent into madness, there was still a good chance that the two kingdoms would go their separate ways after Ferdinand's death. In his will of 1512, Ferdinand named his grandson Ferdinand (younger son of Joanna and Philip) as his heir in Aragon, not the eldest grandson Charles who was heir in Castile. Young Ferdinand, unlike his brother Charles, was Spanish (having been born in Spain in 1502 and brought up there). By contrast, Charles (born in 1500) was a Burgundian born in Ghent and brought up in the Burgundian Netherlands. Luckily for Spain, Ferdinand decided to make Charles his heir in 1515. So, more by luck than judgement, Charles became sole ruler of Castile and Aragon when Ferdinand died in 1516.

Economic disunity

Economically, too, the kingdoms remained separate and different.

Coinage. There were three different coinage systems in operation. Though attempts were made to fix exchange rates – whereby one Castilian gold *ducat* was worth one Valencian gold *excelente*, which was worth one Catalonian *gold principat* – the kingdoms continued to have different coins in circulation.

Customs. The kingdoms of Aragon had many internal customs barriers, while Castile did not. Merchants had to pay tolls when they entered or left the kingdoms, and royal customs officials operated along all the internal frontiers. No attempt was made to change these arrangements, which had resulted from less peaceful times, and trade between the kingdoms remained restricted.

Economies. The Castilian economy prospered, especially in terms of wool production. Castile traded with northern Europe, mainly via Bruges, and began to look for new markets in the western lands across the Atlantic. The Aragonese economy, based on Mediterranean trade to the east, was largely in decline though there is some evidence that Barcelona (the capital of Catalonia) profited from the acquisition of Naples.

Aspects of unity

Although the kingdoms were far from unified under Ferdinand and Isabella, they were, in many respects, united. For a quarter of a century the monarchs acted with unity of purpose to bring peace and stability to their troubled kingdoms.

Shared aims. Both took the business of government very seriously. Both were spurred on by the political instability and conflict they inherited, and they never seem to have disagreed about the policies to be adopted. Both wished to enforce law and order, tame the aristocracy and the towns, and take greater control over the Church.

Financial union. They produced the so-called double *excelente*, a gold coin with both their heads on it. On royal buildings they intertwined symbols representing the two of them.

Dual monarchy. In Castile, they operated a joint monarchy. Although Isabella was the sovereign, Ferdinand was allowed to act and give orders on his own account, if they were not together. When separated, they kept in contact by means of a team of couriers who carried letters from one to the other. In fact, they spent much time together touring their kingdoms to make a reality of personal monarchy. After all, in the marriage contract Ferdinand had sworn to reside in Castile and only visit Aragon with his wife's permission. The Council of Aragon, through which he ruled his native kingdom, attended on him in Castile.

Partnership. The partnership between Castile and Aragon might seem rather unequal in terms of the dominance of Castile. But it was still a partnership and one that Ferdinand actively supported. He encouraged the intermarriage of Catalan and Castilian noble families, appointed Castilian churchmen to important benefices in Catalonia and took it upon himself to revive the medieval Inquisition in Aragon in 1481 and 1482. When Castile was laid low by Philip's death in 1506 and Joanna's insanity, it is not surprising that the *Cortes* of Castile asked Ferdinand to take control. And, despite Ferdinand's remarriage, the kingdoms of Castile and Aragon were bequeathed to the same heir.

Common foreign policy. The kingdoms were also united in great common enterprises such as the reconquest of Granada, the conquest of the New World and the war against France.

In doing this, Ferdinand and Isabella united Spain in the eyes of their fellow monarchs. Foreign powers quickly realised that they were witnessing the great expansion of Spain and its transformation from a collection of small warring states into a great nation with imperial pretensions. With an end to internal fighting and suspicion, Castile and Aragon were perceived as the greatest power in Europe by the time of Charles' accession.

The attitude of the aristocracy. The aristocracy of both kingdoms also shared Ferdinand and Isabella's sense of divine mission. With the aristocracy fired up by projects such as the reconquest of Granada there was little time or energy for the old aristocratic squabbles that had disfigured the kingdoms in the past.

Religious unity. Political purpose and unity was underpinned by greater religious unity. Having taken steps to bring the Church more clearly under royal control, Ferdinand and Isabella unleashed the great potential represented by the religious faith of their people to instil a greater sense of uniformity among them. Theirs was not a passive Christian creed but an active and missionary one. Alien and minority ethnic groups and creeds were persecuted and largely overcome, so that religious uniformity might be imposed. Though not universally popular, the Inquisition operated openly in both kingdoms to root out heresy. Such actions ensured that Spain, unlike Germany, France and England, would not be divided by the religious wars that were a consequence of the Protestant Reformation.

Ferdinand and Isabella thus focused the latent energies of their kingdoms and the latent power of the Castilian monarchy to create a dynamic state united by religious mission and imperial pretensions.

SUMMARY QUESTIONS

1 'The main aim of Ferdinand and Isabella was to enforce religious uniformity on Spain.' To what extent do you agree with this viewpoint?

2 In what ways and to what extent did the power of Spain and Spanish government increase during the reigns of the Catholic Kings?

3 'The partnership between Ferdinand and Isabella was fundamentally unequal.' Assess the validity of this judgement.

4 To what extent can the conquest of Granada be seen as the greatest achievement of the Catholic Kings?

KEY THEME

Contemporary views of Ferdinand and Isabella
Peter Martyr wrote of Isabella that, 'She commands in such a way that she always appears to do it in accord with her husband, so that the edicts and other documents are published with the signature of both.' Ferdinand and Isabella were always referred to jointly as 'the King and Queen', so much so that the chronicler Hernando del Pulgar observed, on one occasion that 'on such and such a day the King and Queen gave birth to a daughter!'

The contemporary court poet and scholar Antonio de Nebrija, who wrote a Castilian grammar dedicated to Isabella, perhaps exaggerated only a little when he penned this epitaph on the joint reign of the Catholic Kings:

And now, who cannot see that, although the title of Empire is in Germany, its reality lies in the power of the Spanish monarchs who, masters of a large part of Italy and the isles of the Mediterranean Sea, carry war to Africa and send out their fleet, following the course of the stars, to the isles of the Indies and the New World, linking the Orient to the western boundary of Spain and Africa.

CHAPTER 2

1516–56: How well did Spain respond to the challenge of empire in the reign of Charles I?

KEY POINTS

In order to cope with a foreign ruler, an expanding empire in the New World and the demands of Charles I's personal empire, Spanish government faced serious problems in key areas. The problematic impact of empire on Spain can be seen in:

- serious unrest and rebellion at the start of Charles I's reign (1516–22)
- administrative reform
- financial and economic difficulties
- advantages and disadvantages of the exploitation of the New World
- Charles' foreign policy commitments, 1516–56.

REBELLION AND ITS CONSEQUENCES

Government in transition

Even before Charles I arrived in Spain to take up his latest inheritance (he was already ruler of Burgundy and the Low Countries, and would become Holy Roman Emperor in 1519), it was clear that the achievements of Ferdinand and Isabella in uniting Spain and bringing internal peace were under threat. This was not surprising as these **achievements** had, at heart, been personal to the two sovereigns as the product of their particular personal and political union.

- They exercised monarchical authority in an essentially medieval way.
- They had no fixed capital but toured their realms incessantly to deal with problems and enforce policies directly and at first hand.

> **KEY THEME**
>
> **Achievements** Some contemporaries and later historians chose to exaggerate Ferdinand and Isabella's achievements by claiming that they were fulfilling a destiny of Messianic dimensions. God, they believed, had sent them first to unite Spain, then to control all of Christendom, before defeating the Infidel and retaking possession of Jerusalem.

With the accession of a foreign prince who inherited and controlled a personal empire in which Spain was only a part, the government of Spain and the New World would need to be modified in order to cope with the new Habsburg imperialism. Naturally enough, these changes and adjustments were likely to cause disorder in the short term.

Problems emerged soon after Isabella's death in 1504. There was wrangling between **Joanna**, Philip and Ferdinand (see page 37), resulting in Ferdinand's rejection by Castile. Although he was later restored, there was further discord when he died in 1516.

Fearful of widespread unrest with the accession of a wholly foreign and unknown ruler, Cardinal Cisneros, now regent until Charles' arrival in Spain, tried to introduce a new voluntarily militia. This force of some 30,000 men would be raised and paid for by the cities and would have the considerable advantage of making the Crown militarily independent of the great magnates. Faced with this threat the magnates managed to stir up opposition and disorder in Tordesillas and other Castilian towns. Realising the weakness of his position without the backing of the new sovereign (who had not yet arrived), Cisneros wisely withdrew the plan.

Reasons for revolt

When Charles did arrive in Spain in 1517, things got much worse. Brought up in Burgundy, he had never been to Spain. He made no attempt to learn the language and he brought with him an entourage of Flemish advisers.

Among these advisers was **Chièvres** who, just to reinforce his position and power, slept in the same room as the young prince.

Even before Charles arrived in Spain, Cardinal Cisneros and the grandees were concerned that Spanish wealth and positions were being used to enrich foreigners. When he did arrive their worst fears were realised.

- Cisneros was sacked – though he actually died before receiving the curt notice of dismissal.

KEY PEOPLE

Queen Joanna (or Juana – 1479–1555) Technically Queen of Castile from 1504 (when she succeeded her mother Isabella) to her death in 1555. After the death of her husband Philip the Fair in 1506, she was increasingly afflicted by some form of insanity. To Spaniards she is known as *Juana la Loca* (Joanna the mad).

Chièvres (1458–1521) Guillaume de Croy, Lord of Chièvres was Grand Chamberlain to Charles I and had been regent in the Low Countries while Philip of Burgundy went, with his wife Joanna, to claim Castile.

- He was replaced as regent by Charles' Dutch tutor, **Adrian of Utrecht**, who would be later rewarded with the **papal tiara**.
- Showing yet more insensitivity towards Spanish pride, Charles allowed Chièvres to appoint his 17-year-old nephew to the late lamented Cisneros' post as Archbishop of Toledo and Primate of all Spain.
- For good measure, Chièvres himself was granted immensely profitable sources of income and the right to nominate to all vacant posts in the New World.

Opposition to the new regime was first voiced at the **Castilian *Cortes***, which met Charles in Valladolid in 1518. Led by Juan de Zumel, who represented the city of Burgos, they first refused to recognise Charles as sovereign, claiming that his mother, Joanna, was the real ruler of Castile. After giving way on this issue, the *Cortes* demanded that Charles:

- divest himself of foreign advisers
- learn Spanish
- give Spanish office only to Spaniards
- respect Spanish laws.

The *Cortes* was not impressed by Charles' agreement to these conditions, as he then proceeded to declare that his advisers were now naturalised Spaniards.

Worse followed as the *Cortes*, lacking the power to refuse Charles money, had to vote Charles 300,000 *ducats* over the next three years without conditions. There were also prolonged wrangles and negotiations with the three *Cortes* in the kingdom of Aragon, where some wanted to choose Charles' brother Ferdinand as king, and where Charles was only recognised as co-ruler with his mad mother Joanna.

Charles Habsburg, officially King Charles I of Spain, but also known as the Emperor Charles V.

Just as matters seemed to be settling down, relations between Charles and the ruling classes in Castile reached breaking point. This was sparked off by the death of Charles' grandfather, the Emperor Maximilian, early in 1519. Charles hastened back from Aragon to Castile in order to raise further funds to secure his election as the next emperor of Germany. In order to beat off competition from the King of France, Francis I, and possibly also

Henry VIII of England, Charles would need about one million gold florins. The Castilian *Cortes* objected to funding this particular project, which also had the demerits of taking Charles away from Spain and of making Spain the paymaster of Charles' personal and essentially foreign empire.

Although money was eventually voted, it was never collected as mobs attacked the tax collectors. The *Cortes* was already in hostile mood as the representatives had been called to distant Santiago and were further enraged when Adrian of Utrecht was named as regent during Charles' absence!

Another cause of concern for the new king's Spanish subjects was the possibility that Spanish wool would now be increasingly exported to the new king's homeland in the Low Countries and that, consequently, the Spanish cloth industry would be seriously undermined. In 1520, even before Charles set sail for Germany, revolt had broken out in Castile.

The Comuneros Revolt, 1520–1

The revolt was based on the towns and cities of central and northern Castile. It began in Toledo where the *corregidor* and other representatives of royal government were expelled. In their place the leading local families oversaw the election of a *Comunidad* (a new governing committee). Other towns quickly joined in and the rebellion was co-ordinated by a central committee called the *Santa Junta de Comunidad*, which met in Avila.

- In Segovia, the representative of the city, who had voted for the second subsidy for Charles, was attacked by a mob and murdered.
- Adrian of Utrecht, the Dutch Regent, fanned the flames when his attempt to keep control of the royalist arsenal in Medina del Campo resulted in half the town being burnt down.
- Many other towns, infuriated by Medina's fate, now joined the rebels. The Comuneros reacted by capturing Adrian and other councillors, as royal government in Castile evaporated.

- Even more worrying for the authorities was the fact that the rebels captured Charles' mother, Joanna, hoping that she would give legitimacy to the rebellion by putting herself at the head of the insurgents. When she refused to do so, some of the rebels declared that Spain was more important than the monarchy and that the *Santa Junta* was the true (and obviously Spanish) government of Castile.

At the height of its power the *Junta* had representatives from fourteen of the eighteen cities that sent representatives to the Castilian *Cortes*. Many other towns joined in, as did many of the peasantry hoping for a lessening of their economic burdens. The rebels even won a battle at Torrelobaton in December 1520. In the same month, the Bishop of Zamora joined the rebellion and captured Valladolid, injecting a dose of religious fervour into the rebel cause. With Charles hundreds of miles away in Germany, it looked as though his possession of Spain might be short-lived indeed.

Reasons for failure of the revolt
And yet the rebellion ultimately failed. In April 1521, the rebels were pursued and cut down by the Constable of Castile, Don Inigo de Velasco, near the village of Villalar. Only 200 rebels and about 20 royalists were casualties in this curiously small-scale encounter, but it marked the end of the revolt as the cause was already close to collapse.

- As the final encounter indicates, the rebellion failed mainly because the grandees of Castile, who had at best shown luke-warm support for the uprising, finally turned against it.
- As the rebellion unfolded, Charles appointed two grandees, the Constable and the Admiral, as co-regents with Adrian, which helped to win over some of the lesser nobles who were wavering. This meant that the rebels would never have the military or political might to create an alternative Spanish government.
- In addition, the nobles quickly became worried about the radical language of some of the rebels. Aristocratic power always depended on the power of the monarchy and usually found itself opposed to the rights of the

towns. So the nobles would not stand idly by as the cities destroyed that monarchy and set up a government answerable to themselves. Besides this, most of the aristocracy claimed authority over the towns bordering their estates and feared the loss of that power.

- The great revolt also failed because the nature of the Comuneros Revolt changed as it engaged more supporters. The original leaders supported the rights of Spain against an alien and corrupt government. Later the leadership within the towns became anti-aristocratic, attacking nobles' rights and privileges in the towns. At that point, the nobility recognised its duty to the old order and was further inflamed when they realised that the rebellion was stirring up the peasantry to demand a lessening of the economic burdens that oppressed them.

- The rebellion also ran into difficulties because the movement was split between radicals and conservatives. The leaders had different ideas about their aims and methods. Some towns wanted to set themselves up as sovereign republics on the model of the Italian city states, independent of all outside authority. Thus, they had little interest in the government of Spain as a whole. For the more conservative leaders, restoration of the good government of Ferdinand and Isabella was their priority. For many of the rebels, failure became inevitable when Joanna refused to take charge of the rebel forces.

- The leaders of the rebellion were powerful men in the towns, who could not easily abandon the principle of monarchical authority. If they could not depose Charles and replace him with his mother, then the most they could hope for were concessions from his Regent. When Adrian promised that Charles would return and marry a Spanish princess, most were won over.

The Germania, 1520–2

Amidst all the excitement of events in Castile, there was a simultaneous uprising in **Valencia**. The first signs of trouble came in August 1519 in the city of Valencia, when armed mobs defied the authorities because they believed the local Inquisition had been rather too lenient on certain individuals. They defied the governor of the city and persuaded Charles to agree that they had the right as a

Valencia The south-eastern kingdom within the Crown of Aragon.

germania (holy brotherhood) to drill and bear arms in the city. It so happened that many of the citizens had been armed in expectation of Turkish raids on the city. This, combined with an outbreak of plague (which led to many of the aristocrats fleeing the city), gave the rebels the means and opportunity to start a serious revolt, which included an **attack on the Moors**.

Led by a local weaver, the rebelling mobs chose a governing committee of thirteen (representing Christ and the twelve Apostles) and took control of the city. Thereafter trouble flared up all over the kingdom of Valencia as the poor and oppressed, sometimes aided by local priests, rose up against the landlords and government officials. The governor of Valencia, the Count of Melito, was forced to flee from the city and an army he raised was defeated by the forces of the Germania at Gandia in 1521. As in many parts of Castile, royal government seemed to be breaking down over a prolonged period of time.

Failure of the Germania
However, the rebels overplayed their hand. While the leader of the revolt, Vincente Peris, ravaged around the south of the kingdom converting and murdering Moors, he left his capital unguarded. The Marquis of Zenete retook the city of Valencia and Peris was defeated outside it as the nobility began to recover their nerve. Five months later, Peris was finally captured and duly executed. By March 1522, the revolt was at an end.

- The Germania failed because it represented too many different interest groups – peasants, artisans and labourers – none of which had any real power.
- It was a general movement of protest relying on the temporary weakness of Crown and aristocracy, essentially in one city.
- The anti-Moorish aspect of the revolt may have roused serious popular support but in time the forces of law and order – Crown, aristocracy and Church – rallied to re-establish the old order.

Consequences of the revolts
In July 1522, Charles returned to his Spanish kingdoms,

Attack on the Moors The Moors were especially targeted by the rebelling mobs, because they were believed to be undermining Christian peasants by working for lower wages. In the aftermath of Ferdinand and Isabella's persecution of *Moriscos* and indeed *Conversos*, an attack on the Moors seemed to be encouraged by both Church and State.

which had been wracked by civil war during his absence. It is clear that he had learnt some **hard lessons** from the experience. The 22-year-old who returned to Spain was rather different from the awkward youth who had appeared in 1517.

The Flemish advisers had gone. Charles replaced the greedy Chièvres and Sauvage with **Mercurino Gattinara** (also a foreigner, an Italian, but a man of sense and vision) and a Spaniard, **Francisco de los Cobos** (an able administrator who was beginning to rise in royal favour). In addition, Charles was now Holy Roman Emperor and deeply imbued with the responsibility to govern all his God-given kingdoms in a responsible way. As Germany became divided in religion with the rise of Protestantism, so the Charles of 1522 realised that Spain must be the stable centre of his personal empire. Returning to Spain rather older and wiser, he was determined to put things right. This time he would:

- stay a full seven years
- learn to speak Spanish
- marry Isabella of Portugal (1526)
- produce a son and heir, Philip (born in 1527).

Charles' response to the revolts

As well as showing Charles the need for good and personal government in Spain, the revolts also showed him the deep divisions that still existed in Castile and Aragon. His sensitivity on this issue meant that the punishments for the rebels were not too harsh.

- In 1522, Charles paraded a force of 4000 German soldiers armed with the latest artillery through the rebel towns of Castile as a show of force. However, only 22 individuals were tried and executed for their part in the prolonged Comuneros Revolt.
- Another 290 were excluded from the general pardon that was proclaimed, but most were reinstated on payment of a fine.
- Meanwhile, royal and aristocratic control of the towns was reasserted and the *corregidores* returned. However, Charles stopped short of any wholesale reform, which might have led to future urban problems.

Charles' hard lessons We know that Charles blamed himself for the disturbances of 1520–2. Later he remarked that in 1520:

I was governed by M. de Chièvres, and I was not old enough or experienced enough to govern these kingdoms. And as I left immediately for Flanders, having spent very little time here, and what is more, being still unmarried and without an heir, it is not surprising that there was scandal and disturbance.

Mercurino Gattinara (1465–1530) Became Grand Chancellor in 1518 on the death of Jean Sauvage. He was an Italian humanist with a broad imperial vision for Charles, believing that God had set him on the road to world monarchy.

Francisco de los Cobos (1477–1547) Unlike Gattinara, de los Cobos was a Spaniard with no intellectual pretensions. As imperial secretary in Spain (1516–47), his ability lay in the practical concerns of administration.

In Valencia it was mainly the Moors who suffered, not only during but also after the revolt. Aristocratic control was re-established and Germaine de Foix, Ferdinand's widow, was sent in as viceroy of Valencia. However, Charles decided that the Moors must now convert to Christianity or leave the kingdom. An edict was passed to this effect in 1525, which meant that no Muslim could openly exercise his faith in Spain. Charles clearly felt that as the defender of Catholicism against heresy in Germany and the Low Countries, he must also be the defender of Christianity against the Infidel in Spain.

Just as the Moors were made **scapegoats** in Valencia, so the Jews were often blamed for the Comuneros Revolts in Castile. In 1521, the Constable of Castile informed Charles that 'the root cause of the revolution in these realms has been the *Conversos*'. This view was echoed a generation later by the Archbishop of Toledo. In government circles as well as in the popular imagination, racial and religious minorities remained convenient scapegoats for the ills of society.

Overall, the revolts cemented the natural alliance between king, aristocracy and the Church. Though he had started life as an alien, after the revolts Charles became Spanish, governing the country with the same serious determination as his grandparents, Ferdinand and Isabella.

The revolts warned him that Spain had the potential for self-destruction and ensured that the reforms in government in the future would not jeopardise the working relationship between the Crown and the nobility. Furthermore, perhaps because of the Germania Revolt, Charles remained sensitive to the different methods of government in Aragon. Just like Ferdinand and Isabella before him, he would accept the political and financial limitations on Crown power in the eastern kingdoms and would not attempt to unify Spain. It is a tribute to **Charles' success in governing Spain** that there was no more excitement during his reign to match that of the Comuneros and Germania.

GOVERNMENT AND ADMINISTRATIVE REFORM

It is easy to assume that Spanish government underwent considerable change and reform during the reign of Charles I as it struggled to come to terms with the imperial pretensions thrust upon it by the acquisition of the New World and Italy, as well as Charles' other possessions.

- A new Council of State for governing Spain and Germany was set up by Gattinara in 1522, and seemed to embody his idea that Charles should establish a central government for his empire.
- Other new Councils also appeared in due course giving the impression of reform and centralisation – in 1523, a *Consejo de Hacienda* (Council of Finance); in 1524, a Council for the Indies; and in 1555, a Council for Italy. A Council for War was set up at the start of the reign.
- Two reformers keen to transform the administrative machinery of Spain from deficient and medieval to streamlined and modern were the Chancellor, Gattinara, and the long-serving Secretary, Francisco de los Cobos, who served on a number of Councils.

Limited efficiency of conciliar government

However, such a picture would seriously exaggerate the scale and impact of administrative changes in Spain in this period. Charles ruled his many kingdoms separately from each other, well aware of the chance of revolt if he tried to introduce wide-ranging changes. Thus the development of new Councils during his reign was but an extension of the **conciliar** policies of Ferdinand and Isabella and they were mainly set up to deal with the new territories.

- The Council for the Indies, for example, was modelled on the Councils of Castile and Aragon, and developed to administer new lands in South and Central America.
- The Council for Italy developed in the same way after Charles added the duchy of Milan (in northern Italy) to his kingdom of Naples. The late date for the formation of the Council for Italy (1555), many years after Ferdinand had acquired Naples, indicates that neither Charles nor his officials thought about administration and Councils in a modern, bureaucratic way.

KEY TERM

Imperial expenditure The total expenditure in all of Charles' dominions. When dealing with Charles I, 'imperial' refers to his personal empire, rather than Spain's empire in the New World.

- The most innovative Council was the Council of Finance established in 1523. This Council diligently drew up budgets for each year and attempted to balance income and expenditure. Since it reported to Charles, it soon came to review **imperial expenditure** as a whole. Although this looked good, the reality was that the Council was a failure. Charles' refusal to curtail his foreign wars or personal expenditure meant that the Council oversaw the collapse of Spain's finances. It did not even know the real scale of the debts, because interest payments on royal debts were not included in the calculation of annual expenditure.

Furthermore, Spanish government and administration still lacked a state capital. It was not until the reign of Philip II that Madrid became the fixed centre of the Spanish empire. Under Charles I, the Councils and officials all had to move around Spain, and indeed Europe, in personal attendance on the peripatetic king, just as they had for the Catholic Kings before him.

Power of the Crown and power of the nobility

Throughout Charles' reign, the government and administration of Spain remained largely medieval.

- The king remained the source of all power, exercising a monarchical power in his own personal way.
- Even those Councils that did exist largely offered advice and attempted only a general oversight of government in the localities. In staffing the Councils, Charles followed the policy of his predecessors. Some nobles like the **Duke of Alva** were given honorary positions in the Council of State but the majority of officials were from classes below the great nobles.
- Francisco de los Cobos, a case in point, was the most powerful official for most of the reign. However, he was more interested in getting the existing structures of government to work more efficiently than in innovation.

KEY PERSON

The Duke of Alva (or Alba) 1507–82 Fernando Alvarez de Toledo y Pimentel. He was an important soldier under both Charles I and his son Philip II. He is best known for his attempts to crush the Dutch Revolt in the period 1567–73.

The real force behind this drive for efficiency was not the ideals of good government and impartial justice but the pressing financial needs of an impoverished monarch.

Nothing illustrates the limited nature of change better than the nobility's refusal on two occasions to pay taxes. They never had in the past and they would not start now! Charles' empire might give them opportunities to exercise power as viceroys or generals, but they had no wish to pay for a foreign policy that rarely seemed to be Spanish.

It was the nobility who continued to rule the countryside and many of the towns. After the Comuneros Revolt, it was often the *hidalgos* (lesser nobles) who benefited from the opportunity to take charge of town government. In many cases, the Crown decided that such local men of independent means stood more chance in the towns than royal officials from the educated elite. *Letrados* were fine as administrators and officials in the federation of governments, which looked after the various parts of the empire, but they lacked the power to control troublesome towns.

Meanwhile, it was the nobility and the Church that continued to hold sway in the rural areas. These groups were the traditional bastions against rebellion and disorder. Under Charles their position was enhanced rather than diminished. For the mass of peasants and labourers, government emanated not from the king but from the local magnate or churchman; they were the natural and time-honoured dispensers of government and justice.

Corruption in government

Just as Charles was naturally conservative in matters of government and administration, so he could not afford to pay for all the new officials he would need if he were to make royal government more effective and absolute at the centre and in the localities. Furthermore, Charles' government was weakened by the fact that he, like all his fellow sovereigns, could not afford to pay those officials, which he did have, decent salaries. Thus, as bureaucracy expanded and more officials were appointed there was the usual rush to supplement income by taking bribes for favours.

The patronage at the disposal of Charles I was immense indeed, so officials did well out of being able to recommend individuals for various posts or preferment. In Spain (as elsewhere) the ruler was flooded with petitions from those who claimed to have rendered *servicios* (special services) and now claimed their due *mercedes* (reward).

As the Emperor's most important and trusted secretary, Cobos did best out of the system. By the time of his death, he had amassed an annual income in the region of 60,000 *ducats* a year. This put him on the same financial level as the richest nobles in Castile. He also ensured that his family did well out of royal service.

- His daughter married the Duke of Sesta.
- His son was ennobled as Marquis of Camarasa.
- His nephew succeeded him as one of the king's main secretaries.

While Cobos was the most successful of all in terms of what he gained from royal service and one of the hardest working administrators, his career reminds us that the administrative system depended on **venality**. Overall then, the burden of a growing empire made little difference to the way in which Spain was governed.

FINANCIAL AND ECONOMIC DIFFICULTIES

Scale of the financial problems

Although the emergence of Spain as a great power had only limited impact on the way in which it was governed, it had a disastrous impact on the country's finances and its economic well-being. In particular the burden of paying for Charles' constant wars in Europe against France, the Turks and the **German Lutherans** fell most heavily on Castile. By the time Charles returned to Spain, royal finances were already at a low ebb.

- Ferdinand and Isabella had mortgaged future income to pay for the conquest of Granada and Naples, and the crushing of the revolts of 1520–2 had also cost the Crown dear.
- As early as 1523, Charles was told that all his next year's revenue had already been spent! Charles' first move was

KEY TERM

Venality Another word meaning 'bribery and corruption'.

KEY PEOPLE

German Lutherans
Followers of one of the first Protestant leaders, the German monk, Martin Luther. Luther's protest against the powers of the papacy began in earnest in 1521, when he refused to renounce his heretical views in front of Charles himself and the papal legate (ambassador) at the Diet of Worms.

to set up a new Council of Finance, but this could do little more than paper over the growing gaps in royal finances by consistently underestimating the size of the royal debt.

In the 1520s and 1530s, the situation was serious. By the 1540s it was nearer to catastrophic. When ordinary income failed to meet Charles' demands for money, he resorted to borrowing. Foreign bankers like the German Fuggers and Welsers were happy to oblige and Charles developed the system of *juros*, first introduced by Ferdinand and Isabella, to pay for the loans. As more loans were taken out so more and more future revenue was pledged away merely to pay the interest payments on these loans.

- By 1546, the income of Castile had already been pledged for the next three-and-a-half years. When Charles wrote to Cobos in that year, asking for immediate funds to pay for a military campaign against the German Lutheran princes, Cobos advised him to make peace! Charles, as always, refused and the debt continued to mount.
- In 1552, Charles borrowed 4 million *ducats* to finance war against France, where the unsuccessful campaign to save the city of Metz alone cost some 2.5 million *ducats*. By the end of Charles' reign the spiralling cost of warfare and the scale of his commitments in Europe and the Mediterranean had rendered him virtually bankrupt.
- In 1557, Charles' son Philip suspended payments from the Castilian treasury. Though this was not technically a declaration of bankruptcy, the Spanish monarchy would never throw off the **legacy of debt** bequeathed to it by the Emperor.

Why did Castile bear the financial burden of Charles' empire?

Castile was the wealthiest part of Charles' inheritance and the one that had the greatest potential for increasing extraordinary revenues. The Netherlands was a great centre of trade and industry but Charles' demands for money left it exhausted by the 1540s, and the local Estates there and the States General jealously guarded their rights to grant extra taxes by not granting them. The tax revolt in Ghent in 1539 was a clear indication that the Netherlands would not continue to increase its contribution.

KEY THEME

The extent of Spanish debt
One estimate by historian Ramon Carande puts total borrowing during the reign at close to 30 million *ducats* and interest payments on the loans at 10 million *ducats*. When ordinary revenue from Spain was about 1 million *ducats*, one can see that the interest payments alone consumed ten years' income.

Naples was a relatively poor part of Italy and Aragon was in economic decline and protected by the rights of its *Cortes*. Thus Castile and its empire in America came to pay an increasing proportion of Charles' income and it was against future Castilian revenues that Charles borrowed from the bankers.

Ordinary revenue

In Castile most of the ordinary revenue came from the *alcabala* (sales tax), usually rated at 10 per cent. This indirect tax at least applied to all Spaniards but during a period of inflation the yield, in real terms, probably dropped during the reign. At the *Cortes* of Madrid in 1534, Charles granted the principal of **encabezamiento**. By 1550, *encabezamiento* brought in about 70 per cent of ordinary Castilian revenue.

Though officially exempt from taxation, the clergy of Spain were more heavily taxed than many laymen. They paid:

- the *tercias reales* (one-third of tithes, granted to the Crown)
- the *subsidio*
- the *cruzada* tax, paid by clergy and laity, which brought in on average about 150,000 *ducats* a year.

In 1523, the Pope boosted Charles' income from the Church still further when he confirmed that the property and revenue of the three great Military Orders (Santiago, Alcantara and Calatrava) belonged to the Crown. The obliging Pope was Adrian VI, Charles' old tutor!

Extraordinary revenue

For extraordinary revenue, Charles had recourse to the *Cortes* of Castile, which was not usually in a position to refuse, provided the taxes did not touch the nobility. In 1523, the *Cortes* of Valladolid voted a **servicio** of 400,000 *ducats*. Such votes increased in value considerably as the reign went on. In the 1520s, they raised about 130,000 *ducats* a year. The equivalent figure for the 1550s was nearer to 400,000 *ducats* a year.

As this tax was a direct tax, it meant that the nobility

(about 10 per cent of the population who claimed or had been granted *hidalgo* status) were exempt. So as the *alcabala* (an indirect tax) decreased in value, it meant that the increasing burden of direct taxes was being paid by those who possessed less wealth. This pattern would continue into Philip's reign and have serious economic consequences.

Though the increasing yield from the *servicio* was a major reason for Castile's importance as the key source of imperial revenue, it was soon to be dwarfed by the increasing revenue from the New World. Revenue was raised there via:

- taxes
- the sale of monopolies on trade and production
- **tribute from the Indians**
- (most importantly) the **royal fifth**.

Across Charles' reign, income from these sources averaged out at 270,000 *ducats* a year, which represented about 20 per cent of total ordinary revenue, derived from Spanish sources. It was a handy shot in the arm, and it increased substantially as the reign went on and economic activity in the New World increased.

Spanish economic problems

On the surface, the reign of Charles was a period of economic boom and prosperity. The population was rising, especially in the towns, and trade with the New World and the import of bullion gave the impression of serious economic progress. Seville's population tripled between 1534 and 1561. Rising population and the import of bullion both led to **inflation** throughout the reign, which was unprecedented. In Andalusia (in the south), the price of wheat more than doubled between 1511 and 1559, while the price of oil tripled in the same period.

- For landowners, merchants and traders, this was indeed a boom period as their incomes probably outpaced inflation.
- However, in the lower orders of society, among the

Increasing average income from the New World (showing yearly figures)

1536–40	324,000 *ducats*
1546–50	382,000 *ducats*
1551–5	870,000 *ducats*

KEY TERMS

Tribute from the Indians
Refers to taxes and other payments collected from the native Indians by the *conquistadors* and Spanish landlords.

Royal fifth A 20 per cent tax on all precious metals (mainly gold and silver) mined in the New World.

Inflation is when there is an increase in the price of goods. This can result in the decline in the purchasing value of money.

landless labourers and those employed seasonally on the land, inflation often spelt ruin and poverty. There were many accounts of **increasing numbers of poor** and vagrants on the streets of the towns.

Above the poor and indigent was a large class of better-off individuals who, as we have seen, were hit not only by rising prices but also by Charles' increasingly heavy tax demands. These people did not share in Spanish prosperity. Small manufacturers complained not only of rising prices, but also of the cheap foreign imports coming into Spain encouraged by the amount of precious metal in circulation.

During Charles' reign, then, Spain was caught in a classic economic trap where the burdens of empire and new economic opportunities led to a growing divide between the few who profited greatly and the many who did not profit at all and who were, in fact, worse off than before.

SUCCESS AND FAILURE IN THE EXPLOITATION OF THE NEW WORLD

As has been seen, the new lands in America contributed importantly to Charles' finances and also to the economic problems that beset Spain by mid-century.

The *conquistadors*
The growth of the Spanish empire can be credited to three men in particular:

- Christopher Columbus
- Hernando Cortés
- Francisco Pizarro.

Christopher Columbus (1451–1506). Columbus was given material backing by Ferdinand and Isabella in 1492, at the second time of asking. He proposed to set out from Spain with three ships in order to reach the Spice Islands and India by sailing west from Europe rather than east. At that time, of course, no European was aware of the existence of the American continent.

Against all expectations, Columbus brought back news of new lands, which, for a long time, were thought to be close to China and India. The Spanish colony he founded on the island of **Hispaniola** had a shaky start. Despite that, the town of San Domingo which Columbus founded would be the capital of the Spanish Indies for the next 50 years.

Altogether, Ferdinand and Isabella funded three expeditions for Columbus. But it was not until the third one in 1498 that he discovered the coast of South America itself when he found the Orinoco River flowing into the sea. The volume of fresh water it produced indicated that it flowed through a mighty continent. However, problems among the colonists in Hispaniola (who wanted grants of lands) and the Indians there led to Columbus' disgrace. He was brought home in irons. Despite this unfortunate end to his career, he must receive great credit for doggedly carrying out the initial exploration and following up an idea that most people thought was insane.

Hernando Cortés (1485–1547). Cortés was responsible, almost single-handedly, for the Spanish conquest of Central America. He was appointed as commander of a Spanish expedition to the mainland fitted out by the governor of Cuba, Diego Velázquez, in 1519. Once he landed with his 600 volunteers and adventurers, Cortés repudiated Velázquez' authority and set about the task of conquering an independent kingdom. Having landed, he burnt his boats (literally!) and began to gather information about the great Aztec empire, which lay inland.

One of the main reasons for Cortés' success was his ability to gain allies against the Aztecs among other Indian tribes. These allies were vital when his peaceful entry into the Aztec capital, Tenochtitlan, resulted in the Spaniards being driven out by force. With the help of his allies the city was later besieged and the Aztecs surrendered in 1521.

Spanish success was based on Cortés' bravery, leadership and organisation, and also on the spread of smallpox. The disease, unknown in America, was brought to the city by the Spaniards themselves and it probably killed thousands

Hispaniola In the Caribbean, now known as the island of Haiti.

Hernando Cortés.

of Aztecs. In this way it was a warning of what was to come. The Indians of Central and South America would be massacred by Spanish diseases.

Cortés called his great land conquest New Spain and returned to his homeland in 1529 when, bearing many gifts, he met King Charles to justify his actions. In his conquests Cortés, unlike Columbus, had acted on his own initiative, not by royal command. As a result the king did not trust him.

- In 1527, the Spanish government had established an *Audiencia* (law court) in New Spain and a civil government to keep an eye on Cortés.
- In 1535, a nobleman, Antonio de Mendoza, was appointed as viceroy. He successfully tamed Cortés and prevented him from leading any further expeditions.

Thwarted in New Spain, Cortés retired to Old Spain in 1539, disillusioned and angry. Charles' government in Castile had shown that the *conquistadors* would not be allowed to run Spain's new empire. That would be the job of nobles and officials sent out from Spain. They, not the wild adventurers, would give the empire real permanence.

Francisco Pizarro (1476–1541). Pizarro conquered the Inca people of Peru and added another large chunk to the Spanish seaborne empire. Arriving in Peru from Panama in 1530 with just 180 men and 27 horses, he surprised even himself by the magnitude of his conquest. He took advantage of civil war among the native **Incas** to launch a surprise attack (while pretending to negotiate) against the reigning Inca, Atahualpa, capturing and killing him and wiping out most of his men. The Incas never recovered from this body blow.

- In 1533, Pizarro stormed and **sacked** their capital Cuzco.
- In 1535, he founded a more suitable capital near the coast at Lima.
- Despite a major Indian rising in 1537, the main worry for the Spaniards was that they might lose the territory through war among themselves.

KEY PEOPLE

The Incas In the 1530s, the Inca empire covered most of modern-day Peru, Bolivia and Equador as well as parts of Argentina. The Inca civilisation was highly advanced. Despite this, the Incas did not develop writing as a form of communication.

KEY TERM

Sack To plunder and destroy.

- Pizarro had his old friend Diego de Almagro strangled in 1538.
- Pizarro himself was subsequently murdered by Almagro's friends in 1541.

Once again the Spaniards had succeeded because they were rather stronger and more ruthless than their opponents. Spain would struggle to keep control of this empire, not because of the opposition of the native Indians for the most part but rather because of the unruly behaviour of the Spanish settlers.

REASONS FOR EXPLORATION AND DISCOVERY

Rivalry between Spain and Portugal

This was a major reason for Ferdinand and Isabella's decision to finance Columbus' expedition in 1492. After all, Columbus thought he was offering a quicker route to India and the Spice Islands, which were already being exploited by the Portuguese. Indeed, the Portuguese flourished as explorers throughout the century.

- Making use of the new fifteenth-century **carrack** with its small foremast and lanteen sail at the rear, together with an improved compass and astrolabe (a navigation instrument), the Portuguese took up exploration with enthusiasm, well ahead of Spain, which was still too concerned with internal problems.
- With its long Atlantic seaboard, Portugal had been quick to sponsor expeditions and exploit the latest technology to explore and trade with new lands.
- At the time of **Prince Henry the Navigator**, the Portuguese sailed southwards exploring the West African coast. The Portuguese discovered the Azores and Cape Verde Islands in 1455. In 1452, the Pope authorised them to enslave the natives of newly discovered territories.
- A real turning point was **Bartholomew Diaz'** voyage in 1486 when he rounded the southern tip of Africa (the Cape of Good Hope). This brought fresh impetus to the long-held Portuguese dream of reaching India by sea. Notably, Diaz' voyage with three ships was funded by the King of Portugal.

Vasco da Gama (c. 1469–1524) A Portuguese explorer. In 1497, he sailed from Lisbon and reached Calicut in India by 1498. On his return he was appointed Admiral of the Indian Ocean. He later returned to India and Africa and helped to establish Portuguese trade with these areas.

Monopoly The Venetian merchants were the only merchants who had access to certain spices from the Far East. In this way they could demand high prices from consumers.

- The success of Diaz' voyage was followed up in 1498 when Portuguese explorer **Vasco da Gama** sailed up the East African coast, crossed the Arabian Sea (guided by an Indian pilot) and landed at Calicut in southern India. He was the first European to land in India since Roman times. Although only one ship of the original four made it back to Lisbon, it was laden with spices, jewels, silks, furs, gold and silver. By 1501, the Portuguese were bringing back valuable spices to Europe and undercutting the Venetian **monopoly** on this trade.

Spanish support for Columbus

Such great success for the Portuguese clearly influenced the Spanish decision to back Columbus. If their lesser neighbour could achieve such feats, then surely Spain could do even better.

- Columbus was not offering to discover America (since no European knew of its existence). His argument to the Catholic Kings was that he would reach India by sailing westwards and get there before the Portuguese, who at that stage had only recently rounded the Cape of Good Hope.
- The Spanish decision to back Columbus also had something to do with the ending of the Granada campaign in 1492. This released Isabella from the great project that had dominated her reign and allowed her to contemplate the expansion of Spain beyond the new frontiers.
- For Isabella, exploration had a lot to do with spreading Christianity beyond Europe and thus it represented a continuation of the crusading spirit of the *Reconquista*. In this case, those being converted would not be Muslims but innocent natives who would thus be given a chance of salvation. The stern, militant and evangelical Catholicism of late fifteenth-century Spain was thus carried over to New Spain across the Atlantic.
- It may be that Isabella also had ideas about Spain establishing a truly global status by acquiring a great overseas empire, which would bring wealth and an imperial title. Spain would then be seen, as some Spanish intellectuals had prophesied, as the greatest power on Earth.

Conquistadors, colonists and friars

Conquistadors. While the Spanish government might be motivated by rivalry and lofty religious idealism, most of the *conquistadors* who carried out the exploration were motivated by other considerations.

- The **lure of wealth** and the hope of finding **El Dorado** certainly inspired many of the early *conquistadors*. These men were not nobles but often the dispossessed or the fighting men whose great conflict against the Moors in Spain had come to an end. Most of them came from Andalusia and were drawn to the capital Seville, which soon became established as the port of departure for the new lands. As well as gold and silver, the *conquistadors* hoped to grow wealthy through the acquisition of great estates of land and large numbers of slave labourers.
- Many *conquistadors* had also been inspired by the great deeds of Spaniards like Cortés and Pizarro, who would overcome incredible odds and dangers to overthrow whole civilisations with just a small band of loyal supporters. It was this search for fame and glory allied to the sense of adventure of life lived on the frontiers of the known world that motivated the *conquistadors*. Francisco de Jerez, *conquistador* of Peru, spoke for many when he asked: 'When in ancient or modern times have there been such great enterprises of so few against so many … to conquer the unseen and the unknown?'
- Some of the more literate among the *conquistadors* were inspired by the romances of chivalry they had read, most notably the *Amadis of Gaul* of 1508. Bernal Diaz de Castillo had read it. 'It seemed,' he wrote later about Mexico, 'like the enchanted things told of in the book of Amadis, and some of our soldiers wondered if it was all a dream.'

Settlers and colonists. The settlers and colonists from Spain who followed in the wake of the *conquistadors* came mainly from the region of Andalusia. They were in search of land, slaves and gold. One contemporary estimate for the number of Spanish colonists claims that by the end of Charles' reign, around 150,000 made the perilous journey across the Atlantic in search of a new life. The risks involved suggest that many were escaping from higher

KEY THEME

Lure of wealth One *conquistador*, Bernal Diaz de Castillo, who documented Spanish expansion in Mexico in his book *The Conquest of New Spain*, admitted that they came, 'to serve God and His Majesty … and also to get rich'. Cortés who later conquered Mexico was even more direct. 'I came here,' he exclaimed when he arrived in Hispaniola in 1504, 'to get gold not to till the soil like a peasant.' Bernal Diaz was a *conquistador* and devoted follower of Cortés.

KEY PLACE

El Dorado The fabled city of gold.

taxes and the rising tide of poverty in Spain, especially urban poverty. Nearly half of the emigrants came from just 30 Spanish cities. As well as economic considerations, many colonists sought freedom and independence from powerful landlords and local government.

Friars. The friars who came were largely in the business of saving souls for God.

KEY PEOPLE

The Dominicans An order of friars who followed the rule of St Dominic. They became the upholders of Catholic orthodoxy, opposing the Augustinian Protestant leader Martin Luther and staffing both Roman and Spanish Inquisitions.

The Franciscans An order of friars who followed the rule of St Francis of Assisi. They wore brown habits.

The Jesuits The Society of Jesus, founded by a Spaniard, Ignatius Loyola, in 1534. It was organised along military lines and Jesuits offered devoted service to the Pope.

• The **Dominicans** first arrived in Hispaniola in 1510.
• The **Franciscans** arrived in Mexico in 1524.
• They were followed later by the **Jesuits**.

The mission of these friars was to convert what they saw as noble and virtuous savages to Christianity. They believed that they could create a true Christian commonwealth in the New World as it was untouched by the corruption of the Old. The native Indians, one Franciscan wrote, were 'of such simplicity and purity of soul that they do not know how to sin'. However, the attempts to create communities of natives living as free Christians were doomed to failure, since the colonists and *conquistadors* were determined to enslave them. In their eyes, these were not noble savages but brute beasts who had to be tamed and made to work for the white man.

Despite long and loud protests from the monks, friars and New World bishops, the colonists largely got their way as the Spanish government, which was sympathetic to the natives, was too far away to make a difference and its colonial government not strong enough to enforce its will.

Advantages of empire
The conquest of the New World did bring great benefits to Spain and especially to the ruling classes.

• The discovery of gold and more especially silver brought Spain and its king great riches that helped to make it the wealthiest country in Europe.
• The New World acted as a kind of safety valve for Spain, somewhere for the restless spirits and the poor to go. As the *Reconquista* came to an end in Spain, those who wished to continue the campaign could do so outside Spain.

- The New World gave the Spanish Church an enormous sense of mission, spreading Christianity to areas where God's message had never been heard before.
- The astonishingly quick and relatively easy conquest of large areas of territory underpinned Spanish confidence in their calling as God's chosen nation. As the rest of Europe became divided by heresy and civil war, the expansion of Spain and its continuing religious uniformity marked it out as the greatest power on earth.
- While Charles' personal empire in Europe divided Spaniards in terms of its desirability and cost, the empire in the New World united Spaniards behind a vision of imperial destiny and civilising mission.

Disadvantages of empire

- The Spanish conquest resulted in the **deaths of millions of Native Americans**, in what really amounted to genocide. Many were killed by the *conquistadors* or murdered and maimed by the cruelty of Spanish landlords. Most were probably killed by European diseases, against which they had no resistance.
- The economy of the empire was based on **slave labour** – first of the native Indians, then of slaves imported from Africa.
- The landscape and ecosystem was changed dramatically as Spaniards introduced new animals (cattle, sheep and horses) and new crops (wheat, vines and olives). The introduction of the animals, particularly cattle, helped to create famine among the Indians, as they lost their lands to great cattle ranches.
- The empire underlined the limited power of the Spanish government. Most of the great conquests were the result of the actions of *conquistadors* acting independently of Spanish government. The settlers and colonists who came after them also managed to defy the wishes of that government. In 1542 Charles passed the famous New Laws abolishing the *encomienda* system and Indian slavery. In 1550, Charles decreed that there should be no further expansion of the Spanish empire in America. Both proclamations proved to be dead letters.
- Spain's conquest and enslavement of the Indians sparked off a serious debate at the highest levels about the morality of what was being done.

KEY CONCEPTS

Deaths of millions of Native Americans The Mexican Indians were reduced from 25 million in 1520 to perhaps 3 million by the end of Charles' reign. In Peru the figures are something like 9 million in 1530 reduced to 600,000 by 1620.

Slave labour By the end of Charles' reign there were more African slaves than whites in Hispaniola, Mexico City, Lima and most areas of Spanish America.

KEY TERM

Encomienda A system of tributary labour established in South America to provide *conquistadors* and settlers with an adequate and cheap supply of labour. It was first used by some Spaniards to control the Moors and later transplanted to the New World.

- The importing of large quantities of silver from America helped to spark off unprecedented and long-lasting levels of inflation in Spain. Economically, Spain became more divided between the few who were wealthy and the many who were poor.

THE BURDENS OF CHARLES' FOREIGN POLICY

The financial burden of Spain's imperialism in the New World were, in some ways, matched by what might be called its European imperialism under Charles I. As a result of his accession, Spain found itself funding a foreign policy that had little in common with the foreign policy concerns of its previous Spanish monarchs. To be fair to Charles, he had no intention of acquiring further territory in Europe in order to dominate the continent, but his possessions did bring with them responsibilities to:

- defend his territories against heresy and the French
- defend Christendom against Islam.

Charles and France

While Aragonese foreign policy had often been anti-French, the causes of that hostility had largely disappeared by the time of Charles' accession in 1516. Ferdinand's guile and diplomacy had secured the counties of Cerdagne and Roussillon and the disputed kingdom of Navarre.

1521. The French King Francis I did launch an attack on Navarre and captured Pamplona, but was soon driven out. The attack was really a diversionary attack to draw Charles away from northern Italy and to take advantage of internal unrest in Spain. Otherwise, the boundary between France and Spain along the **Pyrenees** seemed largely acceptable to both sides. At the same time the wars against France over the kingdom of Naples were largely at an end with Spanish control of the kingdom firmly established by 1516.

1528–9. The French did launch one final expedition against Naples in 1528, but this was defeated at the Battle of Landriano in 1529.

Apart from this incident, Charles' long wars against France

KEY PLACE

Pyrenees A mountain range dividing France from Spain.

had little to do with Spanish interests. From 1516 to 1559 the wars between Charles and successive French monarchs derived mainly from French fears about Habsburg encirclement. After all, Charles controlled not only a newly powerful Spain and Naples (south-west and south-east of France respectively) but also the Low Countries and the Holy Roman empire, which were situated on France's eastern border.

- In the 1520s, the fighting was mainly confined to Italy but revolved around ownership of Milan in the north, not Naples in the south. Charles claimed Milan as an imperial fief, and as the lynchpin to hold together the two halves of his great inheritance, not as a Spanish territory.
- Though successful in Italy by 1529 (the Peace of Cambrai), Charles was at war with France again 1536–8 over Italy, 1542–4 over the border between France and the Netherlands, and from 1552 until Charles' death and beyond, when the main area of contention was France's support for the Lutheran princes in Germany and its attempt to take German cities close to the French border.

For the most part, therefore, the wars against France had much to do with Charles' dynastic and family concerns and very little, directly, to do with Spain.

Charles and heresy

One of Charles' principal aims during his reign was to put an end to the Protestant Reformation. This had started in Germany and Switzerland around the time that Charles became Holy Roman Emperor.

The Reformation was initially led by **Martin Luther** (a monk) in Saxony and Huldrich Zwingli (a priest) in the Swiss city of Zurich. Aided by the support of some princes and city councils, the Protestants (as they were called) gradually became established in parts of northern Germany and threatened Charles' possessions in the Netherlands. Charles devoted much energy to this intractable problem, hoping at first for a negotiated settlement or compromise before eventually deciding on war. Although he defeated

KEY PERSON

Martin Luther (1483–1546) One of the central figures of the Reformation. Born in Eisleben, he became an Augustinian monk in 1507. As a loyal member of the Catholic Church, he visited Rome in 1510. There he witnessed the selling of indulgences – pieces of parchment giving its owner a reduced time in purgatory. Luther objected to the sale of indulgences and, in 1517, nailed his written objections – the Ninety-Five Theses – to the door of the castle church in Wittenberg. This action is seen as the beginning of the European Reformation.

KEY TERMS

League of Schmalkalden
In 1531 a group of German Protestant princes met in Schmalkalden in central Germany to form a league against the aggression of Charles. Led by Philip of Hesse, they represented a clear departure from tradition. Now there was a significant force in Germany prepared to act in defence of their interests and against Charles and the Catholic Church.

The Ottomans The great Muslim empire led by the great Sultan centred on Constantinople, dominating the eastern Mediterranean seaboard. Technically, the Ottomans was the name of the ruling tribe of the empire. During Charles' reign the Ottomans were led by Suleiman the Magnificent, who ruled from 1520 to 1566.

the German Protestant **League of Schmalkalden** at Muhlberg in Saxony in 1547, he was soon faced with revolt in Germany as his allies turned against him. He then had to give in to Lutheran demands for official recognition of their religion at the Peace of Augsburg in 1555.

As Spain remained untouched by the Reformation, it is easy to argue that Charles' determination to destroy heresy in Germany was not in Spain's interests. This view, though, tends to miss the point.

- Spain, as we have seen, was the most deeply and militantly Catholic country in Europe in the late fifteenth and early sixteenth centuries. This was a time of *Reconquista*, the conquest of the New World and the attack on the Jews.
- Furthermore, Spain was always deeply worried that heresy of some sort might spread to its shores.

In this way Charles' crusade against the heretics won approval from the Spanish Church and from many of the nobles and *hidalgos* who fought in his numerous campaigns in Europe. Apart from the threat to Christendom posed by the heretics, campaigning in Germany and the Low Countries confirmed Spain's great power status. Protected by the Pyrenees, it had always been easy for the Spanish to concern themselves exclusively with the affairs of their peninsula. In this way the Renaissance, that great intellectual movement emanating from Italy and spreading to northern Europe, had largely passed Spain by. The wars of Charles I, no less than the acquisition of empire in the New World, opened Spain up to new ideas and cultures and made it the greatest power in Europe.

Charles and the Turks

Even more clearly approved of by the Spanish people were Charles' wars against the Infidel. He fought the Turks on two main fronts in central and eastern Europe as they advanced along the River Danube, and in the eastern and southern Mediterranean where the **Ottomans'** Arab allies sought to destroy Spanish outposts in North Africa set up by Ferdinand and Isabella.

Central Europe. In central Europe the task of repelling the Turks, or at least stemming their advance, was in the hands of Charles' brother Ferdinand. Although the Turks briefly laid siege to the Austrian capital Vienna in 1529, this proved to be the furthest point of their advance westwards. Spanish forces played a minor role in this struggle but the Castilian *Cortes* pointedly refused to vote funds for this war in 1527.

The Mediterranean. Charles' concerns with the safety of Austria left him less time and energy to take on the forces of Islam in the Mediterranean. It was here that Spanish interests were more directly at stake. In particular there was anger at Arab raids on the coast of Valencia in 1529 and the ever-present fear that the Arabs, encouraged by their Turkish allies, might stir up the *Moriscos* in that province. This was one of the reasons why Charles demanded that the Moors convert to Christianity or leave Spain in 1525. In this area Spain was hampered by lack of a Mediterranean fleet until, in 1528, the Genoese mercenary admiral Andrea Doria brought his fleet over to the Emperor. Given all Charles' other commitments, it was not until the 1530s that he did anything decisive in the Mediterranean.

Tunis. In 1535, he organised a great naval expedition, which captured Tunis and expelled the Ottoman admiral Barbarossa. Doria played his part along with some 10,000 Spanish troops in this important victory. However, this was to be the high point of Charles' Mediterranean policy.

Battle of Prevesa. In 1538, his naval forces fought a half-hearted and fruitless naval battle (Prevesa) against Barbarossa in the eastern Mediterranean but in 1541 disaster struck when the Imperial fleet was destroyed by a storm before it could take Algiers.

North African coast. Tripoli was lost in 1551, Penon de Velez three years later and Bougie in 1555. By the end of the reign, Spain had only four outposts left on the North African coast.

KEY PERSON

Barbarossa The Turkish corsair Khayr ad-Din (*c.* 1483–1546). He seized Algiers from Spain in 1518 and placed it under Turkish rule. From 1533 to 1544 he was admiral of the Ottoman fleet, twice defeating the Imperial admiral Andrea Doria.

Conclusion

Overall Charles' foreign policy brought Spain little joy. This was not so much because his foreign policy did not coincide with Spanish interests or aspirations but because it was largely unsuccessful. While northern Italy was captured, France remained a serious menace, the Reformation had become established and the Christians were in retreat in the Mediterranean. However, Spain by now appreciated that empire and great power status came with a heavy price tag. Despite calamities ahead, it was a price that Spain's future rulers never flinched from paying.

SUMMARY QUESTIONS

1 To what extent did Spanish government become more effective during the reign of Charles I?

2 How and why did Spain acquire an overseas empire in the period 1516–56?

3 To what extent, if at all, did Spain benefit from the rule of Charles I?

CHAPTER 3

1556–98: Did successes outweigh failures in the reign of Philip II?

KEY POINTS

- Unlike his father (Charles I), Philip II was Spanish born and bred. He never left Spain after 1559, and all his territories outside the Iberian peninsula now found themselves governed by a Spanish king.
- In 1580, he took control of Portugal. Thus, for the first time, the whole of the peninsula was ruled by one monarch.
- Philip II's great strength as a ruler was as a bureaucrat. He ruled Spain's empire from Castile, unlike his father who travelled throughout his European dominions.
- Philip II was a zealous Catholic who devoted his life to the defence of the faith. This meant a lot of warfare undertaken against Protestants in France, England and, most significantly, in the Spanish Low Countries. It also meant war against the Turks in the Mediterranean and more persecution of the Moorish people still living in Spain leading to a two-year revolt in Granada. The Spanish Church and the Inquisition were used to stamp out new ideas leading to intellectual sterility.
- Persistent warfare brought great triumphs but also huge costs. The Spanish economy was weakened and royal debts increased to the point of bankruptcy on several occasions.

PHILIP II: HIS INHERITANCE, CHARACTER AND FAMILY

Inheritance of Philip II

The burdens of his empire had proved too great for Charles I and, as early as 1530, he had determined that his son Philip should not be asked to inherit all of it. This division of the empire was confirmed when Charles abdicated in 1556.

- Spain, together with its American empire, the Low Countries and Italy, went to Philip.
- Germany and Austria went to Charles' younger brother Ferdinand.

At the same time, Philip would be beguiled by the mirage of Spain's imperial worth into believing that he could shape the future of Europe as a whole. He attempted to hold back the advance of **Protestantism** in the north, while defeating the great Ottoman empire in the east. Such was the dream of empire and Spanish power that Philip inherited from his father. Philip's tragedy was that while he adopted the dreams of empire, he never considered the limitations on Spanish imperialism, which his father's reign and disillusioned abdication had so clearly demonstrated.

Character of Philip II
Philip's character and method of government help to explain his failings and ultimate failure.

- Known as *Il Prudente* (the Thoughtful King), he was a very serious-minded monarch who devoted himself body and soul, night and day, to the serious business of government.
- He ruled Spain from his desk, and spent his life reading papers and reports of all kinds. His obsessive desire to make the right decisions meant that he always wanted more information before making decisions and so decisions were always delayed.
- He could not be forced into making up his mind by more decisive Councillors, since he shunned strong men and usually consulted with the various Councils and Councillors in writing rather than face to face.
- Philip's commitment to the idea of the dignity of kingship, reinforced by a natural shyness, meant that he remained aloof from those around him and spoke only in a whisper – he was **a man of modesty**. These characteristics also meant that he was not a man to command events. Instead he reacted to them (usually slowly) and was a man who lacked political vision.
- His principle aim of defending the Catholic faith against Islam and Protestantism was pursued relentlessly and continuously, even when it was clear that this policy would ruin Spain.

KEY TERM

Protestantism A collective word used to describe all those who rejected papal authority and put forward doctrines at odds with official Catholic theology.

KEY THEME

A man of modesty Philip II was a humble, quiet, thoughtful and pious individual devoted to his family and his gardens. When he built a great new palace, El Escorial near Madrid, it was without the ostentation of its French counterparts. One of its main functions was to act as a resting place for his beloved father, Charles I.

Family life

Philip's seriousness was enhanced by domestic tragedy, especially among his close family.

His first wife. Philip's first wife, Maria of Portugal, died in childbirth two years after their wedding.

His first son. Not only was Philip and Maria's son, **Don Carlos**, physically repulsive with a weak and feeble body supporting an overgrown and ugly head, but also he was mentally unstable. Plans for the prince's marriage were discussed but then quickly dropped. So Philip was faced with the eventual prospect of handing over his great empire to someone totally unsuited for the job. In 1566 and 1567, Don Carlos plotted against his father and attempted to escape to the Low Countries. Sadly for him, the men he asked to help him informed Philip. In 1568, Don Carlos was put into prison, where he died a few months later. The circumstances of his death remain unknown but it was widely rumoured that the king had given the order for his only son to be put to death.

His second wife. Philip's second wife, Queen Mary of England died in 1558, just four years after their marriage.

His third wife. Further tragedy followed for Philip when, a few months after the mysterious death of Don Carlos, his third wife, Elizabeth de Valois (whom he loved dearly), died in her mid-20s. Although she had given him no sons, she did produce two daughters for whom **Philip** had **great affection**. So, by the age of 41, Philip had no son and had been a widower three times.

His fourth wife. Three sons born to Philip's fourth wife, Anne of Austria, died in infancy. Luckily the fourth, Philip, survived to succeed his father in due course.

GOVERNMENT AND FACTION

Impact of faction fighting

Like all serious-minded monarchs, especially those with empires to run, Philip II had a large number of advisers

Don Carlos Philip II's first son was a difficult person. He was prone to outbursts of uncontrolled rage that seemed to grow worse as his father refused to give him the responsibility he craved. Don Carlos was the victim of Habsburg inbreeding. His parents were cousins and two of his great-grandmothers were the same person, Joanna the Mad!

Philip's great affection
The king's affection for his two daughters was clear and well attested in his letters. He was genuinely kind, considerate and concerned for their well-being. He kept them with him as long as he was able. When marriage eventually took them away from him, he was distraught.

who jostled for position, power and rewards. The main rivals in the first part of Philip's reign were:

- **Ruy Gómez de Silva**, the Prince of Eboli
- Fernando de Alvarez de Toledo, third Duke of Alva (see page 51).

Around these men groups formed that saw themselves as rivals and sought to influence the king. Arguments were largely confined to court. However, in 1578 the murder of Juan de Escobeldo in Madrid suggested that **faction fighting** had turned ugly.

The assassins were probably hired by **Antonio Pérez**, the king's chief secretary, who was, since the death of Eboli in 1573, head of the anti-Alva faction. Escobeldo had claimed that Pérez was betraying state secrets and was having an affair with the forceful, aristocratic and one-eyed widow of Eboli. He also knew that Pérez had persuaded Philip unfairly that his governor in the Low Countries, **Don John of Austria**, was planning to stir up trouble between England and Spain in the hope of leading an invasion of England later on. However, Escobeldo's murder represented conflict within one faction, not conflict between the two main groups. Escobeldo had been brought to prominence by Pérez himself, not Alva, and his crime was that he was threatening to expose Pérez' double-dealing to the king.

Alva's disgrace

In 1579, Alva was placed under house arrest for allowing his son to marry without the king's permission. In reality, Alva's influence had been waning since being sent to the Netherlands in 1567. Once away from Madrid, he struggled to contact Philip directly. The situation was made worse by the duke's apparent failure to crush the Dutch rebels, which resulted in his recall in disgrace in 1573. He would be recalled briefly to oversee the invasion of Portugal in 1580, but his political influence over the king was at an end.

Alva's disgrace did not mean victory for Pérez and his group. Philip discovered that Pérez had seriously misrepresented the actions of Don John of Austria and had been involved in Escobeldo's murder. In 1579, he was arrested and replaced by **Cardinal Granvelle**. For good measure, the Princess of Eboli was imprisoned in her own palace for the rest of her life. The destruction of Pérez reinforced Philip's distrust of those around him but it also shows that he would not be ruled by a smooth-talking (but disreputable) favourite.

Junta de Noche

Pérez' replacement, Granvelle, lost influence in his turn by 1585 to a new group of Councillors drawn up in a committee known as the *Junta de Noche*. This group was made up of experienced administrators drawn mainly from the ranks of the lower nobility. Moura, Juan de Idiáquez, Vázquez and, after his death, Idiáquez' cousin Martin met regularly and had overall control of the advice being offered to Philip. While this meant that aristocratic faction fighting had little impact on government, the aristocrats complained that the king was being advised by men with **insufficient experience** of affairs. Although it is true that these men had little experience outside Spain, it is hard to see how they could have acted differently, since, even in the 1590s, Philip continued to make all the decisions.

THE *MORISCO* PROBLEM

The *Moriscos* in the east

The conquest of Granada by Ferdinand and Isabella had created more problems than it solved, especially when Christian promises to respect the Moors' religion and customs turned into persecution and forcible conversion. Under Charles I, the policy of attempting to assimilate the Moors into Spanish society by means of forcible conversion gathered pace.

- In 1525, Charles decreed that forcible conversions during the Germania Revolt and at other times were valid and that the remaining Moors had to convert or leave Spain.
- In Valencia and Aragon, where there were still large and indeed growing numbers of *Moriscos* (converted Moors), the problems were less severe than in Granada. In these

---

An anonymous portrait of the Princess of Eboli.

areas, where the *Moriscos* were mainly tenant farmers, they largely received **protection from their landlords**.

- In 1526, however, the *Morisco* leaders, in return for a hefty sweetener of 40,000 *ducats*, agreed to baptism on the basis that they would not be persecuted by the hated Inquisition for 40 years.
- In 1528, the Aragonese *Cortes* successfully petitioned Charles to agree that the Inquisition should not be allowed to persecute the *Moriscos* until they had been officially instructed in the Catholic faith, a process that was always likely to take a long time.
- Later on, the Aragonese complained long and loudly at the Inquisition's attempts to confiscate the Moorish land. All of this demonstrated that the *Moriscos* in eastern Spain enjoyed protection from the ruling classes who resented the Inquisition and opposed persecution of the Moors, seeing this as Castilian infringements on their *fueros*.

This was seen again under Philip II when attempts to disarm the *Moriscos* by royal edict in 1563 were resisted by landowners who needed their tenants as armed retainers in their local conflicts. Although they did have powerful supporters, the *Moriscos* in the east were certainly unpopular with Christian peasants and many *Moriscos* were enraged by the harsh conditions they lived under. Some certainly did act as allies of their Muslim brethren in North Africa and Constantinople, and many in the coastal regions of Valencia escaped from Spain with their aid.

Reasons for Alpujarras Revolt, 1568–70

The immediate cause of the uprising by the *Moriscos* of Granada between 1568 and 1570 was the government's imposition of still harsher restrictions on the Moorish population.

- After 1559, the government confiscated 100,000 hectares of *Morisco* land on the basis that many Moorish families could not produce proof of land ownership.
- In addition, the government seemed to connive at undermining Granada's main industry – silk production – by allowing cheap imports of silk from other areas of Spain.

- The main cause of widespread anger was the **royal decree of 1567**, which signalled the end of the old patient policy of assimilating the *Moriscos* gradually into Spanish society.
- In addition, the government was becoming aware of the high birth rate among **the *Morisco* population**, which meant that the number of potential opponents was growing not shrinking.

Behind these stringent measures lay the government's renewed anxiety about the possibility of the *Moriscos* aiding and abetting an **Islamic invasion of Spain**.

- In 1558, a force of 4000 Arabs attacked Berja.
- In 1565, Arab pirates defeated Spanish troops at Orgiba, marched inland and carried off several hundred of their co-religionists. Such daring raids on Spain were seen as part of a concerted Muslim advance across the Mediterranean.
- In 1565, the Ottomans besieged Malta. One hapless *Morisco* revealed under torture that the leaders of the *Morisco* community were sending information to the Turks and were ready to seize parts of the Valencian coast in preparation for an Islamic invasion, if Malta should fall. This fuelled government concerns about the *Moriscos* as a security threat and the enemy within. Ottoman success elsewhere in the Mediterranean only made things worse.

The government also became more paranoid in 1566/7 because of the rebellion that had begun in the Netherlands against Spanish rule. Under attack in one area, the government could believe more easily that it was under attack elsewhere. The *Moriscos* represented an even greater threat than the Dutch because they were so much closer to home and had powerful allies. The beginnings of the Dutch Revolt also meant that many of the best Spanish troops had just been sent there with the Duke of Alva. If a rebellion should break out, Spain would be especially vulnerable, so it was best to crack down now rather than be unable to crack down later.

The events of the revolt

After it became clear that Philip II was unwilling to listen

KEY TERM

The royal decree of 1567
This decree stopped the *Moriscos* from speaking, writing or reading Arabic. Instead, they were all to learn Spanish. *Morisco* dress, literature and traditional rites were likewise banned, and the decree went on to advise that children should be brought up away from their parents.

KEY THEMES

The *Morisco* population In Granada, for example, which had recently been an independent Moorish state, the concentration of *Moriscos* was higher than anywhere else in Spain. Despite expulsions, they still amounted to 54 per cent of the population.

Islamic invasion of Spain
There was no such plan for an Islamic invasion but the government was worried about links between the *Morisco* community and their co-religionists in Morocco and Turkey. The Barbary pirates were often welcomed when they raided the Spanish coast and gangs of *Morisco* bandits roamed the countryside.

to *Morisco* grievances, the frustrations of the people boiled over into outright rebellion, which started on Christmas Eve 1568.

Based at first on the silk-producing areas of the Alpujarras, rebel numbers grew to some 30,000 – in other words, most of the *Morisco* population of Granada. The government seems to have been taken by surprise and, with Alva away in the Netherlands, it was rather short of troops. At its height in 1570, the rebellion was supported by some 4000 Turks and Berbers, and there were rumours that *Moriscos* in Valencia and Aragon would rise as well.

After two years of difficult fighting in the mountains of Granada, reminiscent of the long wars of Ferdinand and Isabella, government troops under Don John of Austria put the rebellion down. Atrocities were committed on both sides.

- In 1570, all 2500 inhabitants of the town of Galera were slaughtered when Don John finally captured it.
- On the *Morisco* side were the *monfies* (brigands and fanatical fighters), who terrorised whole districts and tortured and killed every Catholic priest they could find.
- As part of the official campaign to starve the rebels of support, 3500 innocent *Moriscos* from the city of Granada were rounded up and forcibly distributed to other parts of Spain.
- The end came in 1570, when the *Morisco* leader was stabbed to death in a cave by his own supporters.

Aftermath of the revolt
The idea of spreading the *Moriscos* of Granada over the rest of Castile became Philip's main solution to the *Morisco* problem after 1570.

- Some 80,000 *Moriscos* were deported between 1569 and 1571. This process involved long columns of chained and fettered men being led away to towns and villages across Castile.
- Around 20–30 per cent did not even survive the journey.
- Those who did arrive faced hostility and discrimination from their new Christian neighbours.

- Another 3000 or so were deported in the purge of 1584–5, which still left some 10,000 living in Granada.

This brutal policy was only partially successful. **The dispersed *Moriscos*** tended to group together in certain towns where their hard work and apparent accumulation of wealth caused hostility. Granada's *Morisco* problem had now been spread across Castile to areas that had not seen racial and religious tensions before. In both Aragon and Valencia, the *Moriscos* were still very much in evidence and growing in numbers. Certainly the revolt and its aftermath helped to make Christian Spain a narrow and intolerant society. The wholesale expulsion after 1609 reflected the government's inability to solve the *Morisco* problem, but it was a problem largely created by Spain's abandonment of the old policy of *convivencia*. Just as in the New World, the development of a more Christian Spain was accompanied by the slaughter of non-Christian outsiders.

THE DUTCH REVOLT, 1566–79

As far as Philip II was concerned, the Dutch Revolt, like the Alpujarras Revolt, was a domestic Spanish issue. Armed opposition to Spanish policies in the Low Countries was no different from opposition in Castile or Italy or Aragon. Just as Philip refused to compromise with the *Moriscos*, so he never considered compromise with the Dutch rebels. In this way the Dutch Revolt developed from a minor headache into a running sore and finally to a great open wound that would helped to destroy Spain's status as a great power.

Reasons for revolt

The Spanish Netherlands was a collection of thirteen contiguous provinces (now known as Holland and Belgium), which lay in a kind of wedge shape north-east of France (the borders were never quite clear!) and west of what is now Germany. The provinces were economically important for Spain and especially important to Philip, who had an **attachment to the Spanish Netherlands** through his father, Charles I.

The dispersed *Moriscos*
One of Philip II's officials commented after the event, 'It was a great mistake to expel the *Moriscos* of Castile from the Alpujarras. It would have been better to have kept them there under guard at their own expense.'

Attachment to the Spanish Netherlands Philip II had a special attachment to these provinces. They were his father's patrimony and indeed the land of his father's birth (Charles I was born in the city of Ghent). Philip revered his father and knew that, when Charles divided up his empire, he deliberately handed these provinces to his son (Philip), not his brother (Ferdinand). This helps to explain why Philip fought so hard to keep them.

The most important reason for the revolt was Spain's reaction to the spread of heresy in the Low Countries. With its large numbers of cities and printing presses and its proximity to Germany, where Luther had begun his attack on the Catholic Church, the Low Countries were always likely to absorb Protestant ideas.

By the 1560s, several different types of Protestantism such as Lutheranism, **Calvinism** and **Anabaptism** were making headway. In 1566, there were outbreaks of **popular iconoclasm** in many areas and it was this that sparked off Philip's determination to suppress **heresy** in his Dutch domains as quickly as possible. An Inquisition was set up and, in 1567, the Duke of Alva was dispatched to the area with the best Spanish troops to crush heresy and rebellion.

- He executed two prominent Dutch noblemen (Egmont and Hoorne) and set up a special court, which he called the Council of Troubles (and which the Dutch called the Council of Blood).
- To add insult to injury, he demanded special taxes to pay for his troops and when the provincial parliament, the **States General**, refused to approve them he collected them anyway.
- Further damage was done when his troops massacred all the inhabitants of one or two towns such as Naarden to show they meant business.

Although largely successful by 1572 in crushing the revolt, Alva had done more than anyone else could to ensure widespread hatred of Spanish government. He made a reality of their fears that Spanish control of the provinces would amount to **tyranny**. Alva's uncompromising stand ensured that the revolt would continue.

By this time, Spain's brutal suppression of heresy in the Low Countries meant that it had cut across the rights and privileges of the ruling classes. Philip and Alva's policies resembled those employed in the destruction of the *Moriscos* of Granada. However, unlike Granada, the Low Countries were not a recently conquered kingdom. They were a federation of independent provinces, which, like Aragon, were jealous of their traditional rights and laws.

KEY TERMS

Calvinism Emerged from the ideas of the French Protestant reformer John Calvin (1509–64).

Anabaptism Originally a Protestant doctrine, which replaced infant baptism with adult or 'believers' baptism. Later it became a term of abuse for the more radical Protestants who seemed to threaten the political and social order.

Popular iconoclasm Outbreaks of vandalism by groups of ordinary people, usually directed towards church buildings or property.

Heresy In this context (that is, from the perspective of Philip II), the word refers to religious beliefs that denied or condemned important Catholic doctrines such as the papal headship of the Church and transubstantiation (the belief that in the Mass the bread and wine change into the actual body and blood of Christ, only the appearance of bread and wine remaining).

States General Rather like the *Cortes* in Spain, this was an assembly of people representing each of the thirteen different provinces in the Low Countries. Opposition to Philip's policies could be voiced here.

Tyranny A system of government that is both brutal and illegal.

Dutch hatred of Spanish tyranny, exemplified by Alva, now combined with Protestantism to produce a powerful nationalism, which would prove difficult to eradicate.

Course of the revolt, 1572–9

In 1572, a second revolt was sparked off by an unlikely group of Dutch pirates called the Sea Beggars. This revolt began in the provinces of Holland and Zeeland, away from the centres of Spanish power in Flanders and Brabant. Led by **William of Orange**, this revolt was not so easily crushed.

- Alva had no navy to blockade these maritime provinces and his failure to suppress the revolt led to his disgrace and recall to Spain in 1573.
- After that, Spanish efforts to end the revolt were handicapped by Philip's refusal to consider any kind of religious toleration and by mounting financial difficulties. In 1575, he announced that he was bankrupt and the next year his troops mutinied for lack of pay and sacked the city of Antwerp. Some 8000 civilians were murdered and Spain's authority reached a new low.
- For the first time all the provinces acted together and in 1576 signed the **Pacification of Ghent**, which committed them to raising troops in order to see off the Spaniards.
- By 1579, the divisions between the provinces became obvious and the united front broke up. Fearful of French intervention, the three southern provinces agreed to take back Spanish troops and to maintain Catholicism as the only true religion. Six provinces in the north, led by Holland, signed the Union of Utrecht, which bound them together to resist Spanish oppression. By 1579, Spain's fortunes in the Low Countries had recovered sufficiently for Philip to believe that all the provinces could once again be brought to heel.

THE CONQUEST OF PORTUGAL, 1580

Peaceful acquisition of Portugal

Rather more successful for Philip II was his peaceful conquest of Portugal in 1580, which meant that, for the

William of Orange (1533–84) Also known as William the Silent, he was the first great leader of the Dutch Revolt. Although lacking success early on, he managed to hold some of the rebellious provinces together against Spain and saw the need to enlist foreign support. He was assassinated in 1584.

Pacification of Ghent The year 1576 marked a turning point of the Dutch wars. For the first time all provinces of the Low Countries were united, regardless of their religious differences, to drive out the Spanish. As a result the Spanish governor Don John of Austria was unable to control the region.

KEY PEOPLE

King Sebastian of Portugal (1554–78) King of Portugal from the age of three (1557) when his grandfather, John III, died. Philip II was his uncle twice over as Sebastian's mother was Philip's sister and Philip's first wife, Maria of Portugal, was Sebastian's aunt.

Cardinal Henry (died 1580) The fourth son of King Manuel of Portugal, who died in 1521. He was younger brother to John III of Portugal and technically great uncle of King Sebastian. Cardinal Henry's mother was Maria, daughter of Ferdinand and Isabella. He was made a cardinal in1545 and acted as Regent for King Sebastian. He was king from the death of Sebastian until his own death two years later. As a cardinal he was unmarried and had no children. The Avis dynasty came to an end with his death.

KEY THEME

Philip's charm offensive
This involved a lot of Spanish silver and one of his top advisers, who happened to be Portuguese. Philip pointed out that a weak and vulnerable Portugal really needed a strong ruler. More specifically, he agreed that if he became king, Portugal would retain its traditional rights and laws and would be treated, like the Crown of Aragon, as an equal partner in a Spanish federation, not as a conquered country.

first time since the Romans, the whole of the Iberian peninsula was under the control of one ruler. The opportunity for annexation arose when the Portuguese king, **Sebastian I**, rather unwisely decide to launch a great crusade against the Arabs of North Africa. He took the nobility of Portugal with him, burnt his boats when he landed in Africa and was promptly defeated by Arab forces at Alcázarquivir on 4 August 1578. Sebastian, together with the flower of the Portuguese nobility, was killed.

- For Portugal this was a great national disaster.
- For Spain it represented a chance to take control of a colonial rival and gain a navy.

Sebastian's heir was his uncle, the aged **Cardinal Henry**, but as he had no children or brothers, his heir would be Don Antonio, the Prior of Crato, or Philip II himself. Philip's claim seemed strong as his mother was Sebastian's grandmother, but the Portuguese were traditionally hostile to the Castilians. Philip launched a **charm offensive**. Unfortunately this diplomatic pressure did not lead to him being adopted officially as Cardinal Henry's heir.

When the King Cardinal died, early in 1580, Philip decided to use the army to win over finally the reluctant Portuguese. Resistance from the Prior of Crato was minimal. Lisbon surrendered easily and the rival candidate fled the country. Once in charge, Philip was scrupulous in maintaining Portuguese customs and rights. He agreed that:

- viceroys of Portugal should always be natives
- the administration of both Portugal and its growing overseas empire should be left intact
- no attempt would be made to introduce Castilian forms of taxation.

Results of the acquisition of Portugal

For Spain the annexation of Portugal to the Spanish Crown had advantages and disadvantages.

Advantages
- On the one hand, Spain now had complete security within the Iberian peninsula with no need to worry

about a Portuguese invasion. By and large the Portuguese ruling classes accepted the situation with good grace and many felt that with Spanish patronage they would be better placed to defend Portuguese interests.

- The addition of the Portuguese colonial empire in Brazil, Africa and the East Indies was also a major bonus allowing for closer economic collaboration between the two and the end of colonial rivalry.
- Spain also gained control of a long Atlantic seaboard, a strong navy and an excellent port in Lisbon.

Disadvantages

- On the other hand, this takeover bred increased fear and hostility from those powers like France and England, which were concerned at this addition to Spanish power.
- Philip's easy annexation of Portugal strengthened his belief that Spain had been empowered by God to defeat both Islam and Protestant heresy. Having gained Portugal there seemed no limits to what Spain might achieve. The results of this overconfidence were disastrous for Spain. Just when the Dutch Revolt encouraged Philip to think that there were serious limitations on what Spain could achieve, the annexation of Portugal and the increasing flow of silver coming to Spain from the New World boosted Spain's confidence in its own power and ability, with fatal consequences.

CONTINUATION OF THE DUTCH REVOLT, 1580–98

Spain's great triumph in Portugal helped to convince Philip that the Netherlands in general and the provinces comprising the **Union of Utrecht** in particular could be recovered. Throughout much of the 1580s, this optimistic view was for once borne out by events there.

With the death from typhus of Don John of Austria in 1578, Philip appointed **Alexander Farnese, Duke of Parma** as governor. His blend of diplomacy and military brilliance meant that, during the 1580s, he won over many of the southern Catholic aristocrats to Spain's cause on the

KEY UNION

Union of Utrecht Formed in 1579. It brought together the northern provinces of the Low Countries in common cause against Spanish rule.

KEY PERSON

Alessandro (or Alexander) Farnese, Duke of Parma (1545–92) The Duke proved to be Philip's most able commander during the Dutch Revolt. He was the son of Margaret of Parma, illegitimate daughter of Charles I, who had earlier been Philip's regent in the Low Countries.

basis that the Union of Utrecht represented heresy and chaos. On the battlefield he gradually won back for Spain many of the central provinces, so that by the time of his death in 1592, Spain controlled most of the provinces, leaving the Union of Utrecht liable to attack from both the north and the south. Parma would have done even better but for Philip's decision effectively to abandon his campaigns at crucial times.

- Parma lost most of the campaigning season of 1588 as Parma's troops were preparing themselves for the invasion of England.
- Then, in 1590 and 1591, Parma was forced to use his troops in France. So when Parma died the next year, Spain had probably lost its last chance to defeat the rebels.

Thereafter the Spanish were overwhelmed once again by financial difficulties, mutinies and divided leadership. By contrast the Dutch:

Maurice of Nassau (1567–1625) Second son of William of Orange. He became the most important military commander of the Dutch rebels after his father's assassination in 1584.

- were increasingly well organised under **Maurice of Nassau** (William of Orange's son)
- enjoyed help from abroad
- enjoyed a prospering Dutch economy.

Although they could not push the Spanish out of the Low Countries altogether, they enlarged the territory under rebel control, so that by the time of Philip's death in 1598 it was already clear that the end result would be the partition (division) of the Low Countries. Spain would retain the southern provinces but would lose the northern area centred on Holland and Zeeland, the storm centres of revolt in 1572.

THE REVOLT OF ARAGON, 1591

This revolt, like the one in the Low Countries, indicated the limitations of Philip's authority within his own realms. Apart from a few brief visits, Philip neglected the three kingdoms comprising the Crown of Aragon as they were relatively poor and since their special *fueros* (rights, or laws) protected them from too much royal intervention. However, Philip II was concerned at the increasing lawlessness in the area as rural poverty, feudal aristocrats and a *Morisco* minority combined to produce outbreaks of civil unrest and a big growth in the number of bandits.

KEY TERM

Corsair A kind of pirate.

- In 1582, contravening Aragonese laws, Philip sent eighteen companies of infantry to Valencia to defend the coast from Arab **corsairs** and disaffected *Moriscos*. Five years later, bandits seized a whole shipment of silver on its way from Madrid to Barcelona, *en route* for Italy.
- In 1589, prolonged disorder in the Aragonese county of Ribagorza (close to the French border) led to another military intervention by Philip, and the county was re-incorporated into the Crown in 1591.

In 1590, Aragon witnessed the most serious dispute with the government in Madrid during Philip's reign. At the centre of the problem was Philip's former secretary, Antonio Pérez. Facing serious charges relating to the murder of Escobeldo (see page 73), Pérez fled from Court. As a Catalan, he had escaped to the city of Saragossa in Aragon, where he claimed the right to be tried by the *Justiciar* rather than the king.

- Aragonese opinion was very much on his side, as many believed that Philip, not Pérez, had given the order for Escobeldo's murder in Madrid in 1578.
- Philip responded by using the Inquisition to claim, quite falsely, that Pérez was a heretic and should be handed over to the Inquisition for trial.

Attempts to transfer Pérez to the Inquisition provoked a riot in which the *Justiciar* was wounded and Philip's viceroy, Almenara, was killed by the mob. A later attempt to transfer him provoked a similar outburst. Aragon's ruling class was determined that Pérez would be tried by Aragonese justice, not Castilian. This defiance only provoked Philip into a military response.

In October 1591, an army of 14,000 marched across the border into Aragon. Philip claimed that he respected the *fueros* of Aragon and was merely destroying those who resisted his will. The rebels in Saragossa claimed that

A portrait of Philip II in armour.

KEY PERSON

Pope Paul III (1534–49)
The first Pope to realise that the Catholic Church should put its own house in order, so that the Protestant threat could be eradicated.

KEY INSTITUTION

General Council of the Church Made up of leading Catholic churchmen from across Europe, this body could only be called together by the Pope and could act as the supreme authority in Church affairs. Popes were nervous that General Councils would claim to be superior to the Pope. This is why earlier Popes had refused to call one.

Philip's action in sending troops was unconstitutional. However, Aragonese opinion was won over by Philip's claim that his troops were merely on their way to fight France. Outside Saragossa, the rebels attracted very little support apart from two noblemen. Saragossa fell easily and Pérez fled to France. In the aftermath, Philip acted with severity.

- The new *Justiciar* was immediately beheaded without trial.
- The two noblemen who had supported rebellion died mysteriously soon after being sent to Madrid.
- Several others were publicly executed in Saragossa.
- Just for good measure, the Inquisition held a huge *auto de fé* in the city with over 80 victims, just to ensure that the royal will was clearly understood.

Later, Philip called the *Cortes* of Aragon and imposed changes, which increased his power a little. The *Justiciar* in future could be removed by the king who could now choose non-Aragonese as viceroys. These were limited gains in reality. They matched the revolt, which was really very limited indeed. No attempt was made to oppose the royal army and the rebel leaders were easily rounded up. Compared to the revolt in the Netherlands, the Revolt of Aragon of 1591 was something of a non-event.

PHILIP II AND THE CATHOLIC CHURCH

Problems facing the Catholic Church

By the time of Philip II's accession to the Spanish throne in 1556, the Catholic Church in Europe was in the process of fighting back against the spread of Protestant heresy in Europe. In 1555, Philip's father had been forced to tolerate Lutheranism in Germany. Lutheranism and other forms of Protestantism were making headway in the Netherlands, Sweden and Denmark, while Calvinism, centred on the Swiss city of Geneva, was spreading into France, England, Scotland and parts of Germany.

Faced with this disturbing situation, the Catholic Church had at last begun to stir itself. **Pope Paul III** called together a **General Council of the Church** made up of leading Catholic churchmen and theologians to the town of Trent in northern Italy. In three separate sessions (1545–8, 1551–2 and 1562–3), this great Council sought to reform the Catholic Church's personnel and liturgy. In terms of **theology**, it was very conservative, defining Catholic orthodoxy in a way that would outlaw the heretics and demand their destruction.

In 1534, the Spaniard **Ignatius Loyola** founded the Society of Jesus (the Jesuits), which was given papal approval by Paul III in 1540. The Jesuits were designed to reinvigorate the Catholic Church with a sense of missionary zeal and enthusiasm. The original plan to recapture Jerusalem from the Turks had to be shelved. But later Jesuits would spread the Christian word to all corners of the (then) known world – from South America to India and even Japan. Within Europe the Jesuits came to be seen as a major part of the **Counter-Reformation**, the Catholic Church's fight back against Protestantism. Initially, however, the Jesuits attempted to reinvigorate Catholicism with some of its lost spirituality.

It was this spiritual revival of the Church that Philip II would attempt to foster during his reign. Personally devout, he would use his control over the Church in Spain and the New World to reform and improve the Church that had been entrusted to his care. Being Philip, he naturally took the task seriously and he enjoyed considerable success at least within Spain. Outside Spain, his support for the Counter-Reformation, which attempted to push back the frontiers of Protestantism, met with rather less good fortune.

Reform of the Spanish Church

During Philip's reign there were some 40,000 secular priests and 50,000 **regular clergy** in Spain. The Spanish Church was the third largest in Europe (after Italy and France) and, thanks to the concessions wrung out of the papacy by Ferdinand and Isabella and by Charles I, the Church of Spain was almost wholly controlled by the King of Spain. At the same time the Church was clearly in need of reform. Since one Church office at the lower end of the spectrum rarely generated enough income to live on, many clergy held several offices in plurality, which often meant

KEY TERM

Theology Refers to beliefs about God put forward by the Church.

KEY PERSON

Ignatius Loyola (1491–1556) Founded the Jesuits after surviving serious injury at the Battle of Pamplona, fighting against the French. He devoted his life to the service of God and the Pope, and gathered around him a small band of followers. At first they hoped to reconquer Jerusalem for Christianity but then decided to devote their efforts to helping the poor and needy. As the Counter-Reformation unfolded, the Jesuits were often leading advisers to the Catholic rulers in Europe.

KEY CONCEPTS

Counter-Reformation Term given to the work of all those institutions and individuals that aimed to restore the spirituality and power of the Catholic Church when it was faced by the growth of Protestantism in Europe.

Regular clergy Refers to the monks, friars and nuns who lived by the rule (in Latin *regula*) of their individual orders.

KEY TERMS

See Another word for a bishop's diocese, the area under his administration.

Clerical celibacy Refers to the fact that Catholic clergy were not supposed to engage in sexual activity as they were 'married' to the Church.

Conventuals Orders of regular clergy (monks or friars) who had lapsed from the strict rule of their founders and followed a more relaxed regime.

Erastian monarch Refers to a monarch who controlled the Church in his kingdom, even if, officially, it was controlled by the Pope.

Foreign mother house A religious order that has its headquarters in another country.

absenteeism. In the diocese of Barcelona in 1549, for example, only six out of 67 parish priests were resident. Bishops took no action, as they themselves were often absentees. Fernando de Valdes visited his **see** of Oviedo only once in a twelve-year period and rarely visited the bishopric of Seville after being elevated to that position.

As well as absenteeism, Church rules about **clerical celibacy** were openly flouted.

- Perhaps one in five parish clergy actually lived with a woman.
- Rather more may have been guilty of occasional sexual lapses.

As well as this, the parish clergy, like so many of their brethren, were ill-educated and unable to meet the spiritual needs of their parishioners. Some Spanish reformers likened the situation in some parts of their homeland to that of the New World, in terms of the ignorance and superstition of the common people.

So what of Philip's reforms of the Church?

- One of the first was to reorganise the dioceses, or bishoprics, so that they took account of the centres of population. By the end of the reign, Castile had five archbishoprics and some 30 bishops, while Aragon had three archbishops and fifteen bishops. Six of Aragon's bishoprics were new. In Castile in 1572, Burgos was upgraded to an archbishopric.
- Philip was also concerned to improve the life of the regular clergy. He took action against those monks known as **conventuals** who lived without reference to their original rule. He received papal approval to carry out drastic reform of the conventuals in 1566 and proceeded to dissolve some houses while merging others with those of more committed monks.
- Meanwhile, as an **erastian monarch**, who realised that reform could not be well directed unless the impulse came from one centre, Philip also removed the Cistercians and other monks from obedience to a **foreign mother house.**

Impact of the Council of Trent

The decrees of the Council of Trent were welcomed by Philip II and proved a real spur to further reform of the Church.

Uniformity. In particular, the decrees introduced greater uniformity in ceremonies and liturgy and helped to eradicate regional variations. In this way Spaniards and their king could feel themselves part of a more universal church. The imposition of the **Roman Missal** in 1568 and **Breviary** in 1570 made liturgical practice uniform across Spain. Naturally there was some opposition at times but greater uniformity was soon achieved.

Increased power of bishops. The Council of Trent also helped to strengthen the power of the bishops over their clergy and encouraged them to hold reforming synods (assemblies of clergy) within their sees on a regular basis. There were a number held in the 1560s soon after the Council of Trent's decrees were promulgated but they tended to tail off thereafter.

Education. Trent also put renewed emphasis on the importance of education for clergy and laymen alike. Bishops were encouraged to set up **seminaries** for the training of clergy and some 20 or so were founded during Philip's reign.

Sermons and instruction. In addition parish clergy were told to preach a sermon every Sunday, to give religious instruction during the mass and to set up Sunday schools for local children.

Keeping records. At the same time the parish clergy had to keep strict records of births, marriages and deaths in their parishes, and to record the attendance of their parishioners at mass every Sunday.

Improving spiritual contemplation. In a development very similar to the views of more extreme Protestants, churches were also encouraged to rid themselves of any religious images deemed sensual and to whitewash interior walls so that spiritual contemplation might be improved. Diocesan

KEY TERMS

Roman Missal A missal is a book that contains all of the texts used in the Catholic Mass throughout the year. The significance of the Roman Missal was that it was to be used throughout the Catholic world.

Breviary A book that contains the service to be held every day in the Catholic Church.

Seminaries Schools that are set up to educate and train Catholic clergy. The Jesuits had their own seminaries, which helps to explain their success.

synods in Granada (1573) and Pamplona (1591) gave orders for the destruction of unseemly images.

The end of secular functions. In similar vein, the churches in Spain were supposed to rid themselves of secular functions. In many parishes the church had been used for secular festivities and meetings – those would now cease. As if to emphasise the point further, the secular clergy were encouraged to wear **vestments** as a sign of the special nature of their order.

Spanish reformers

As well as encouraging these types of reform, provided they were controlled by himself or his bishops, Philip also ensured that worthy men were chosen as bishops. **Gaspar de Quiroga** is a good example. Trained as a canon lawyer, he was keen on reform but was also an uncompromising supporter of royal rights and powers over the Church. Philip made him President of the Council of Italy in 1567, Bishop of Cuenca in 1572, Inquisitor General in 1573, Archbishop of Toledo and, thus, Primate of Spain in 1577.

In all this we see that Gaspar de Quiroga's career was controlled by Philip and that he was expected to carry out secular as well as religious functions. He was a resident bishop who lived frugally and used funds from his see to sponsor **diocesan synods**, education and patronage of the arts in the service of religion. In his reforming work he made use of the Jesuits and Augustinians, and he produced a new *Manual of the Sacraments* in 1581. A year later he called together a number of Spanish bishops to a synod in Toledo, where new regulations were drawn up to encourage clergy to reside in their parishes and to punish them if they failed to do so.

Amid this reform of the Church, Spain produced a number of **mystics** who proved to be extremely influential. **St Teresa of Avila and St John of the Cross** founded a new order of nuns called the **Discalced** Carmelites. Between 1562 and 1576, they founded a number of reformed houses before falling foul of the Inquisition. With Philip's help they survived this investigation, though not before St John had been kidnapped and periodically flogged by his enemies.

The Jesuits

The Jesuits, founded by a Spaniard Ignatius Loyola, also played an important part in the spiritual regeneration of Spain. In the 1560s and 1570s, Philip encouraged the **work of the Jesuits** in Spain. Here they undertook important missionary work among the common people.

While Jesuit work continued on the ground, Philip II found himself in conflict with Jesuit leaders. Although the early Jesuits were mainly Spanish, the constitution of the Society stressed that it was an international order, which owed obedience to the Pope rather than to any secular ruler. Encouraged by national divisions within the Order and his own desire for control of all aspects of religious life and personnel in Spain, Philip attempted to take control of the Jesuits in Spain. In 1588, he obtained the Pope's approval for the appointment of the Spanish bishop of Cartagena to carry out a visitation of the Spanish Jesuits in an attempt to remove them from papal obedience and control. In the end the attempt failed, but Philip still found that most Spanish Jesuits remained compliant to the royal will.

Impact of reforms

Overall the impact of these reforms and reformers should not be exaggerated. Philip had many other matters to distract him and even reforming bishops had trouble with vested interests such as those laymen and monasteries that controlled large parts of Church patronage and wealth. In Orense, the bishop controlled only 70 out of 700 benefices, while in Oviedo all the monasteries were lay foundations and did not acknowledge the authority of the bishop. Local customs and inertia also played their part in limiting the impact of reforms. Nonetheless, by the end of Philip's reign, the Church was an improvement on the one he inherited.

The Spanish Inquisition

The Inquisition, or Holy Office, had been established with papal permission in Spain by Ferdinand and Isabella primarily to deal with those who had converted to Christianity from their Moorish or Jewish faith (*Moriscos* and *Conversos*) but who were suspected of lapsing from their adopted Catholicism.

Work of the Jesuits One Jesuit reported that the people he worked with lived in caves without priests or sacraments, and some were so ignorant that they could not even make the sign of the cross. Another Jesuit, Pedro de Léon, devoted himself to missionary work in Andalusia and Estremadura.

- In Philip's reign the Inquisition is traditionally seen by non-Spanish historians as a terrible instrument of repression, which brought prosecutions by means of informers and regularly persecuted by means of torture, *auto de fé* and burnings.
- The reality of the Inquisition's operations under Philip II was rather more mundane and less severe, though it played its part in the revival and reform of the Catholic faith in Spain.

In all there were only fifteen Inquisition tribunals, or courts, in Spain during Philip's reign, and each was staffed with about three inquisitors. These were hardly the numbers to make for serious persecution. Most cases were brought by individuals and not by the officials, and 60–70 per cent of accusations were directed at ordinary Catholics, not Moors or Jews. Most cases brought before the Inquisition were not about heresy but concerned rather less serious crimes – commonly blasphemy, sacrilege, scandalous behaviour or sex outside marriage. While many were punished, fines and public penance were much more common than executions. In addition the Inquisition made efforts to educate the offenders and the community at large in terms of proper Christian behaviour.

In the area of witchcraft persecution, the Inquisition proved to be much more enlightened than many other religious and secular authorities in Europe. While Germany, France and Switzerland experienced increasing persecution of witches, which some historians have dubbed a 'witch-craze', the Spanish Inquisition was much more liberal. In a special conference in Granada in 1526, inquisitors had concluded that witchcraft was little more than a delusion. In 1610, after an exceptional case in Navarre, the Inquisition ruled out further persecution of witches.

Nonetheless, the Spanish Inquisition had its harsher side and can be accused of **anti-intellectualism**. It stifled theological debate and academic research, leaving Spain an intellectual backwater. When Philip returned to Spain from the Netherlands in 1559, the Inquisition, led by **Hernando de Valdés**, the Inquisitor General, laid on two

KEY THEMES

Protestantism in Spain
Protestantism hardly touched Spain at all. Perhaps six or seven people were executed for heresy between 1562 and the end of Philip's reign in 1598.

The Inquisition's anti-intellectualism Writing in 1566, the humanist scholar Hernán Nunez complained that the inquisitors 'discourage the study of letters because of the dangers said to be present in them ... These and other similar problems drive me insane and take away from me the wish to carry on.'

KEY PERSON

Hernando de Valdés (1483–1568) Inquisitor General from 1547 to 1566. He saw heresy everywhere. A ruthless careerist, he was Archbishop of Seville from 1546. Seville was seen as particularly prone to heresy as it was at the centre of international trade.

great *autos de fé* in Valladolid and Seville to welcome him home. These ceremonies were deliberately stage-managed for maximum effect and to impress Philip with the zeal of the Inquisition, which hoped for better times under the new king. In truth, few *autos* had been held in the previous 40 years after the demise of the *Converso* problem. Now Valdés wished to secure his position by rooting out suspected Lutherans, who were not really Lutherans at all.

Bartolomé de Carranza

Valdés followed up this success in 1559 by arresting, on suspicion of heresy, none other than the Primate of all Spain, the Archbishop of Toledo, **Bartolomé de Carranza**. He was suspended from office and imprisoned in August 1559, just a year after he had been elevated to the archbishopric.

Valdés, a long-standing adviser to Prince Philip, was also a long-standing enemy of the Dominican Carranza. He accused him of being a Protestant because of statements made in his book *Commentaries on the Christian Catechism*. Carranza was kept imprisoned for some seven years before being sent to Rome. Here the case dragged on for another nine years before he was found not guilty of heresy but guilty of putting forward sixteen 'highly suspect' propositions. The Inquisition's part in this extraordinary case, in which the Primate of Spain was brought low, did it little credit and the long-drawn-out affair certainly made Spanish intellectuals think twice about discussing new ideas.

The case of the Augustinian scholar, Alonso Gudiel, Professor of Scripture at the University of Osuna, also gave Spanish scholars pause for thought. The Dominicans who staffed the Inquisition always regarded Augustinians as suspect. After all, Martin Luther, who had started the Reformation in Germany, was an Augustinian monk. In this case, the Augustinian Gudiel was arrested by the Valladolid Inquisition at the instigation of another theologian and found guilty of heresy. He died in prison a year later and Augustinian houses were told that he had died outside the faith.

Ten years later, the Inquisitor General, Quiroga, who had originally condemned Gudiel, reopened the case and promptly reversed his decision.

Another Augustinian, Luis de León, theologian and poet, fared little better, being imprisoned for five years on charges of heresy, even though the case against him was rather weak. Once again, it was Quiroga's direct intervention that saved him. As with the Gudiel case, the charges and imprisonment seem to have developed from personal grudges borne against the accused by the accusers.

The Index

Alongside the Inquisition was the Index of forbidden books. This was seen as a vital defensive measure against the spread of heresy. Although the Iberian peninsula had proved near-impervious to the Reformation, the new militant form of Protestantism, **Calvinism**, which was about to make itself felt among the artisans and aristocracy of France, might be more problematic.

The first edition of the Spanish Index was produced by the Inquisition in 1551/2 and based on one produced by the University of Louvain (in the Spanish Netherlands) in 1546. This was updated and renewed by Inquisitor General Valdés in 1559 following the apparent discovery of groups of Lutherans in Valladolid and Seville.

The Index naturally banned works by heretics of all descriptions but also banned the writings of a number of others who questioned the actions of the Church. These included the works of the following people.

- **Desiderius Erasmus** and other humanists who, though good Catholics, had helped to stir up anticlerical sentiments before and during the Reformation.
- In addition, a number of recent Spanish devotional works were placed on the list even though the authors were undoubtedly orthodox enough. John of Avila's *Audi filia* and Luis de Granada's *Book of Prayer* (1544) and *Guide of Sinners* (1556) were works in this category, which fell foul of the Inquisitors.
- Even works by Catholic martyrs, such as the Englishmen Sir Thomas More and Bishop John Fisher, who had

---

been executed for their faith by Henry VIII, found their way on to the Index on the grounds that their works might be misused or misinterpreted.

The Index was updated and seriously expanded by Quiroga in 1583–4. The number of books had now quintupled, though only a small percentage were Spanish works. Overall the existence and expansion of the Index made Spanish intellectuals nervous and cautious. Intellectual developments in Spain were also blighted by tight controls on access to non-Spanish literature. A decree of 1558 made it an offence punishable by death to import a book without a licence. A year later, Philip announced that Spaniards were not to study at foreign universities. These measures may seem **draconian** but it is easy to understand Philip and the Inquisition's caution in the face of what they saw as the terrifying spread of heresy in the rest of western Europe.

Relations with the papacy

Philip's relations with the papacy were often stormy and this is, in many ways, unsurprising.

- Firstly, Popes were very concerned about the extent of Philip's control over the Spanish Church and his determination to exclude papal influence of any kind. For Philip, it was obvious that royal control of the Church in Spain had led to the triumphs over the Jews and the Moors, and had imposed religious uniformity in Spain.
- At the same time, the same royal control had kept Protestant heresy successfully at bay.
- Furthermore, Philip was not prepared in the least to compromise the rights and privileges he had inherited from his predecessors. To do so would, in his eyes, compromise Catholicism in Spain itself.
- In the same way, Philip's great struggle in the Low Countries proceeded from the fact that he would never rule over heretics.

From the papacy's point of view, Philip's control over the Church in Spain was seen as an affront to the power of the papacy. In this period of Counter-Reformation, the papacy liked to emphasise the supremacy of the Pope above all other earthly powers.

> **KEY TERM**
>
> **Draconian** Refers to the actions of the ancient Greek tyrant Draco, and thus means harsh and repressive.

List of Popes during the reign of Philip II

1555–9	Paul IV
1559–65	Pius IV
1566–72	Pius V
1572–85	Gregory XIII
1585–90	Sixtus V
Sep 1590	Urban VII
1590–1	Gregory XIV
Oct–Dec 1591	Innocent IX
1592–1605	Clement VIII

Tension between Philip and the papacy

At the beginning of Philip's reign, king and Pope clashed over the case of Bartolomé de Carranza, Archbishop of Toledo (see page 92).

(see page 92)

Pope Pius IV succeeded the fanatically anti-Spanish Pope Paul IV in 1559 and died in 1565. He was responsible for calling the third session of the Council of Trent, 1561–3.

Pope Pius V was Antonio Ghislieri. He was a model of monastic virtue and austerity and set the pattern for future Counter-Reformation Popes. He was Pope from 1566 until 1572. After his death he became Saint Pius V.

- Philip claimed that all matters of heresy arising in Spain could be dealt with in Spain. Even the docile **Pope Pius IV** objected to this and demanded that the case of such a distinguished and high-ranking churchman as Carranza must be referred to Rome.
- In 1563, Philip withdrew his ambassador in Rome and the next year Pius hit back by refusing to renew the subsidy tax (*subsidio*) on the Spanish Church, which was an important part of Philip's revenues.
- **Pope Pius V** was even more determined to get the case taken to Rome and, in the end, Philip accepted a compromise. The case went to Rome but Philip was allowed to send members of the Spanish Inquisition as members of the court to try the Archbishop. Philip effectively won the argument as his representatives proceeded to stall the case for nine years, by which time the not-guilty verdict was of little value.
- Furthermore, the Carranza case was exceptional. No other appeals to Rome from Spain were allowed during Philip's reign. In 1572, Philip issued a decree declaring that any attempts by the papacy to transfer a case from Spain to Rome were to be disregarded and that no Spaniard should be cited to appear before any tribunal outside Spain.
- Unwisely, as it turned out, Pius V issued an edict in 1567 against bullfighting, declaring that all those who took part should be excommunicated. Philip and his bishops ignored the decree! An attempt by the papacy to get Spanish bishops to publish a Papal Bull without royal permission likewise failed dismally.

Nomination to vacant sees An important privilege guarded by Philip and other Spanish rulers. It meant that when an important churchman or woman died, it was the right of the monarch to name the successor. The importance of this is that it allowed the monarch considerable control over the Church in Spain.

Meanwhile, the papacy could do nothing to undermine Philip's rights to **nominate to vacant sees** and abbeys or to tax the Church. Throughout the Carranza case, for example, Philip pocketed a share of the Archbishop's revenues as though the see were vacant and he always expected considerable financial rewards from newly appointed clerics. The decrees of the National Council of the Spanish Church had to have the Crown's approval and when taxes were needed more quickly, Philip could use the Catholic clergy to encourage prompt payment from their flocks. Philip's control of the Spanish Church remained absolute.

Tension over foreign policy

Philip and the papacy also came into conflict over their respective foreign policies. Only at the time of the Holy League and the great naval victory over the Turks at Lepanto in 1571 (see pages 100–1) did their foreign policy aims appear to be in harmony. Typically, such harmony was short-lived. After the battle, Philip refused to be drawn into Pius V's hopes for a great crusade against the Ottoman Turks but instead looked to consolidate Spanish power in the western Mediterranean.

- At the outset of his reign, Philip was at war with the violently anti-Spanish Pope, Paul IV. From 1556 to 1559, Paul was allied to France in a war fought against Spain and England in the Low Countries.
- While later Popes stopped short of such extreme measures, they remained concerned at the growth of Spanish power in the Italian peninsula and attempted to gain diplomatic credibility and independence by backing Spain's enemies. In this way Philip and the papacy fell out over attitudes to **Henry of Navarre** in France. In 1585, soon after his elevation to the Holy See, Sixtus V declared that Henry of Navarre as a relapsed heretic could not inherit the French throne. However, when it became clear that the alternative might be Philip's daughter, both Sixtus and his effective successor Clement VIII had second thoughts. The last thing they wanted was for Spain to take control of France since this would leave the papacy powerless. Accordingly, in 1595, much to Philip's annoyance, Clement officially recognised Henry as the true king of France, even though he had previously failed to honour his conversion to Rome.

The issue of England

Philip and the papacy were also at odds over England. An important feature of Philip's foreign policy was the aim of returning England to the Catholic fold.

KEY TERM

Bull of Excommunication
A papal decree, or command, announcing that the individual is now excluded from the Church. Excommunication was a very grave penalty indeed for practising Catholics. Papal Bulls are named by reference to their opening Latin words. This Bull of 1570 was thus called *Regnans in excelsis*.

KEY THEME

Philip and the papacy The Venetian ambassador claimed that Pope Sixtus thought that, *The king and his armada are becoming ridiculous while Queen Elizabeth knows how to manage her affairs. If that woman were only a Catholic, she would be loved by us more than any other sovereign, for she has great qualities.*

Philip II's testy reply to a letter from Sixtus V does much to explain his frustration with the Holy See during his reign:

Nothing surprises me more than to see your Holiness leaving time for the heretics to take root in France. The Church is on the eve of losing one of its members, Christendom is on the point of being set on fire by the united heretics, Italy runs the greatest danger, and in the presence of the enemy we look on and temporise. And the blame is put on me because, looking at those interests as if they were my own, I hasten to your Holiness as to a father who I love and respect and, as a good son remind him of the duties of the Holy See ...

Differences about excommunication. Pope Pius IV's attempts to excommunicate the Protestant **Queen Elizabeth** were successfully blocked by Philip in 1561 and 1563. Even when Pius V excommunicated her in 1570, Philip refused to allow the **Bull of Excommunication** to be published in his domains and also tried to stop it from reaching England. Philip claimed that the excommunication would make England more Protestant and would lead to more persecution for the dwindling band of English Catholics.

In fact, Philip opposed papal moves against Elizabeth because he hoped to preserve the Anglo–Spanish alliance against France, which had been such an important part of his father's policy.

Differences about invasion. The retention of good relations with England was especially important for Philip, since, in Catholic eyes, the true Queen of England was the **Queen of Scots**, who was half-French and (briefly) Queen of France! In the 1570s, Philip consistently refused to listen to papal appeals for an enterprise against England to unseat the heretic Queen Elizabeth.

When he did finally attempt an invasion of England, the Armada of 1588, it was a reaction to English aggression against Spain in the Netherlands and the Caribbean, rather than a crusade against heresy. What was even more galling to Philip was that when he did finally take up the papacy's call for an attack on England, a new pope, Sixtus V, seemed to be against the venture. He thought that persuasion would be more effective than war and hoped that Elizabeth might agree to conversion to Catholicism. Even when Philip was preparing his great Armada against Elizabeth, Sixtus made a point of complaining at Philip's slowness and took every opportunity to compare Philip unfavourably with Elizabeth. Faced with this attitude, it is easy to see why **Philip distrusted the papacy**.

Disagreement over the Spanish Netherlands

Even when papacy and king agreed on the aims of Spanish policy, as in the Netherlands, there was still room for them to disagree about methods and to blame each other for the problem. When Philip came to see that a military solution was needed in the Low Countries to quell rebellion and heresy, the papacy demanded negotiation with the rebels. In 1566, Pius IV urged Philip to go to the Netherlands in person and sent a special *nuncio* (ambassador or legate) to investigate the situation there. Philip ignored the advice and objected to the legate. Each side blamed the other for not doing enough to halt the spread of heresy in the Netherlands and when the Pope saw the problem as religious, Philip declared that he was fighting against rebels not heretics.

PHILIP II'S FOREIGN POLICY

Aims

Due to the extent of his empire Philip II's aims in foreign policy were complex.

- His primary aim was to protect Spanish interests at home and abroad and, if possible, to wage war against the Infidel. Philip wished to push back the forces of Islam, which were spreading westwards across the Mediterranean and were a combination of Turkish Ottoman power based in Constantinople and Arab pirates based in various outposts along the North African coast.
- As the Dutch Revolt dragged on, so Philip's aims widened considerably. He wished to deflect and oppose those countries that helped the Dutch rebels, directly or indirectly. This aim widened again to involve a war on several fronts at the same time against the forces of international Protestantism. Philip came to see Spain as the natural, armed wing of the **Counter-Reformation.**

The scale and duration of Philip's wars were too great for Spain to bear. By the end of the reign, Spanish finances were close to collapse and, perhaps more importantly, Spain's foreign policy had proved a costly failure.

War against the Infidel

Philip, like his father Charles I, saw war against Islam as a crucial part of his God-given duty. In the Mediterranean the struggle was ideological but also defensive. The

KEY TERM

Counter-Reformation is the term given to the attempts of Catholics to crush the new Protestant religion.

Ottoman Turks, led by Sultan **Suleiman the Magnificent**, expanded their influence westwards across the Mediterranean, aided by powerful allies in the shape of the Barbary Pirates and other assorted corsairs. Furthermore, as already seen, there was a genuine fear in Spain that these forces would join up with the Spanish Moors and invade Spain itself.

Tripoli. Philip's determination to wage war against the Infidel in the Mediterranean got off to a bad start. In 1559, he attempted to capture the North African port of Tripoli, which had been lost to Spain in 1551. This attack provoked a swift and decisive response from the Ottoman navy whereby Spain lost 42 of its 80 vessels, and its commanders scuttled home leaving 18,000 assorted Spanish troops to be captured and taken back to Constantinople. Philip had attacked too soon, before he had built up sufficient forces. His youthful mistake had unnecessarily provoked his enemy.

Malta. As a result Spain built up its naval forces in the Mediterranean in a more methodical and determined manner, using the shipyards in Barcelona to produce new ships. By 1564, Philip had 100 vessels at his disposal. This led to success in 1565, when Garciá de Toledo successfully dislodged a Turkish invading force from the island of Malta.

Spurred on by this victory yet more ships were produced but the expected major assault on the Ottoman fleet was then delayed as Philip became embroiled in the Dutch Revolt. In 1567, troops from Italy, earmarked for war against the Turks, now moved north with the Duke of Alva. Spain did not have the manpower to fight two major campaigns at once. Luckily for the Spanish the Turks themselves were in some disarray when Sultan Suleiman died in 1566 and was succeeded by the rather less impressive **Selim II**.

Cyprus. The cause of Spain's next conflict with the Turks was the capture of Cyprus by Ottoman forces in 1570. The island was owned by the Italian city-state Venice, and it tried to get Spain's help to dislodge the attackers on the basis that the Turks were preparing to sweep across the Mediterranean, in the same way that they had swept up the Danube to the gates of Vienna in the 1520s.

Nonetheless, Philip II was not really interested in launching a lengthy crusade against the Turks or in helping the Venetians and it took the persuasive abilities of the saintly Pope Pius V to convince him that joint action was necessary. Still alarmed by the Revolt of the Alpujarras (1568–70) and finding that Alva had brought the Low Countries under control, Philip finally agreed to supply half of the ships, men and resources for a huge naval alliance with Venice and the Pope himself, to fight the Turks over a three year period.

Lepanto, 1571

Led by the king's half-brother, Don John of Austria, the 'allied fleet' achieved a wondrous success by smashing the Turkish fleet at Lepanto, off the Gulf of Corinth in Greece. The Turks lost some 200 out of 230 ships along with 30,000 dead and 3000 taken prisoner. The Christian side was delighted and writers such as **Cervantes** celebrated Don John's success.

Despite the psychological uplift this generated, the victory at Lepanto did not really alter the balance of power in the eastern Mediterranean. The Turks rebuilt their fleet with astonishing speed. Despite a further expedition the next year, the Turks refused to offer battle. No attempt was made to recapture Cyprus, which remained in Ottoman hands. Philip then retired from the Pope's Holy League and launched an attack on Tunis in 1573, showing that his priority remained the North African Arab states. Although the city was captured, the Turks retook it a few months later.

The papal vision of a great Christian Crusade that would do serious damage to the Turks effectively died with its greatest **apologist**, Pius V, in 1572.

- Spain and the Turks agreed not to fight seriously at sea any more.
- By 1578, the two sides had agreed a truce, which was renewed at regular intervals until 1590.

KEY PERSON

Miguel de Cervantes (1547–1616) The most famous Spanish writer of his day. *Don Quixote*, which tells of the strange adventures of Don Quixote and his servant Sancho Panza is seen as a commentary on the disillusion widespread in Spanish society at the end of Philip's reign. In reaction to victory at Lepanto he wrote: 'That day, which was so happy for Christendom, because all the world then learnt how mistaken it had been in believing that the Turks were invincible at sea.'

KEY TERM

Apologist Someone who argues vigorously in favour of a person or course of action.

- Even then there was no serious conflict between the two, as both had other problems.

Critics of Philip claim that after Lepanto he gave up on the idea of a crusade against the Turks. Yet this misses the point. Philip did not *abandon* the idea of a crusade against Islam in the Mediterranean because he was sensible enough never to envisage any such thing. While he opposed Islam in theory, he soon appreciated the practical difficulties of launching crusades. Lepanto was a success, not because it actually pushed back Ottoman influence in the eastern Mediterranean (which it did not) but because it had probably done enough to help convince the Turks not to take on Spain in the western Mediterranean.

War against France: aid for the Catholic League

Spain's natural enemy in Europe was France. It was fortunate indeed for Philip II that for much of his reign France was embroiled in terrible and debilitating civil wars known as the 'Wars of Religion'.

After 1560 a combination of weak monarchs, factious nobles and the spread of Protestantism led to whole series of spectacular civil wars and the occasional massacre of Protestants, culminating in the terrible massacre of St Bartholomew's Day in Paris in 1572. For much of the period, Philip was a spectator but he grew increasingly worried that French Huguenots (as the French Protestants were called) or the French government might try to intervene in the Low Counties against Spain.

In 1581, this happened. The **Duke of Anjou**, brother of King Henry III of France, accepted the position of 'prince and lord of the Netherlands' at the request of the Dutch rebels, and turned up with an army of 17,000 men. Disappointed at his lack of real power and diverted by an attempt to marry Queen Elizabeth I, his intervention ended in spectacular disarray with the so-called French Fury when his troops failed to seize the city of Antwerp. His intervention naturally caused annoyance in Spain but worse was to follow when he unexpectedly died in 1584. His death meant that the heir to the childless Henry III was his cousin, Henry of Navarre. The problem for Philip was that Henry of Navarre was a Huguenot.

KEY PERSON

Francis, Duke of Anjou (1555–84) The youngest of the sons of Henry II and Catherine de Medici, and the only one who did not become king. He intervened ineffectually in the Dutch Revolt on the side of the rebels and his premature death in 1584 made the Huguenot Henry of Navarre, heir to the throne.

The prospect of a Protestant France led Philip to intervene directly in the Wars of Religion. In the secret Treaty of Joinville of 1584, he promised 50,000 crowns a month to the French Catholic League, run by the **Guise family**, and pledged to prevent the accession of a Protestant. In 1589, Henry III was assassinated and the League fought to prevent Navarre's succession.

- Faced with this crisis, Philip dispatched Parma and his army to France in 1590 and 1591 to help the League militarily.
- Just for good measure, he pressed his own daughter's claim to the French throne as being preferable to the heretic Navarre.

The outcome was a qualified success for Philip. In 1590, Parma forced Navarre to lift his siege of Paris. In 1593, Henry of Navarre decided to convert to Catholicism, in order to secure his Crown. However, he followed this up with a declaration of war on Spain in 1595. Philip had a brief success with the capture of Calais in 1596 so that, too late, he had a decent Channel port. However, this success led to a military alliance between France and England against him.

By 1598, Philip's new governor in the Netherlands, the **Archduke Albert**, negotiated peace with France at the Peace of Vervins by which Spain gave Calais back to France and got little in return.

War against England: the Armada, 1588

Spain's war against England (1585–1604), culminating in the sending of a great fleet or Armada to invade and conquer Queen Elizabeth's realm, has often been seen as an inevitable conflict between Catholic Spain and Protestant England. It is also thought that this attempted invasion shows Philip to be a man of extraordinary, not to say presumptuous, ambition.

- Here was a king oppressing Protestants and freedom-fighting Dutchman.
- At the same time, he was backing the deadly and oppressive Catholic League in France.
- In addition, he wanted to conquer England.

The Guise family From Lorraine, the family were fiercely Catholic and very ambitious. Mary of Guise was Mary Queen of Scots' mother, and the family usually boasted one duke and one cardinal. Throughout the Wars of Religion, they took an uncompromising stance in favour of the total destruction of Protestantism in France.

Archduke Albert (1559–1621) Son of the Emperor Maximilian II and Philip II's nephew. He was appointed governor of the Low Countries in 1583. In 1598, he became the official ruler of the Spanish Netherlands with his wife, Philip's daughter Isabella.

Since Spain was a great Catholic power it was felt that the conflict with Protestant England was therefore inevitable and that Philip was being rather greedy.

Early relations with England

The reality of Anglo–Spanish relations was rather different. At the beginning of his reign, Philip was anxious to be on good terms with England. His chief enemy in Europe was clearly France, and France was allied to Scotland. In 1560, Francis II (1559–60) married the young Mary Queen of Scots, daughter of James V and the French princess, Mary of Guise. Philip's fear was that England might join this alliance and thus act as a powerful anti-Spanish alliance, which could be a serious threat to Spanish control of the Low Countries.

Treaty of Edinburgh As part of the religious wars in Europe, France sent an army to Scotland and laid siege to the town of Leith. By the terms of the treaty, signed on 5 July 1560, both England and France committed themselves to a policy of non-interference in Scotland.

This fear was reinforced when England made a peace with Scotland in the **Treaty of Edinburgh** 1560 and when Scotland became a Protestant country during Mary Queen of Scots' absence in France. For Philip there was the added threat of a Protestant alliance in northern Europe, which might spread to Protestant Scandinavia. So in the 1560s and 1570s, Philip was keen to remain on good terms with Protestant England. He intervened with the Pope to stop him excommunicating Elizabeth I (see page 97) and he even offered her his hand in marriage, without getting too upset when she turned him down.

Anglo–Spanish relations worsen: the Netherlands

When relations between the two countries did deteriorate in the 1580s, it was rather more to do with Elizabeth I's provocation of Spain than Philip's ambition.

Elizabeth's intervention. Elizabeth intervened in the Netherlands on the side of the rebels. At first her aid was indirect. In 1569, a Spanish squadron carrying money to the Low Countries to pay the Duke of Alva's troops was attacked by French pirates and forced to shelter in Plymouth harbour. Elizabeth promptly confiscated the money, which seriously undermined Alva's ability to pay his troops.

Later on, as the rebel cause in the Low Countries seemed on the brink of collapse, Elizabeth went even further. In

1584, the rebel leader William of Orange was assassinated in Delft and, at the same time, Philip's most successful general, the Duke of Parma, was making excellent progress in his gradual re-conquest of northern territory. He recaptured the all-important city of Antwerp in 1585, and seemed poised to launch an attack on Holland and Zeeland, the two provinces at the heart of rebel territory. In the same year, faced with the prospect of Spanish victory, Elizabeth sent a military expedition to the Low Countries under the **Earl of Leicester**. He arrived with some 7000 men and promptly made a rather minor contribution to rebel success in holding out against Parma's onslaught. Leicester's expedition represented an English invasion of Spanish territory and could hardly be overlooked by Spain's king. So war between England and Spain was started by England.

Why Elizabeth's intervention was curious. Elizabeth's intervention was all the more curious as she did not wish to oust Spain from the Netherlands. Indeed, she was most worried that if Spain lost control there, then France would expand into the vacuum, thus presenting England with a dangerously French and Catholic Channel coastline opposite Kent. In addition, Elizabeth, as a monarch, had no sympathy with those who wished to see the overthrow of monarchy – even Spanish monarchy – in the Low Countries. Elizabeth was finally swayed into open aggression against Spain by some advisers who were more keenly Protestant than she was and who feared that Philip might unite somehow with France and launch a joint invasion against the country that was clearly seen as the main champion of international Protestantism.

Anglo–Spanish relations worsen: the Caribbean

From Philip's point of view, Leicester's intervention, however limited in terms of its military achievements, was an invasion of Spanish territory and should not go unpunished. In addition, Philip had been upset and goaded into fury by the attacks of English pirates on Spain's New World empire. At first, the attacks took the form of infringing on Spain's demand that no one should trade with Spanish colonies without permission.

- In 1562–3, **John Hawkins** infringed Spain's rules by selling African slaves in the Caribbean without a licence.
- A second expedition by Hawkins, two years later, clearly had Queen Elizabeth's approval.
- The third expedition in 1567–8 led to violence. Hawkins' second in command, **Francis Drake**, opened fire on the Treasurer's house at Rio de la Hacha (modern-day Columbia) and captured a Spanish vessel. In retaliation, a Spanish fleet gave Hawkins a severe mauling at San Juan de Ulua (Mexico) in 1568.
- After 1571, Drake launched a series of piratical raids on the Spanish empire.
- In 1573, he returned to Plymouth with a cargo of precious metals stolen from Spain.
- During 1577–80, he circumnavigated the globe, returning with yet more booty. Elizabeth's response was to throw diplomatic caution to the wind and knight him. Philip was naturally furious.

Philip strikes back

By 1583, encouraged by his acquisition of Portugal (1580), which gave Spain easier access to northern Europe and the English Channel, Philip decided that it was time to strike back at English attacks in the New World. At this time there were vague plans either to launch a sea-borne invasion from Spain or to transport the Spanish army from the Low Countries to Kent.

In 1584, diplomatic relations between Spain and England were broken off. Elizabeth expelled the Spanish ambassador for alleged involvement in a plot to overthrow her in favour of her Catholic cousin, Mary Queen of Scots. Following Leicester's expedition to help the Dutch rebels in 1585, Philip ordered the seizure of all English ships trading in Spanish ports. Drake then led a further expedition to the Caribbean, which netted more booty, but missed out on two treasure fleets with large cargoes of precious metals.

During 1586, Philip began to make more concrete plans for the invasion of England, which would pay back English aggression and result in the re-conversion of England to Catholicism. At first it was hoped to replace Elizabeth with

Mary Queen of Scots. However, with her execution at
Fotheringhay Castle in 1587, Philip sought to press his
own claim in the person of his daughter, Isabella. As Philip
began to build his great fleet, his preparations were
disrupted by Drake's daring raid on the Spanish port of
Cadiz in April 1587. Altogether some 24 Spanish vessels
were lost and this helped to delay the great enterprise
against England until the following year.

The Spanish Armada, 1588

Unfortunately, Philip's plan for the invasion developed as a
mixture of two plans.

- One was formulated by his admiral, Santa Cruz.
- The other originated with his general in the Low
  Countries, the Duke of Parma.

The new master plan was to send a great Armada of new
ships that would neutralise or destroy the English navy and
then transport Parma's troops, unopposed from the Low
Countries, across the Channel to England. The confusion,
or rather conflation, of two plans left unresolved the
problem of how Parma and his troops could rendezvous
with the fleet, when Spain did not possess a harbour in the
Low Countries with water deep enough to accommodate
the huge ships. A rendezvous at sea was unthinkable, yet
this is what the plan seemed to demand.

Although Philip was warned often enough about this fatal
flaw by Parma, he seems to have trusted in God to smooth
out such difficulties. The reality of the situation was that
even a country as powerful as Spain faced huge problems
in mounting a serious invasion of England. The English
Channel allied to the English navy made the chances of a
successful invasion remote. Just to tip matters against
Spain a little more, Santa Cruz died before the Armada
sailed and was replaced by the **Duke of Medina Sidonia** –
a great soldier but a man with no naval experience.

Into battle. The great Armada, with 130 ships and 22,000
assorted sailors and soldiers, set sail in May 1588 from
Corunna. By July it was off Cornwall, after which it
proceeded up the Channel harassed but little damaged by
the English navy.

KEY PERSON

**Duke of Medina Sidonia,
Alonso Pérez de Guzman
(1550–1615)** He tried to
turn down command of the
Armada on the basis that he
knew nothing of ships and
was often seasick. He has been
unfairly blamed for the failure
of the great enterprise.

Then disaster occurred. Without a harbour on the Spanish side of the Channel, the Armada dropped anchor off Gravelines to wait for Parma's troop transport vessels to reach them. In stormy conditions, the English unleashed eight fire ships. The Spanish cut their anchor cables and the English fleet, now 150 ships strong, attempted to take advantage of the confusion and disarray. In the ensuing battle only four of the great vessels were sunk but most were severely damaged and soon ran out of shot.

A storm then added to their difficulties, driving the battered Armada up the North Sea from where some of them, including Medina Sidonia's ship, limped around Scotland and Ireland and returned to Spain.

Aftermath of disaster. Philip II received the news of the disaster calmly. To his credit he refused to blame his admiral. Medina Sidonia continued to be shown favour in the future and Philip never asked him to go to sea again. The king took the view that it was God's will. In reality, the disaster had a mainly psychological impact on the two sides. England had not defeated Spain and war between the two sides continued with Spain holding the upper hand.

A year after the disaster, Philip was planning another armada. This time, to avoid problems in the Channel, he decided to launch an invasion of England via Ireland. The Protestant English were in the middle of a reconquest of rebellious and Catholic Ireland, and there was a real chance of Spain finding willing allies there. The new armada sailed in 1596 but was partially destroyed by a storm before arrival. Undeterred, another attempt was made in 1597, with an armada almost as big as that of 1588. This time the destination was Cornwall but once again the fleet was dispersed before it could land.

Results of Anglo–Spanish rivalry
The failure of the armadas indicated not that Spain was weak nor that it had been defeated by England but that a seaborne invasion of a hostile land was a very difficult business, even for a great power.

- While Spain had failed to conquer England, that was always a distant prospect.

- More worrying for Spain was that it was unable to take control of the Channel, so that supplies for the Spanish army in the Low Countries and supplies from the Baltic area for Spain were very expensive.
- But Philip had managed to defend his empire as far as he was able. The empire in the New World was raided and looted by pirates of various nationalities but no colonies were lost to hostile powers.
- If Spain had little success against the English, the English had little real success against Spain.

THE IMPACT OF EMPIRE: ROYAL FINANCES

Two things are clear concerning the financial impact of empire in the reign of Philip II.

- First, that royal income rose but expenditure rose faster.
- Second, the financial burden of that empire and its foreign policy of increasing warfare, fell increasingly on Spain itself rather than the other territories making up the Spanish empire. Within Spain the burden fell disproportionately on Castile.

The Crown's income

Philip II's income from regular sources of revenue probably tripled during his reign from 3 million *ducats* in 1559 to 10 or 11 million in the 1590s. While Aragon's contribution remained fairly static, income from the Church increased.

- From 1561, the *subsidio* tax on Church lands and clerical incomes became permanent.
- The *cruzada*, first granted to Ferdinand and Isabella for the conquest of Granada in 1492, continued to be collected and was renewed every three years by a compliant papacy.
- In 1567, the papacy added to royal revenue by inventing a new Church tax, the *excusado*, levied on the income from property in each parish.

Taken together this meant that regular revenue from the Church in Spain and the New World increased fourfold during the reign to 1.4 million *ducats* a year in the 1590s. In addition, the Crown could hope to enjoy occasional windfall payments from the Church.

- It collected the revenues from vacant bishoprics and, as the Crown retained control of new appointments to bishoprics, it could ensure that vacancies were quite long.
- One further windfall was the income from the see of Toledo during the long imprisonment of Archbishop Carranza throughout most of the 1560s. Overall the Church may have contributed about 20 per cent of all Crown revenue by the 1590s, indicating that the Church was being more rigorously taxed as the reign went on. Certainly there were complaints to this effect by some bishops from the 1570s onwards.

The **laity** of Castile suffered the same fate. As soon as Philip returned to Spain in 1559 and became aware of the Crown's financial problems, he began to increase tax rates. Income from the *encabezamiento* increased accordingly, while increased taxes on trade boosted income from customs duties. In the wake of the Armada crisis, the *Cortes* of Castile was persuaded to vote a special new subsidy, called the *millones*, levied on four basic foodstuffs: meat, wine, oil and vinegar. The total amount of the *millones* was increased by the government in 1596, as yet another financial crisis unfolded.

As well as more taxes, Philip increasingly raised revenue through the sale of noble titles and the sale of government office.

- The first was relatively harmless but not very popular.
- The second was more significant and contributed greatly to the administrative inefficiency, which would continue to blight Spain in the next century.

Income from the New World also showed a healthy increase during Philip's reign. In the 1560s, it stood at around 90,000 *ducats* a year. This figure had tripled on average by the 1590s. Not only did the Crown enjoy increased income from the royal *quinto*, or fifth, but also it levied traditional Spanish taxes such as the *alcabala* (sales tax) and the *cruzada* in the New World.

Royal expenditure

Although Spain was much more heavily taxed during Philip's reign, royal expenditure rose much faster than income. This resulted in bankruptcies being declared by the Spanish government in 1557, 1560, 1576 and 1596. These bankruptcies meant that the Crown suspended payments on its bills and borrowings until:

- agreements were made with the creditors
- the debts were rescheduled.

Philip inherited enormous debts from his father and a large part of annual income was always spent on servicing this debt via interest payments or by granting his creditors financial privileges.

- The Genoese creditors, for example, were granted a monopoly on the sale of playing cards in Spain and control of some of the salt works in southern Spain.
- The Fuggers of Augsburg, who did so much to prop up Charles I's empire, were allowed to administer silver and mercury mines in Spain and also took charge of the lands of the three great military religious orders (see page 10).

The cost of servicing the debt went up as Philip's reign progressed and the debts continued to grow. The greatest cause of the increasing debts was, of course, the spiralling cost of Spanish warfare.

- Expenditure on the Dutch Revolt started in earnest in 1567 and continued for the rest of the reign. As the revolt progressed, Philip went to war with both England and France, thus increasing military expenditure still further.
- Looking at the period 1587–90, we can see how enormous Spain's military expenditure was. In that period, the French Catholic League received 1.5 million *ducats*, the Armada cost a further 5 million and Parma, in the Low Countries, received in excess of 21 million. At an exchange rate of roughly 4 *ducats* to the pound

that meant an outlay of more than £7 million in a four-year period. While it is right to remember the debts, it is also astonishing that the King of Spain could marshal and deploy such vast sums of money.

- Similar sums continued to be spent throughout the 1590s. Between 1590 and 1598 a further 30 million *ducats* went to fund the Spanish army's campaigns in France.

Did Philip mishandle Spain's finances?

There are arguments both for and against whether Philip II mishandled Spain's finances.

Argument for. It might be argued that Philip II paid too high a price in attempting to keep control of the Low Countries. The bankruptcy of 1596 was the most serious of the reign and was largely caused by Spanish expenditure in the Netherlands and other related theatres of war. For the third time in his reign, Philip suspended payments of interest on existing debts as a means of forcing his bankers into making further loans. Negotiations took up most of Philip's final months and it was not until February 1598 that a new agreement was signed with the Crown's creditors.

Argument against. While the total debt by the end of the reign was reckoned at 100 million *ducats*, we should not perhaps be too critical. We should not expect Philip or any other monarch to 'balance the books'. Philip believed that he was appointed by God, incurred various God-given responsibilities and should not give up those burdens on the advice of finance ministers. In the case of the Netherlands, Philip could not bring himself to offer religious toleration, since that would mean caving into heresy, which he could never do.

Despite the bankruptcies, Spain did not renounce or refuse to pay its debts. It merely rescheduled them. In view of the enormous income to be expected from the New World and the terrible losses if they refused to advance further money, the bankers and financiers continued to lend and the Crown continued to borrow. Empire brought enormous expenditure but Philip continued to pay the price.

SPAIN'S ECONOMY UNDER PHILIP II

Spain's imperial expansion and extensive warfare had a serious impact on the Spanish economy in the reign of Philip II. This was largely because economic growth had not kept pace with Spain's meteoric rise to great power status.

- That status was achieved not so much through the economic strength of Spain and its monarchy as through the unification of the peninsula, the sudden and unexpected acquisition of a huge overseas empire, the need to defend the Netherlands from internal and external subversion, and the eclipse of France in the second half of the sixteenth century via long-drawn-out and bloody civil wars. In this way Spain under Philip II achieved a status, with its resulting economic and financial burden, that its economy was unable to sustain.
- Nonetheless, economic problems and weaknesses should not be exaggerated. All European economies were fairly primitive at this time and the problems were not really serious until the reigns of Philip IV and Charles II in the seventeenth century. At the same time, it would be disingenuous to blame Philip II for all Spain's economic difficulties at a time when governments did not really have economic policies to speak of.

Economic improvement

In the first part of the reign, the economy seemed to be improving. Across Spain and particularly around Seville, there was sustained growth in the population. In Castile the population may have grown by 10 per cent in the second half of the century, with rather more growth in the south and in Granada than in the north of the region.

This population growth, probably less pronounced elsewhere in the peninsula, led to an increase in agricultural production, achieved through ploughing up fresh land. In the valley of Bureba, output of wheat increased by 26 per cent, wine by 50 per cent and rye by 54 per cent in the 20 years after 1560. A rising population also meant increased demand for woollen cloth and silks produced in Spain. By 1580, the city of Segovia boasted

600 looms and a system that had moved on from domestic to factory-style production. In the early years of the reign, the Spanish empire also encouraged a growth in manufactures that led to economic improvement.

Economic problems

Later in the reign, it became clear that the Spanish economy was little suited to the burdens of empire and economic recession set in.

Inflation. On the one hand, the import of precious metals from the New World helped to bring about serious price inflation in Spain. Professor Hamilton gave the classic explanation of his **theory of price revolution** back in 1934 and it is now generally accepted that the huge imports of precious metal (mainly silver) coming into Spain and often being spent outside Spain, led to a sustained increase in commodity prices during the sixteenth century.

Interest rates. At the same time, Philip's huge debts and reliance on foreign financiers meant that interest rates were high, which stifled borrowing and investment and also meant that, increasingly as the reign went on, important parts of the Spanish economy were in the hands of foreigners.

Relative weakness. In addition, as Spain's economy became part of a wider European economy, its weakness compared to the likes of the Dutch, French and English economies gradually became apparent. Spain lacked a large and expanding middle class, so that its banking and insurance, its manufactures and trading lagged behind those of other countries. In Spain, most successful merchants aspired to move out of commerce and buy up landed estates and a title to nobility. After all, the nobility had all the advantages of high status, exemption from taxation and the security of landowning at a time of rising agricultural prices and rents. As a result of this, Spain's merchants and merchant vessels were limited in number and failed to expand sufficiently at a time of increasing trade. Much of the important trade between Spain and the Baltic, for example, was carried in Dutch vessels, even while Spain was at war with the Dutch provinces!

KEY THEME

Hamilton's theory of price revolution This phenomenon was so unusual that Professor Earl J. Hamilton gave it the name of 'price revolution'. In essence it meant that those at the lower end of the social scale were worse off as wages always lagged behind the prices of essential goods. By looking at 'real wages' during Philip's reign, Hamilton calculated that from 1530 to 1600 most Spaniards could buy 20 per cent less goods than before or after. While allowing for the inexact and partial nature of the statistics available to him, it is clear from Hamilton's work that American silver left most Spaniards worse off.

Agricultural problems

Spain during the reign of Philip II suffered a series of **demographic crises** brought about by poor harvests and disease. These were made worse by the generally poor state of Spanish agriculture. While agricultural output did go up in some areas, this was achieved by farming more land, not by making farming more efficient. Ploughing was often done by mules, which meant a shallower furrow and quicker exhaustion of the topsoil. In addition there were long-term structural problems, which undermined increased agricultural output and put Spain at risk of periodic food shortages.

- Much Spanish land was of limited fertility and the long, hot summers often led to drought when water was most needed.
- Furthermore, most of those working the land were landless labourers at the mercy of any economic downturn. Even where there were peasant proprietors, they often had insufficient land to sustain their families.
- Much of the land continued to be owned in great *latifundia* (estates) by the aristocracy or the Church, neither of which was keen to introduce new agricultural methods to bring about greater efficiency.
- Their ownership of **land held in entail**, meant that the amount of land on the market was very limited, so that a class of improving farmers could not develop.

As a result, Spain continued to be prone to periodic mortality crises when hit by disease and bad harvests. With birth rates falling after 1580, the situation was made worse by serious outbreak of the plague in Andalusia (1582), Catalonia (1589–92) and throughout Spain (1596–1602). The last plague alone is thought to have resulted in 600,000 deaths. Overall it is clear that grain production in Spain was insufficient to meet the normal demands of the population.

This meant that Castile in particular had to rely increasingly on imported grain, which created yet higher bread prices. Much of this grain came from the Spanish possessions of Sicily and Naples in Italy. Philip's foreign policy and his serious need for soldiers may also have undermined the situation.

KEY TERMS

Demographic crisis A crisis which results in an increase in the death rate. Such crises could have serious economic and social consequences.

Latifundia Very large farms or estates, as opposed to smaller farms tended by individual families.

Land held in entail Land that, by means of a legal device known as an entail, cannot be sold or alienated from the family that owns it.

- His demand for soldiers removed men from the land, thus creating a labour shortage.
- At the same time, Philip's response to higher grain prices was to put an upper limit on those prices.

It is clear that the king was very concerned about the impact of rising food prices and much of his correspondence testifies to his paternalistic approach to the problem. While price ceilings may have helped the poor and needy, they stopped producers from enjoying reasonable profits. In a similar way, the Crown's high rates of taxation helped to produce economic stagnation. Burdened with crippling taxation and over-regulation, there was little incentive for the entrepreneur to invest or embark on a risky speculation, if profits would be wiped out by taxes.

At the same time the 1590s saw other changing economic trends that hampered the Spanish economy for years to come.

- The Dutch and English were increasingly active in trading directly with the New World, thus undermining Spain's trading monopoly there.
- At the same time the New World economy was hit by severe labour shortages and began to produce similar goods to those manufactured in the mother country.
- Increasingly, the trade between Spain and the New World slumped and the Spanish empire looked to other countries for its needs.

Overall there were clear signs that the Spanish economy was unable to take advantage of the advent of empire and instead found the burden of great power status too great to bear.

DID PHILIP'S SUCCESSES OUTWEIGH HIS FAILURES?

Philip's reign clearly enjoyed mixed fortunes both for Spain and for Philip himself.

Successes

In the first half of the reign, perhaps up to 1580, Spain can be seen as broadly successful. At home, the *Moriscos* were dealt with and ceased to be a problem; Portugal was acquired via a bloodless *coup* while both Church and State remained firmly under Philip's control. Abroad there was success against the Turks at Lepanto; the expansion of the New World empire and the arrival of increasing shipments of silver. Up to 1572, there was even success, under Alva, in putting down the Dutch Revolt. With France troubled by civil war and even the Turks less interested in European expansion after the death of Suleiman in 1566, Spain could be seen as the greatest power on earth, with the largest overseas empire ever seen.

Failures

After 1580, however, the problems began to mount up. The Dutch Revolt dragged on with the northern provinces poised to break away from Spanish control. Attempts to invade England and change the succession in France resulted in dismal failure and ever-increasing royal debts. Even inside Spain there was discord with the Revolt of Aragon, economic recession and serious epidemics and outbreaks of plague.

Conclusion

For Philip himself, the question is perhaps rather unhelpful as a means of assessing the reign. Equally passive and aloof in the face of triumph and disaster, he felt that the great affairs of society and history were in God's hands and were little influenced by humble princes. Philip would not have assessed his reign in terms of success or failure, but rather in terms of how diligently and conscientiously he had carried out what he regarded as God's will. In this way, historians must give Philip great credit for his unflagging efforts at ruling his empire.

He worked tirelessly, perhaps because he couldn't see the difference between the trivial details and the vital principles. He was a simple man of simple habits but he was equally the slave of duty. This meant that he was always his own first minister. He never delegated power to favourites, as his successors would, but stuck to his own motto, often repeated, that 'it is as well to think of everything'. He is often criticised for taking too long over decisions. One Spanish ambassador remarked that 'if death should come from Spain, I should be immortal'.

On the other hand, he ruled his kingdoms with justice and, judging by the circumstances faced by all sixteenth-century governments, he ruled them well. Internal revolts were kept down to a minimum, while Spanish arms were feared throughout the world. While he bestrode the world like a Titan, Philip was never ambitious for power or conquest but remained humble and withdrawn. His sense of duty was underpinned at all times by his religious faith and his inherited sense of the majesty and importance of his position. Judged by these criteria, Philip's reign, in its own terms, was decidedly a success.

Sadly for Philip, his son would not prove to be as conscientious as his father. As he lay dying in his beloved Escorial Palace, Philip confided to the distraught onlookers, 'God, who has given me so many kingdoms, has not granted me a son fit to govern them.'

SUMMARY QUESTIONS

1 How extensive and serious were domestic problems during the reign of Philip II?

2 'A colossus with feet of clay.' How accurate is this description of Spain in the second half of the sixteenth century?

3 'Philip II's main difficulty was that he took the business of government too seriously.' To what extent do you agree with this judgement.

4 How successful was Spain's foreign policy during the reign of Philip II?

CHAPTER 4

1598–1665: Why did Spain face so many problems in the reigns of Philip III and Philip IV?

KEY POINTS

- Philip III was less committed to government than his father. He ruled through a favourite, or *Valido*. His reign saw the final expulsion of the *Moriscos* from Spain.
- Philip IV was more involved in government, and for most of his reign his favourite, Count-Duke Olivares, attempted to institute wide-ranging reform.
- Spain remained a great power in Europe. Under Philip III, the country made peace and was less involved in conflict in Europe. Under Philip IV, Spain restarted the war against the Dutch rebels and was sucked into the Thirty Years War 1618–48.
- By the end of Philip IV's reign, Spain had lost the Dutch provinces as well as Portugal.
- Traditionally, Spain is often seen as being in decline during this period, but the scale of that decline is debated.

THE REIGN OF PHILIP III, 1598–1621

Methods of government
Philip II's dying premonition made in 1598 that he had not produced a son fit to rule the Spanish empire proved well founded.

How Phillip III was different to Philip II. Unlike his father, who had been a model of engaged monarchy, ploughing through mountains of paperwork with an unflinching sense of duty, **Philip III** devoted himself to harmless pleasures and a determination not to govern.

- It is said that he often posted guards at the palace gates to prevent ministers or officials from troubling him.
- At the same time he tried to avoid meeting his subjects.

> ### KEY PERSON
>
> **Philip III (1578–1621)** A sickly and pale youth, aged 20 at the time of his father's death. The only one of four brothers and one sister to survive infancy, he was much given to the pleasures of hunting and feasting and the avoidance of work. Philip was a deeply religious man and throughout his reign between 1598 and 1621 he devoted himself primarily to the interests of the Church. Very much a family man, he and his wife, Margaret of Austria, plus their five children, just wanted to divert and amuse themselves and enjoy the privileged position they occupied.

- Although he travelled quite extensively, often going on pilgrimage, he avoided going on progress through Spain.

In this way Philip III practised a kind of aloof withdrawal that, in the end, would undermine the power and prestige of the monarchy.

How Philip III was similar to Philip II. Like his father, Philip III was at least devoted to the Catholic Church and was personally devout. At least he did not interfere in the business of government or dream up interventionist policies that might have cost Spain dear.

Luckily for Philip III, he had a friend who was happy to take away all his responsibilities so that the king could enjoy his leisure. Don Francisco Gomez de Sandoval y Rojas, a rather poor Valencian aristocrat, had befriended Philip before his father's death.

- In 1599, he was raised to the position of **Duke of Lerma** and became *Valido* (the king's favourite).
- In 1602, the Venetian ambassador commented, 'To obtain one's suit, it is more important to be in favour with the Duke of Lerma than with the king … for it truly appears that the king has no other will than that of the duke.'

Lerma's position remained informal until a decree of 1612, which declared that the duke's orders carried the same weight as the king's. Lerma himself was easygoing and affable, bored by the routine tasks of administration but keen to map out the broader lines of royal policy at home and abroad. In order to safeguard his position, he brought in friends and relations, and rewarded them with patronage.

- His uncle became Archbishop of Toledo.
- His wife became chief lady-in-waiting to the queen.
- His son became Marquis of Cea.
- His uncle became President of the Council of Portugal.
- His brother became Viceroy of Valencia.

Added to these were two favourites of the favourite, **Rodrigo Calderón** and **Pedro Franqueza**. As the new men were brought in, so the old guard, who had served Philip II loyally, tended to depart. Don Cristóbal de Moura was sent off to Portugal as viceroy. Rodrigo Vázquez was sacked as President of the Council of Castile.

Once in power, the favourites soon acquired great fortunes as they traded their influence for bribes and position. Lerma's annual income had reached 200,000 *ducats* by 1602 and by the time of his fall, some contemporaries (usually his enemies) put his personal fortune at 44 million *ducats*! When Rodrigo Calderón was eventually arrested in 1619, his goods alone were valued at 2 million *ducats*.

Position of the aristocracy

The advancement of the Duke of Lerma and his friends also heralded the return of the Spanish aristocracy to court. Philip II had kept them at arm's length allowing them to rule the provinces but not to dominate central government. Under Philip III this process was largely reversed. This came about because the new king wanted the aristocracy at Court to reflect his power and position.

During his reign, **Madrid**, now established as the capital, grew from a population of around 40,000 to perhaps 70,000. The aristocracy themselves were keen to return to Court. They were desperately in need of further patronage to boost their fortunes, which were being undermined by inflation and declining food prices. The **aristocracy had been hard hit** by the inflation of the sixteenth century, which may have seen a quadrupling of prices while incomes barely doubled. Under Philip III they came back to Court in the hope of plundering the royal treasury, and they were often successful. At the same time Philip III created more titles for the great men of the realm. He created three dukes, 30 marquises and 33 counts.

Clear evidence for the renewed wealth of the grandees comes from the increasing size of their households.

- Count-Duke Olivares boasted some 200 servants.
- However, he was outdone by the Duke of Osuna, who had 300 personal servants.
- Even he was also surpassed by the Duke of Medinaceli, who had a massive 700 personal servants.

KEY THEMES

Madrid as capital Philip II had definitively established Madrid as capital of Spain in 1560. Three years later he began the construction of the Escorial Palace near the city.

Financial plight of the nobility The Venetian ambassador, perhaps not the most reliable source, claimed that many grandees, like the monarchy itself, spent four-fifths of their annual income servicing their debts.

Overall the aristocracy clearly made political and financial gains under Philip III that served to accentuate, once again, the imbalance between rich and poor. This feature undermined and weakened Spanish society. Although they gained a higher profile, the influence of the aristocracy should not be exaggerated. While they gained influence through honorary posts in the many Councils, the importance of these Councils was diminishing as Lerma made all the major decisions. Although he was not a bureaucrat in the mould of Philip II and thus left rather fewer written records, his power should not be underestimated. He ruled informally through his own favourites and with the king's full backing, thus excluding the aristocracy from real influence in central government. Luckily for Spain, the *letrados* (army of officials) who actually carried out administrative duties continued to ensure that Spain was effectively governed.

FOREIGN POLICY 1598–1621: DECLARATIONS OF PEACE

Although it is easy to be critical of the Duke of Lerma as the easygoing and greedy favourite, he should be given credit for redirecting Spanish foreign policy towards peace.

- Though Spain was involved in minor wars in Italy and aided enemies of the Turks, Lerma's regime ended Spain's military commitments in northern Europe and consequently reduced military expenditure quite considerably.
- At the same time Spain remained influential and was still regarded as the greatest power in Europe.

Lerma showed how Spain could achieve peace with honour. Sadly, those who overthrew him in 1618 returned to aggressive policies, which would hasten Spain's decline.

Peace with France
Peace had already been made at Vervins (1598) before the death of Philip II. Although relations worsened thereafter as France recovered from its long period of civil war, the assassination of Henry IV in 1610, when war seemed imminent, led to more peaceful relations as France tried to

cope with the minority of **Louis XIII**. In 1612, the two
countries agreed to a double marriage alliance where Philip
III's daughter, Anne of Austria, would marry Louis XIII
while Louis' sister, Isabella de Bourbon, would marry
Philip III's son (the future Philip IV).

The marriage ceremonies took place in 1615 thus further
enhancing the peace between Spain and France.

Peace with England

Although at peace with France, the war against England
had carried on in a desultory way.

- In early 1601, Lerma organised an armada of 50 ships to
  attack England but this was beaten back by fierce
  storms.
- In late 1601, an armada actually landed in Ireland with
  orders to team up with the rebellious Irish Catholics
  against the hated English forces of Queen Elizabeth.

This second plan had some chance of success. The
Spaniards landed in Kinsale in southern Ireland and,
although blockaded by the English governor, Lord
Mountjoy, a large Irish force soon appeared on the scene
to help out the Spanish forces. If the Spanish had managed
to link up with their Irish allies, then Mountjoy's limited
resources of money and men might have been seriously
stretched. However, the Irish forces under the Earl of
Tyrone, so successful in their native Ulster, achieved little
and the Spanish were forced to surrender Kinsale in return
for safe passage back to Spain.

After this setback, Lerma's thoughts turned towards peace.
With war in the Low Countries ongoing, it seemed
sensible to cut back on foreign policy expenditure. The war
with England finally came to an end in 1604 at the Peace
of London. Elizabeth's death in 1603 had led to the
accession of James I, the King of Scotland. Although he
was a Protestant, he lacked Elizabeth's long-term hatred
and fear of Spain, and he took the sensible view that
England could not afford war against Spain. As he also
lacked Elizabeth's flair for interfering in the Dutch Revolt,
Philip III's government was quite prepared to consider
making peace, which would bring some relief to the over-

Louis XIII (1601–43) Son
of Henry IV of France. He
ruled from 1610 to 1643. In
this period, led mainly by
Richelieu, France recovered its
international position after the
debilitating Wars of Religion.
Louis was succeeded by his
grandson Louis XIV.

pressed Spanish treasury. At the same time, Spain realised that the real threat to its interests was now France, reunited after years of debilitating civil war. Therefore, peace with England might bring with it an English counter-weight to French aggression.

Relations with England remained cordial for the rest of Philip's reign. The Spanish ambassador in London, **Count Gondomar**, was one of the great diplomats of his age and won a huge amount of influence with King James. He secured the execution of Sir Walter Raleigh in 1618 for his attacks on the Spanish empire and encouraged the idea of a marriage between James' son Charles and a Spanish princess. Although this failed to materialise, Spain remained at peace with England during Philip III's reign.

The Truce of Antwerp, 1609

Five years after the peace with England, Spain finally agreed a truce with the Dutch rebels. Although Spanish fortunes had improved under **Ambrogio Spinola** with the capture of the important port of Ostend in 1604, Spain was clearly not in a position to defeat the rebels. Its forces continued to mutiny for lack of pay and the government of the Archduke Albert advised Lerma that peace of some sort was the only option.

In the event, Philip III agreed to a truce in 1607 – just a few months before another Spanish bankruptcy. This truce was finally ratified and made official in 1609. However, even after more than 40 years of trials and tribulations in the Low Countries, the Spanish government could not bring itself to admit defeat. As a great power, Spain was too concerned about its image in the world to allow it to be seriously undermined by a heretic republic. Instead of agreeing to recognise the Dutch Republic as an independent nation, Spain only agreed to a Twelve Year Truce and, sure enough, hostilities between the two countries recommenced in 1621 as part of an even wider European conflict known as the Thirty Years War.

- The Spanish government would have seen such an admission of defeat as a betrayal of Spain's imperial and religious imperatives. After all, the Low Countries were not just part of the Spanish empire but part of Philip

KEY PEOPLE

Count Gondomar (1567–1626) He was Diego Sarmiento de Acuña, one of the foremost diplomats of his age. Improved relations between England and Spain can largely be attributed to his good work.

Ambrogio Spinola (1569–1630) An Italian who became Spain's leading general in the Low Countries. In 1604, he took the port of Ostend and in 1609, he negotiated the Twelve Years Truce. In 1620, he invaded the Palatinate in Germany. Returning to the Low Countries in 1621, he took Breda but his conciliatory policy lost him the favour of Philip IV and he was appointed governor of Milan in 1629.

III's patrimony, his inheritance from his father and grandfather.

- To give away half of it after so much effort would have been a betrayal of those men who had fought and died to win it back, a betrayal of family as well as of Spain, and the end of Spain's greatness.
- If the Dutch were allowed to break away then so might the Catalans. Spain's empire might come to an end, betrayed by its leaders.
- Spain was a great power and thus could hardly avoid warfare. Europe was divided by religion and a rising tide of nationalism. Under these circumstances, Spain was always going to be dragged into conflict. Nonetheless, the decision to restart hostilities in 1621 was a mistake, which would cost Spain dear.

THE EXPULSION OF THE *MORISCOS*, 1609

Reasons for expulsion

While Lerma should be given credit for his largely peaceful foreign policy, he should be criticised for his decision to expel forcibly the *Moriscos* from Spain. As long ago as 1582, Philip II's Council of State recommended that the *Moriscos* should be expelled from Spain. Yet no action was taken. The reality of Spanish society was that the converted Moors, though often oppressed and despised on racial and religious grounds by their Spanish neighbours, were tolerated and often protected by Spanish landowners who relied on their labour.

The *Moriscos* had not caused trouble since the Revolt of the Alpujarras in 1569 and as late as 1607, two senior ministers, Don Juan de Idiáquez and the Count of Miranda, were recommending teaching followed by genuine conversion to Christianity as the best way to assimilate the *Moriscos* into Spanish society. Previous attempts at genuine conversions had conspicuously failed to bear fruit. There had never been enough money to pay for the massive educational effort, which would have been needed to convert 300,000 Arab-speaking Muslims to Christianity. **Archbishop Ribera** of Valencia, where the *Moriscos* were most densely settled after their dispersion

KEY PERSON

Juan de Ribera (1532–1611) Archbishop of Valencia. He was very concerned about the possibilities of a Moorish uprising in the kingdom.

from Granada, did more than most to set up seminaries and schools for *Morisco* youths. Yet in the end, he had to admit defeat and was subsequently one of the most influential voices recommending expulsion.

The idea of expulsion had been buttressed by the dispersal of the Moors from Granada after the Revolt of the Alpujarras (see pages 75–8). This had created a Castilian dimension to the *Morisco* problem that had not previously existed.

- In Castile, the Moors were often rootless, scattered and poor, the object of Castilian hostility.
- By contrast, in Valencia they lived in communities and were valued by landlords as industrious and exploitable workers.

If the *Moriscos* had only been a Valencian problem, they might not have been expelled. In 1599 and 1604, Philip III was in Valencia. On neither occasion was the idea of expulsion of the *Moriscos* raised.

However, in the early years of Philip's reign, the *Moriscos* continued to be seen as a serious threat to Spain's security. In 1602, a group of *Moriscos* was discovered plotting with the French government to assist a French invasion of Spain.

- They offered to raise a force of 80,000 men, who would help the French if they invaded northern Spain.
- Three cities would be handed to the French as bases for the proposed invasion.
- In 1604–5, *Morisco* plotters handed over 120,000 *ducats* to the French as a token of their good faith.

Nonetheless, these hopes came to nothing. Perhaps more serious as a cause of their expulsion was the plot hatched in 1608 by *Moriscos* in Valencia to assist an invasion of Spain by Moroccan forces under Muley Cidan. This time the *Moriscos* claimed that they could raise 100,000 troops to help in the dismemberment of Spain. The Spanish government was seriously worried about this conspiracy, particularly as the Turkish Sultan, Ahmet I, had just ended his war with Persia and might be in a position to help his fellow Muslims.

The Moroccan conspiracy brought the *Morisco* problem to the top of the political agenda. Some suggested mass slaughter and others enslavement, but it was expulsion that won the day, perhaps because **Lerma hoped to gain** from the process. He ensured that the day on which Philip III approved the decree of expulsion (9 April 1609) was the same day as he signed the Twelve Year Truce with the Dutch. In other words the expulsion, designed to stir patriotic feelings, was used cynically to cover the humiliation of defeat. This way, 1609 would be remembered not as a year of defeat but as a year of victory.

The expulsion and its results

Between 1609 and 1614, the government carefully organised the expulsion of the *Moriscos* from Spain. Safe passage to the coast was enforced and ships for the voyage were hired. While some contemporaries estimated the numbers of those expelled at more than a million, most historians now think that about 300,000 *Moriscos* departed from Spain. Most went to North Africa – to Morocco or Tunis – while some took up an offer from Henry IV to settle in southern France. Many were welcomed; some were not. In the end many went happily, pleased to leave a land where they were an oppressed minority with little hope of advancement, power or riches.

The immediate **economic results of the expulsion** were serious, especially in Valencia and Aragon where most of the *Moriscos* had lived. Most were landless labourers or craftsmen, sorely needed in the local economy. Efforts to replace them largely failed.

- In Valencia only 14,000 new settlers came to take over land vacated by some 114,000 who had been expelled.
- Some 205 *Morisco* villages in the province remained deserted by 1638, often in the less fertile parts of the region, but it meant a serious reduction in grain production in the area.
- Certainly the Church was worse off in former *Morisco* areas. Income for the bishopric of Saragossa fell by 40

Lerma's motives He may have been swayed by the opportunity to enrich himself further at the *Moriscos* expense. Most of his estates were in Valencia and it was now determined that all *Morisco* lands would be confiscated by the Crown. The final nail in the *Morisco* coffin was the Truce with the Dutch rebels.

Economic results of the expulsion Studying price rises in Spain, Professor Hamilton showed that increasing prices had much more to do with importing gold and silver bullion than with the expulsion of racial and religious minorities.

Contemporary responses to expulsion of the Moors One royal confessor writing in 1633 was certainly convinced that the expulsions had been a grave mistake. 'It is a very short time ago,' he wrote, 'since the *Moriscos* were expelled – an action which did such harm to these kingdoms that it would be a good idea to have them back again, if they could be persuaded to accept our Holy Faith.'

per cent, while that of Valencia dropped by 30 per cent, thanks to the expulsions.

Nonetheless, the long-term economic impact of the expulsions should not be exaggerated. It was easy, after the event, to claim that Spain's economic decline in the seventeenth century was all linked to the expulsion of the Moors.

- One official report claimed that the volume of wool passing through the city of Cuenca had dropped by 95 per cent between 1601 and 1625, while the number of cattle in Spain as a whole had fallen by 12,000,000. Such reports may well be exaggerated and certainly cannot be linked exclusively to the expulsions.
- In the long term, the removal of the *Moriscos* only served to underline and possibly speed up decline, which was already evident. The expulsions were only one factor explaining Spain's economic troubles.
- Many parts of the western Mediterranean where there were no such expulsions also suffered economic decline in this period.

HOPES OF REFORM: THE *ARBITRISTAS*

The expulsion of the *Moriscos* and Spain's continuing economic problems led to many complaints from literate intellectuals. They produced hundreds of pamphlets throughout the seventeenth century analysing the ills of society and offering advice on how solutions might be brought about. Some 165 such pamphlets were produced during the reigns of Philip III and Philip IV. The writers of these pamphlets were called the *arbitristas*. The government was surprisingly tolerant of their *arbitrios* (suggestions). It set up the first *Junta de Reformación* in 1618 and the famous *consulta* (report to the king) of the Council of Castile in 1619.

- One of the first to appear in front of the *Junta* was Martin Gonzalez de Cellorigo's *Memorial* of 1600.
- One of the most famous was Sancho de Moncada's *Political Restoration* of 1619. He based his ideas on an

KEY THEMES

Views of the *arbitristas*

One of the *arbitristas*, **Saavedra**, claimed that 'the main duty of the prince is to conserve his realms'. He did not think that the government was doing enough. Fajardo Diego de Saavedra (1584–1648), incidentally, was a statesman and author. He studied at the university of Salamanca and became Spanish ambassador in Rome.

A contemporary view of the distribution of wealth

In his *De Rege et regendi ratione* of 1616, Mateo Lopez Bravo, a Madrid magistrate, observed that 'great wealth in one person plunges many into poverty'.

Cervantes' view of the *arbitristas*

He made great fun of the *arbitristas* in his book *Coloquio de los Perros* (1606–9) in which the *arbitrista* ends up in hospital and suggests that the government's financial problems could be overcome if everyone from fourteen to 60 'shall be compelled to fast once a month on bread and water on a day specially chosen'. The money that they would otherwise have spent on food that day could then be sent to the government and the financial ills of the nation would soon be overcome.

analysis of parish registers in Toledo. This seemed to show that fewer people were getting married, the population was stagnating and the cause of the problems was poverty.

While some thought that decline and difficulties were a natural and unalterable consequence of Spain's rise, others took the view that the government should do more to bring about reform and end corruption.

The *arbitristas* and their complaints

Economic problems were often at the heart of *arbitristas* critiques. They complained about the weakness and decay of industry and agriculture, and an unwillingness to work or to foster enterprise and investment. The cost and corruption of government was also an easy target to identify.

- Most *arbitristas* disagreed with the expulsion of Jews and Moors and deplored the extremes of wealth and poverty in Spanish society.
- In addition, there were serious attacks on the war in the Low Countries and calls to remember that Spain's first priority should be its empire and the Mediterranean, not northern Europe.
- Others rejected the empire itself, arguing that the discovery of the New World had been the start of Spain's undoing.

The *arbitristas* and their solutions

While it was easy to identify problems, the *arbitristas* were less convincing when it came to solutions. Many looked to the past, back to the days of Ferdinand and Isabella as a supposed Golden Age but had few ideas of how to reform society of their own day. Scapegoats could always be found – for example, the Jews, the *Moriscos* and foreign merchants – but there was little by way of practical suggestion. More often than not the solutions were impractical. Although some of the *arbitristas'* suggestions were of little value, their ability to criticise the regime shows that Lerma's government and those which came afterwards were not unduly repressive. Indeed it was Lerma himself who responded to the suggestions of the *arbitristas* by setting up the *Junta de la Reformación* in 1618.

THE FALL OF LERMA, 1618

Reasons for Lerma's fall

Lerma's new *Junta* proved largely ineffectual and may have been merely a device to hold on to power a little longer. By 1618, it seemed that the *Valido*'s days were numbered. The favourite had always had his critics and had never been far from scandal.

- As early as 1608 two important Royal Councillors, Alonso Ramirez de Prado and the Count of Villalonga, had been prosecuted for financial misdemeanours and forced to pay back a total of some 2 million *ducats* of ill-gotten gains.
- More worrying for Lerma were the rumours that one of his main favourites, Rodrigo Calderón, had actually poisoned the queen (who died in childbirth) because he had just been relieved of his court offices by Philip III. It seems Calderón blamed his misfortunes on the queen's increasing influence with the king. With her sudden death aged only 26, the king was heartbroken and vented his anger on Calderón. Once again Lerma weathered the storm and indeed promoted Calderón to new positions of power.
- The main cause of the *Valido*'s downfall seems to have been the return to Spain of **Don Baltasar de Zúñiga** in 1617. He had served as Spanish ambassador, since 1599 in Brussels, Paris and, most recently, Vienna. Lerma's determination to keep him away from Madrid for so long is perhaps a clear sign that he feared Zúñiga's power and ideas.

Threats to Lerma

Even before Zúñiga's arrival there were signs that Lerma's position was under threat.

- In 1615, one of Philip's chaplains had published a book arguing that Philip should abandon the *Valido* and rule through his ministers.
- This same chaplain spent the summer of 1618 with Philip, when news came through of the Protestant rebellion in Bohemia. This revolt threatened the position of Ferdinand II, Catholic Habsburg Emperor of Austria, who expected to rule that part of the Holy Roman

KEY PERSON

Don Baltasar de Zúñiga (d. 1622) A powerful Spanish aristocrat, diplomat and politician. He came to power when Lerma fell and, five years later, on his death, handed power to his nephew, Olivares.

empire but who had now been apparently ousted by the **Calvinist Elector of the Palatinate**.

- In fact, the Elector Frederick in his turn would soon be expelled from Bohemia but, in 1618, this turn of events was seen as the chance for Zúñiga and his friends to attack Lerma's peaceful and defensive foreign policy. They argued convincingly that if the Emperor's power was diminished by the loss of Bohemia, then Spain's position in Italy would also be undermined, as well as its control of the all-important **Spanish Road**, which would be needed in case of further conflict with the Dutch.
- In the Spanish Netherlands, Archduke Albert added his voice to Zúñiga's party by claiming that military intervention in Germany would frighten the Dutch into renewing the Twelve Year Truce on terms more favourable to Spain. In this he was wrong, but the argument seemed convincing. Others claimed that Spain's problems arose from its lethargy in foreign affairs and that a successful war at this point (which of course would be short!) was the only way to revive Spain's imperial fortunes. In 1618, the Council voted some 700,000 *ducats* to assist the Emperor – a clear sign that Lerma had lost influence.

Lerma's legacy

Lerma was right to argue that involvement in war in aid of the Emperor would be a disaster. There would, he foresaw, be no way out and the enemies of Spain, including a more powerful France, would interpret help to the Emperor as a deep-laid Habsburg plot to control western Europe and destroy Protestantism. In fact, Spain was embarking on a war which would last for 40 years and leave it very much weaker than when it started. In this way Lerma's peace policy would be vindicated in the light of future events.

- He gave Spain a valuable breathing space between 1609 and 1618 and arguably left the country stronger in 1618 than it had been at Philip III's accession in 1598.
- What cost Spain dear was not the idleness of the king and the corruption of his courtiers but the reimposition of war and the demands of war.

Nonetheless, Lerma's sound policy could not save him. He left court in October 1618 and retired to his estates. His

The Calvinist Elector of the Palatinate, Frederick V
Known as the Winter King, Frederick was a zealous Protestant who believed that God intended him to become Emperor of Germany. He was married to James I's daughter, Elizabeth. His title of Elector meant that he was one of the seven men who, when the Emperor died, chose his successor.

The Spanish Road The name given to the routes taken by Spanish troops from northern Italy to the Low Countries.

son, the **Duke of Uceda**, gave him the final push in an act
lacking in filial kindness and Lerma would later be forced
to give up some of his ill-gotten gains. That said, he had
taken out one important insurance policy. He persuaded
the Pope to make him a Cardinal, which gave him
immunity from serious prosecution.

PHILIP III'S FINAL YEARS, 1618–21

Fall of Calderón

Rodrigo Calderón was not as fortunate as his master,
Lerma. He was made the scapegoat of the old regime by
Lerma's son and the new favourites, who crowded around
him.

In February 1619, he was taken off to gaol in Valladolid
amid cries of 'Death to the traitor'. His goods, thought to
be worth some 2 million *ducats*, were seized and he was
faced with a formidable list of 244 charges, among
them that of having murdered the queen, Margaret of
Austria, back in 1611. Calderón was tortured but the
charge of murdering the queen was later dismissed and
the judges officially acquitted him of all charges in
December 1620.

Just when Calderón thought the king would release him,
Philip III died and his successor was persuaded to renew
the case against him. This time there was no escape.
Calderón was executed in October 1621.

Meanwhile, the realities of Spanish politics in Philip's later
years remained the same as before. Uceda acted very much
like his father, and the rewards and patronage continued to
flow. Although the Council of Castile produced its famous
consulta of 1619, which listed the ills of society rather
graphically, Uceda quietly ignored its message and
recommendations.

Foreign policy

However, there were important changes in these years in
terms of foreign policy.

The Emperor. Committed to a more interventionist role in

European politics, the new regime sent aid to the Habsburg Emperor, Ferdinand, to help his cause in Bohemia. In November 1620, Spanish forces were present at the **Battle of the White Mountain**, which saw the decisive defeat of Frederick, the Elector Palatine.

At the same time other Spanish forces occupied Alsace, the Palatinate and the Valtelline passes in order to secure the Spanish Road to the Netherlands (see map on page 161). Such a show of strength at this time clearly antagonised Spain's opponents.

The Dutch situation. Meanwhile, negotiations began with the Dutch to see if the truce of 1609 could be extended past 1621. The Spanish wanted to persuade the Dutch to lift their blockade of the River Scheldt (which served the port of Antwerp) and to give an undertaking that they would not attack Spain's New World empire or interfere in its colonial commerce. Spain was worried about the recent expansion of Dutch trade. The Dutch had expanded their commerce at the expense of Portugal as well as Spain, establishing forts in India, West Africa, Indonesia and Brazil. In addition, in the period before 1621 they were making approaches to and alliances with Spain's enemies, Morocco, Algiers, the Turks, the German Protestants, Sweden and the **Hanseatic League**. By 1621, then, the Dutch were in a strong position and were not prepared to compromise. This made renewal of the war with Spain inevitable. Unfortunately for Spain, that war would be fought not only in Europe but in the far-flung parts of its empire as well.

Problems in Portugal

The monarchy also faced mutterings of discontent in Portugal. There had been various sightings of King Sebastian, leading to speculation that he had perhaps not been killed at the Battle of Alcazarquivir after all. This showed that there was residual hostility to Spain's control of Portugal.

- In 1619, Philip III travelled to Portugal anxious to have his young son Philip recognised as heir to the Portuguese throne. The Portuguese *Cortes*, in truculent mood after

years of neglect, expected to have their grievances listened to.
- Instead the king cut short proceedings after the recognition of his son and hurried back to Madrid to oversee the problems in Germany. The Portuguese *Cortes* was far from happy with this cavalier treatment and their hostility would boil over into outright revolt 21 years later.

Having reached Madrid, Philip was taken ill. Although he rallied the next year, he did not recover. He died in 1621 at the age of 43, and was succeeded by his 16-year-old son as Philip IV.

PHILIP III'S ACHIEVEMENTS

The historian J.H. Elliott noted that Philip's life had been 'as blameless as it was unprofitable'. In retrospect, Elliott's judgement seems harsh.

- Philip avoided work as much as possible but the government of the country carried on in a similar way to the days of the workaholic Philip II. For all Philip II's hard work and over-developed sense of conscientiousness, it is not clear that Spain was better governed under the second than under the third Philip. Furthermore, Philip III at least was no tyrant.
- The ideas and criticisms of the *arbitristas* are a clear indication that Spain was a more open society than might be supposed by looking at the power of the Church and the expulsion of the *Moriscos*.
- Corruption, or what we would call corruption, was endemic in all the courts of Europe at this time. All kings and ministers were surrounded by those seeking patronage, power and office in a society where office holders remained largely unsupervised. In addition, some of the most notorious courtiers were arrested and fined, even though most were not.
- Philip's *Valido*, Lerma, might have done more to reform Spain but the problems facing it were enormous and its empire was unwieldy and far too spread out.
- Furthermore, it has been too easy for historians, like the

arbitristas, to exaggerate the scale of the problems. No one had access to statistics about the number of vagrants or the number of those dying of plague. We do not know the size or paucity of harvests with any great precision. Even the movement of prices is still a matter of guesswork and inference.

What we can say is that Spain remained the greatest power in Europe at the end of Philip's reign. Though it was not well equipped to withstand simultaneous attacks from many quarters, at home and abroad, over the next 40 years it was still a power to be reckoned with.

THE REIGN OF PHILIP IV, 1621–65

The rise of Olivares: Chief Minister, 1622–43

With Philip III's untimely death, there was another change of ministers. Uceda, son of Lerma, was ousted, and Zúñiga quickly assumed overall control of affairs. In **influencing the young Philip IV**, aged only sixteen, Zúñiga was helped by his nephew, Gaspar de Guzmán, Count-Duke Olivares, who had been intimate with the young prince since joining his household in 1615. With Zúñiga's sudden death in 1622, Olivares came to assume the greatest power until his disgrace and fall some 21 years later.

- Unlike Philip III, who so often ran away from government, Philip IV was encouraged to become a true king of Spain by Olivares, who believed that only with a hard-working and effective king could Spain regain its 'reputation'.
- Once in power, Olivares showed himself as an energetic reformer. He wished to reduce corruption at court and in administration, weaken the power of the regional *Cortes* and create a more centralised government for Spain.
- Notoriously corrupt men from the old regime were made an example of. Calderón, as we have seen, was executed while Uceda and even Lerma (despite his cardinal's hat) were imprisoned and fined. Lerma died on his estates in 1625, bereft of most of his great fortune. Uceda died in prison.

KEY THEME

Relationship between Olivares and Philip IV
Being some eighteen years older than the young and rather uncertain Philip IV, Olivares' relationship with the king was like that of teacher and pupil, with the king usually content to follow Olivares' advice.

Junta de la Reformación

In 1622, Olivares set up a new *Junta de la Reformación*. Unlike the token body set up by Lerma in 1618, this Junta was a real chance for the *arbitristas* to offer solutions to Spain's problems. At last Spain had a first minister who seemed serious about tackling corruption and graft. The proposals put forward by the new Junta were wide-ranging.

- Ministers would be more closely supervised with checks on their accumulation of property.
- All those taking high office would have to give a sworn inventory of their goods when taking office and when leaving it.
- Taxes would be reformed; a single tax would replace both the *alcabala* (sales tax) and the hated *millones* (more recent sales tax on basic consumer goods).
- To encourage population growth, married men would be given tax breaks and no one would be able to emigrate without a royal licence.
- Nobles were to be penalised by **sumptuary laws** if they overspent.
- Many municipal offices would be abolished where it was

An oil painting of Count-Duke Olivares on horseback.

clear that new offices had been recently created merely for gain.

- An army of national defence would be established, drawing upon all the regions of Spain according to their wealth.
- Brothels were to be abolished.

These proposals became law as the 23 Articles of Reformation.

The drive for greater unification

A further drive for reform was seen in 1624, when Olivares drew up the *Great Memorial* for the king. In the *Great Memorial*, Olivares revealed that his central aim was now to enhance and drive forward Spanish unity.

Like many Castilians before him, Olivares believed that Spanish weakness derived from the **disunity of the peninsula**. Writing to Philip IV, Olivares noted that the king 'should direct all his work and thought to reduce those realms which make up Spain to the same order and legal system as Castile'. Looking at developments in France, Olivares could see that Spain's great rival for European power had the potential to become more powerful than Spain because its government was more centralised.

In attempting to end the centuries of independence or *quasi* independence enjoyed by the regions outside Castile, Olivares' regime and his hopes for Spain's future greatness would be dashed.

- At first Olivares tried to sugar-coat the bitter pill by claiming that a more unified realm would mean that the rulers of the peripheral regions would gain by being granted posts and offices in Castile.
- In addition, if he was serious about the future economic unity of Spain, then Castile's monopoly over New World trade would have to be ended.

However, despite the hopes of many, the reality of Olivares' actions was rather less heroic.

KEY THEME

Disunity of the peninsula
Because of the way in which Spain as a country had been put together by the marriage of Ferdinand and Isabella and the conquests of Granada and Portugal, it was a geographical but not political unity. Ever since unification, each region had retained its government, *Cortes* and *fueros*. In practice this meant that Castile had always borne a disproportionately heavy part of the overall burden.

The Union of Arms, 1626

One further reform to be attempted along these lines was Olivares' great Union of Arms introduced in 1626. This was a scheme to raise troops to defend Spain and its empire from foreign invasion, should the need arise. It was part of a broader effort to ensure that areas outside Castile played a greater part in sustaining the burden of Spain's empire. Ever since the reigns of Ferdinand and Isabella there had been a strong feeling among Castilians that they were paying too much and the others too little. So, in the Union of Arms, Olivares devised targets for the numbers of soldiers which were related to each area's wealth and population.

In order to sell the idea of the Union of Arms to Aragon, Philip IV and Olivares travelled to that kingdom in 1626 to preside over the three *Cortes* in Valencia, Aragon and Catalonia. They hoped to receive the assent of these bodies to the new scheme. Unfortunately such consent was not forthcoming.

- All three areas had long-standing grievances against the government, which they felt had deliberately neglected their interests and now wished to destroy their rights with Olivares' Union of Arms.
- The scheme meant that if any part of the monarchy, including Italy and Flanders, was attacked by an outside power, then the Crown of Aragon would have to pay for troops for as long as they were needed.
- More specifically, the Crown of Aragon had clear laws about the use of its troops outside its boundaries. These laws would be swept aside by the new scheme.

Olivares' determination to press on regardless of the *Cortes'* grievances (remember they had not been called for some 27 years!) meant that the royal party abandoned the *Cortes* in mid-session without any formal agreement on the new plan. Despite this, Olivares announced the official launch of the Union of Arms in July 1626. Once again it sounded as though reform had been successfully instituted when in fact it had not. More trouble was being stored up for the future.

Union of Arms, 1626 – the figures show the number of men to be raised by each region of Philip IV's dominions

Castile and the Indies	44,000
Catalonia	16,000
Portugal	16,000
Naples	16,000
Flanders	12,000
Aragon	10,000
Milan	8,000
Valencia	6,000
Sicily	6,000
Mediterranean and Atlantic Islands	6,000
TOTAL	140,000

Bankruptcy

In January 1627, Olivares announced the suspension of all payments to the royal bankers. Coming 20 years after Lerma's bankruptcy, it might seem to be something of a triumph that Spain had gone so long without such a declaration. Olivares attempted to put his announcement in a positive context, as he had lined up a group of Portuguese businessmen who had agreed to take on part of the debt at lower rates of interest. The **reforming measures** undertaken by Olivares, together with his natural optimism and high self-regard, meant that by 1627, it was easy for him to convince himself that reform was being instituted successfully on a number of fronts. Despite his best efforts, these reforms had a limited impact on Spain's problems. Those problems would be increased by the return to war in the 1630s.

FOREIGN POLICY UNDER OLIVARES

Spain's ability to introduce reform would depend largely on foreign policy. Success in short-term wars or a long period of general peace might have consolidated Spanish power since Spain was no longer fighting an aggressive war against the Dutch.

- As chief minister, Olivares inherited renewed conflict with the Dutch after the expiry of the Twelve Year Truce in 1621. In reality, Spain's leaders had given up the hope of recovering the Netherlands from the Dutch, but they did hope to gain some territory from the Dutch, in order to strengthen their position at future peace talks.
- Spain's problem was that its large and sprawling empire was hopelessly overstretched and too tempting a target for its many enemies.
- France, whose power had been so long eclipsed by civil war, was now recovering its strength and was convinced that Spain was plotting to enhance its power and prestige in alliance with the Habsburg Emperor of Austria. Faced with this danger, which was, in reality, more apparent than real, France was prepared to ally with and fund Spain's enemies, even if they were

Cardinal Richelieu Armand Jean du Plessis (1585–1642). He adopted the name Richelieu from the name of his family estate. He was a Cardinal of the Catholic Church and rose to be chief minister to Louis XIII of France. He was energetic, intelligent and a very shrewd politician. Hated by the aristocracy, he believed in the importance of strong government.

Protestant. This was rather ironic since France was a Catholic country and Louis XIII's chief minister, **Richelieu**, was a cardinal.

Spanish success, 1621–5

At first, Spain did get the wars it wanted – brief, small in scale and successful.

- Despite Spinola's failure to take Bergen-op-Zoom in the Netherlands in 1622, successes soon followed.
- In 1625, the port of Bahia in Brazil was recaptured from the Dutch, the English were repelled from an attack on the port of Cadiz led by the Duke of Buckingham, Spinola captured Breda from the Dutch and the French were forced to agree to withdraw from the Valtelline, an Alpine pass that lay across the Spanish Road (see map on page 161), which had been occupied by the Spanish in 1622.
- At the same time a three-pronged attack was planned against the hated Dutch. An attempt was made to block all Dutch trade with the Spanish peninsula, raids on Dutch shipping in the English Channel and North Sea were launched from Dunkirk in the Spanish Netherlands and attempts were made to create a Spanish/imperial fleet (using Spain's alliance with the Habsburg Emperor of Austria), which might attack Dutch trade in the Baltic.

Setbacks for Spain, 1626–35

Despite this bright opening, matters soon turned against Spain. Even the successes of 1625 had cost a great deal of money, and spending at that level could not be sustained – particularly in view of the failure of the Union of Arms.

Renewed wars. While the French made peace in 1626, this was unlikely to last and Spain was still nowhere near making peace with the Dutch.

Buoyed up, perhaps, by the successes of 1625, Olivares allowed Spain to renew hostilities with France in the War of the Mantuan Succession (1628–31). This was an unsuccessful attempt to oust the new French duke, Charles of Nevers, from his two duchies in northern Italy that bordered on the Spanish duchy of Milan. The war cost some 10 million *ducats*. By the Treaty of Cherasco in April 1631, Nevers' claim to the Duchy was fully recognised.

Dutch demands. Worse still, Spain's involvement in Italy against France gave the Dutch time to counter-attack in the Low Countries. By 1628, however, when Spinola returned to Spain, there seemed a real chance of making a new truce with the Dutch. Philip IV was impressed, but Olivares was not. As a result, the chance for peace slipped away. The Dutch renewed hostilities. They captured a great Spanish silver fleet off Cuba later that year (which resulted in the trial and execution of the Spanish admiral) and launched a successful campaign against the Spanish Netherlands the next year, capturing two more towns. Four more were lost to Spain in 1632. Peace negotiations reopened later that year but Dutch successes now inflated Dutch demands to include the complete withdrawal of Spain from the whole of the Netherlands.

Campaign in the Low Countries. This was quite unacceptable to Spain and meant that Olivares now had to make a further great effort to launch a campaign in the Low Countries. This he did in 1634. Philip IV's brother, the so-called **Cardinal Infante**, was the new commander. He set off from Milan, linked up with the new imperial commander, the Archduke Ferdinand, and together they inflicted a crushing defeat on a **Swedish army** of 25,000 at Nördlingen in Germany. Although a great triumph for Spain, Nördlingen was in fact a sideshow. The victory did nothing to help Spain's precarious position in the Low Countries. The real result of Nördlingen was to push France into a declaration of war on Spain in 1635. Allied with the Dutch and now fully recovered from the debilitating Wars of Religion, France had the wealth and power to defeat Spain and, possibly worse, **continue the conflict** for many years to come.

Continuing setbacks, 1637–43

After the French declaration of war, Spain enjoyed little success.

- In 1637, the Dutch recaptured Breda.
- In 1639, they destroyed a Spanish fleet at the Battle of the Downs in the English Channel. This was a desperate blow to Spain's hopes in the Netherlands, as their troops' supplies now had to be brought via the English Channel since the Spanish Road from Milan to Brussels had been cut in 1638, when Bernard of Weimar took the fortress of Breisach.
- Further afield, off the coast of Brazil, in 1640 the Dutch repeated the feat against an even larger Spanish fleet.
- Finally in 1643, Spain suffered a crushing defeat on land at the hands of the French. At Rocroi, close to the Spanish Netherlands, an invading but largely bankrupt Spanish army was destroyed. The auxiliary troops fled but the Spanish *tercios* stood their ground and were slaughtered.

Tercios The Spanish infantry, the best troops in the Spanish army.

With the flower of its army gone, Spain could not create a new army and so could not hope to continue the war against the Dutch. Thanks to the magnitude of its unexpected defeat, Spain at last pursued peace with the Dutch in earnest. As always the negotiations were long and protracted. Even now, Spanish *reputación* (reputation) had to be defended. Peace did not come until 1648 but when it did, Spain had to agree to recognise, officially, Dutch independence. It was a massive blow to Spanish morale of course, after the outpouring of so much blood and treasure fighting the hated and heretical Dutch rebels, but long-term peace with the Dutch did allow Spain to continue the war with France on more even terms.

KEY REGION

Catalonia The region was, and is, one of the most distinct of the Iberian peninsular. In the ninth century it was fully independent. By the twelfth century the Counts of Barcelona had holdings to the north of the Pyrenees and even islands such as Majorca. In 1137, Catalonia united with Aragon and gradually it became dominated by Castile. Such domination was generally not welcomed.

THE REBELLIONS OF 1640: CATALONIA AND PORTUGAL

Catalonia: causes of revolt

Spain's foreign policy commitments of the late 1630s, allied to long-term resentment of government from Madrid, led to two spectacular revolts in 1640. The first was in the province of **Catalonia**. The strategic importance of this province, which bordered on France, became even more significant after 1635 when Spain and France were officially at war. In 1639, a French army invaded Catalonia and took the border town of Salses. Faced with this

Olivares moved in an army from Castile and seized his chance to demand fresh troops from the Catalans, who seemed rather reluctant to repel the enemy. These moves led to a serious increase in tension in the province.

- The Castilian troops naturally expected to receive support (billeting, supplies and so on) from the Catalans they were defending but found the Catalans hostile. In April 1640, the local inhabitants burnt one royal official to death in the town of Santa Coloma de Farnes. In retaliation the Spanish *tercios* sacked the town and set it ablaze.
- At the same time, Olivares' demands for Catalan troops to help the war effort were ignored. The Catalan *Diputació*, which represented the ruling classes when the *Cortes* was not called, declared Olivares' move unconstitutional. In Pau Claris, a clergyman from the cathedral chapter of Urgel, the *Diputació* had a fiery leader who demanded that Castilian oppression should be resisted.
- In January 1640, the Catalan *Audiencia* (high court) declared that the billeting of Spanish troops was illegal and **contrary to their constitutions.**

One further element in this explosive Catalan situation was the widespread social problems, poverty and misery in the province. In addition, the local aristocracy were disaffected by Madrid's constant demands for money and perhaps by the fact that some 25 per cent of their number had been killed in the long siege to retake Salses.

Course of revolt in Catalonia

Although the frontier town of Salses was retaken from the French by January 1640, the cost was full-scale rebellion. After the destruction of Santa Coloma, peasant bands mobilised and took several towns. The Spanish army itself was attacked and forced to retreat as native rebels assaulted it on all sides. Some of the insurgents disguised as harvesters entered the capital Barcelona. Here even the *Diputació* could not control the situation and the rebels **sacked the city.** A rebellion infused by regional hostility to government in Madrid had become a social revolution against all government. For much of 1640 the situation

Contrary to their constitutions Olivares was beside himself when he heard that the billeting of troops had been declared unconstitutional. 'I am nearly at my wits' end,' he said, 'but I say and shall still be saying on my deathbed, that if the constitutions do not allow this, then the devil take the constitutions!'

The sacking of Barcelona (1640) Rioting and plundering, the mob rampaged through the city. Government officials were murdered and even the native-born governor of Catalonia was hacked down as he attempted to escape by boat.

was largely anarchic as the poor took their chance to extract vengeance on the rich.

- Olivares' attempts to raise a fresh army to bring peace to the province failed miserably and demonstrated that it was not only the nobility of Catalonia who possessed only limited loyalty to the Crown.
- Worse news was to follow in 1641, when the Catalan *Diputació*, having regained a measure of control, transferred their allegiance to France. At first Claris hoped to renounce monarchy, just as the Dutch had, by declaring **Catalonia an independent republic** under French protection. When the French refused to help out on these terms, Catalonia handed itself over to the French without conditions.
- The final blow for Olivares, in this particular drama, came in January 1641 when a combined Catalan and French force defeated a relieving Spanish army at Montjuich, just outside Barcelona. The Spanish commander immediately retreated and Catalonia remained in French hands for the next eleven years.

KEY THEME

Catalonia as an independent republic Back in Madrid, Olivares was in despair. 'Without reason or occasion,' he fumed, 'they have thrown themselves into as complete a rebellion as Holland.'

Portugal, 1640

The loss of Catalonia was far from the end of Olivares' woes in 1640. As well as rebellion in the east, there was also rebellion in the west, in Portugal, and this time the loss was permanent. The Portuguese, unlike the Catalans, had been a nation in the past, but were swallowed up by Philip II as recently as 1580. Their resentment at government from Madrid was consequently fuelled by a sense of outraged nationalism. Their complaints grew more serious in the 1630s as Olivares' attempts to squeeze more money out of them gathered pace.

- In 1633, the Portuguese Church was taxed and a new tax on office holders was imposed.
- Nobles were being bullied to contribute to the war effort and a new range of sales taxes was brought in.
- As well as this, the government in Portugal became more Castilian when a new administration was brought in by Philip IV in 1634. The new governor was Philip's cousin, Margaret of Savoy.
- Furthermore, the Portuguese seaborne empire in South

America (chiefly Brazil) and in the East Indies was under constant attack from the Dutch. Many blamed Spain, perhaps unfairly, for this undermining of the Portuguese empire.

The spark that set off revolt in Portugal was undoubtedly the outbreak of revolt in Catalonia. Ironically, it may have been Olivares' attempts to avoid rebellion that sparked off the trouble. Realising that the **Duke of Braganza** had a claim to the throne, Olivares ordered that he and other members of the Portuguese aristocracy should join the army being sent to put down revolt in Catalonia.

KEY PERSON

Duke of Braganza (1604–56) A Portuguese aristocrat related to the royal family. He became King John IV of Portugal and reigned from 1640 to 1656.

The cunning plan backfired when Braganza and friends, helped by strong encouragement and money from Cardinal Richelieu of France, staged a rebellion. With very few Spanish troops left in Portugal, it was a largely bloodless *coup*.

- A few guards at the royal palace in Lisbon, together with Olivares' chief agent in Portugal were assassinated.
- Margaret of Savoy was escorted to the Spanish border.
- Braganza proclaimed himself King John IV of Portugal.

Olivares' claim that the Portuguese were 'essentially faithful' to the Spanish Crown proved wide of the mark.

Andalusia, 1641

As well as Portugal and Catalonia, there was also trouble in Andalusia, though it proved to be much less of a threat to the monarchy. Here the threat was from Castilian grandees and proved something of a damp squib.

Riding on the tide of regional separatism, the Duke of Medina Sidonia and the Marquis of Ayamonte (both related to Olivares) hatched a plan to get rid of the hated *Valido* (the king's favourite) and turn Andalusia in the south of Spain into an independent state. Their schemes were aided by the fact that the region bordered on Portugal where Medina Sidonia's sister was the new queen and, of course, the rebels thought they could rely on direct aid from France and the Dutch.

As the king had asked them to raise troops in Andalusia to help against Catalonia, they hoped, like the Portuguese the year before, to use these troops to further their cause. Interestingly the plotters also hoped to restore an aristocratic chamber to the Castilian *Cortes* so that the king would be forced to take more notice of his aristocracy. It was easy for the aristocracy to blame an indulgent king and a hated royal favourite for the current humiliations being heaped upon their homeland.

The plot was betrayed and came to nothing, but Medina Sidonia was pardoned. The government dared not risk alienating the Castilian aristocracy at this time of multiple crises.

THE END OF OLIVARES, 1643

At first the disasters of 1640–1 only seemed to strengthen Olivares' position as first minister. There were no great men queuing to take on his power, as the situation seemed so hopeless and they had no alternative remedies to offer. Many felt that only a man of Olivares' energy and determination could avert the total dissolution of the Spanish monarchy. However, the defeats led to increasing pressure on Philip IV from the nobility to sack his *Valido*.

- At first the nobility signalled their disapproval by abandoning the royal court, so that on Easter Day 1641 only one grandee was available to accompany the king to chapel! Then they persuaded the king to go on campaign at the head of an army to recapture Catalonia.
- In 1642, king and minister suffered further disasters – defeat at Lerida at the hands of the Catalan rebels and the loss of the city of Perpignan to the French. These events effectively sealed Olivares' fate.
- When king and minister returned to Madrid, Olivares' carriage took a roundabout route to avoid popular demonstrations of anger at the apparently never-ending defeats. Popular opposition combined with pressure from the rest of the grandees forced Philip's hand and, in January 1643, he relieved Olivares of his offices.

KEY THEMES

Olivares' attitude to his own failure Even as the end drew near, Olivares' hopes revived when Cardinal Richelieu died in December of 1642. Olivares pinned the blame for all the disasters on the Cardinal's policies. 'Without our wanting war or offering the least pretext for it' he claimed when he heard of Richelieu's death, 'France against all right and reason has attacked us on every front, and has stripped Your Majesty of entire kingdoms in Spain by resorting to hideous treachery …'

Olivares' loyalty 'After religion,' he wrote, 'I have always put first, the honour, authority, reputation and success of His Majesty.'

Olivares' attitude to France The Count-Duke always realised that Spain was at a basic disadvantage compared to its powerful neighbour. He himself noted, 'The soil of France [is] so rich, and ours so dry and rugged.'

OLIVARES: AN OVERVIEW

There are many positive points one can make about Olivares.

His commitment. He was deeply attached to the ideas of reform and genuinely sought to improve the efficiency of government and administration.

His disinterest in wealth. He, unlike so many of his contemporaries, acted in a disinterested way, opposed to the accumulation of private wealth at the expense of the public good.

His loyalty. He remained devoted and loyal to his king. Collaborating with a weak king, he bore the burdens of high office with great fortitude and stoical resolve when other men might have buckled.

His ability to take the blame. In the end, he blamed himself for the disasters and did not seek to find scapegoats. His will, which he drew up in 1642, dwells on his own sinfulness and he hoped to use his wealth to continue reform after his death. Among the specific bequests he made was one for 100,000 *ducats* for rebuilding and repopulating the town of Algeciras on the Andalusian coast and one for maintaining a squadron of galleons to defend the Straits of Gibraltar. By contrast, Olivares' great rival Cardinal Richelieu left money to found a town named after himself.

His defensive foreign policy. So there is no doubting the Count-Duke's integrity and energy, and it is easy to argue that the defeats should not be blamed on him. He never sought war as a way of extending Spanish influence and power at the expense of another country. Instead war came about as Spain sought to reconquer the Low Countries and defend all the other parts of its extensive empire.

Olivares' ministry and problems demonstrated that all great powers are likely to face attack from fearful lesser neighbours. In addition, Olivares was faced with a reborn France under Richelieu. The Dutch, too, were powerful opponents and even Olivares realised that Spain had never had sufficient forces and resources to reconquer the lost provinces.

Spain's problems were deep-rooted and could not easily be overcome. Successful revolts in Portugal and Catalonia tell us more about the structural weaknesses of Spain than they do about Olivares' failings. Monarchical weakness in the Crown of Aragon in general and in the province of Catalonia in particular, stretched back to Ferdinand and earlier. Even the combined might of two hugely successful and revered native rulers, Ferdinand and Isabella, had been unable to change that and subsequent rulers had been wise enough not to try. For Olivares this meant that Spain was always fighting with one hand behind its back. The defections of Portugal and Catalonia, both with help from France, represented a betrayal of the Spanish ideal. In addition the pressure of constant warfare was least likely, it turned out, to secure greater loyalty and contributions from these regions of the peninsula where they still saw the government as Castilian not Spanish. Olivares could not draw on national unity.

The historian should not dwell on the scale of the disasters too much. In 1640–2, matters were very serious indeed but by the end of Philip's reign there were signs of recovery. The revolts did not lead to the dissolution of the Spanish state or the Spanish empire. Olivares made few mistakes and did as much as any man could to maintain Spain's claims to be a great power.

SURVIVAL AND RECOVERY, 1643–65

After the demise of Olivares, Philip IV promised to play a **more active part in government**, thus removing the need for a *Valido*, who single-handedly controlled policy and patronage. In reality, the direction of affairs was given to Olivares' nephew, **Don Luis de Haro**. Although Philip attended the Council of State, for all his intelligence and good intentions he was wracked by doubt and indecision, feeling himself unworthy of the burdens placed upon his shoulders by God. In his long **correspondence with the**

KEY THEME

Philip IV's more active part in government 'Such a good minister [Olivares] must be replaced only by me myself.'

KEY PERSON

Don Luis de Haro (1598–1661) Effectively principal minister from 1643 to his death in 1661. Kindly, generous and rather less heroic than his uncle, Haro, even with his mediocrity, was quite a good man to steer Spain on to the road to recovery. Rather more modest and discreet than Olivares, he avoided heroics and lavish display. Where Olivares tried to master the king, Haro was always his friend.

KEY THEME

Correspondence with the mystical nun Sister Maria de Agreda Philip's troubled letters to the nun amounted to some 600 in a period of approximately 20 years.

mystical nun **Sister Maria de Agreda**, he poured out his troubles and unworthiness. Unfortunately, he failed to follow the nun's chief desire, which was peace.

- In 1656, against the advice of his ministers he rejected French peace terms.
- More pardonably, after 1657, he insisted on war to recover Portugal. But the war consumed Spanish resources to no good effect, at a time when the burden of taxation might have been lessened.

Despite Philip's failings, Spain in this period, though exhausted, began to recover its fortunes. Though Portugal was lost, Catalonia was recovered in 1652, gains were made in northern Italy and peace made with France in 1659 at the Treaty of the Pyrenees. At last Spain had the peace it needed to recover its strength. However, it was most unfortunate that Philip's only surviving son, Charles II, was sickly, mentally retarded and aged just four. He could never hope to play a serious role in government.

Philip IV of Spain.

Troubles in Italy, 1647–8

In the late 1640s, Spain faced further revolts, this time in its Italian possessions of Sicily and Naples.

Sicily. In Sicily, where the trouble started in 1647, the Spanish governor faced riots and disorder in the capital Palermo. As with Catalonia, the rioters were mainly from the lower orders complaining at high prices, high taxes and food shortages. However, they remained loyal to Philip and were easily put down by the local nobility who feared extended social unrest.

Naples. All the trouble was over before the arrival of forces from Spain under **Don Juan José** and indeed Sicilian forces helped to put down the more serious problems in the kingdom of Naples. Here revolt broke out in towns across the kingdom, just a few months after the start of trouble in Sicily and for very similar reasons. The kingdom had seen an eight-fold increase in taxation levels over the last 100 years and many were angry that their money was sent to pay troops in far away places. The Italians had little interest in Spain's struggles against the Dutch or the Catalans. Once again it was at first a revolt by the common

KEY PERSON

Don Juan José of Austria (1629–79) An illegitimate son of Philip IV. He was a reasonably capable military leader but politically he was less astute. He briefly held power during the reign of his half brother Charles II.

people – the leaders including one Tommaso Aniello, a fish vendor nicknamed Masaniello.

When the Spanish viceroy fled, the aristocracy took matters into their own hands, proclaimed a republic and, just like Catalonia, offered their allegiance to France. The Duke of Guise and a French fleet duly appeared but, after a sharp battle and a siege, Don Juan José saw off the French and retook the city of Naples. By April 1648, the revolt had been crushed after less than a year. Spanish success was underlined by the fact that a second French fleet, sent in August 1648, was beaten off by combined Spanish and **Neapolitan** forces.

Though the revolts had been crushed, the Spanish had been forced to make concessions, which in reality meant less revenue from their southern Italian possessions in the future. Given that these lands were Italian, not Spanish, their retention by Spain at this difficult time must be seen as something of a triumph.

Peace with the Dutch, 1648

Even before the Catalan problem had been brought to a satisfactory conclusion, Philip and Haro had at last brought an end to the conflict, which was the single most important cause of Spain's misery, the Dutch Revolt. Since its inception with the Iconoclastic Fury of 1566 and the despatch of the Duke of Alva's army in 1567, the Dutch Revolt had proved to be Spain's **nemesis**. It took the disasters of 1640–3 and the revolts in Italy – in other words the prospect that the whole Spanish monarchy was about to self-destruct – to bring the Spanish to accept the inevitable – **Dutch independence**.

It is easy to see how much better off Spain would have been if peace had been made a generation earlier but for Spanish leaders only total exhaustion would be sufficient to justify humiliating defeat.

- After all, Spain was recognising a state whose official religion was the heretical theology of Calvinism and whose political system was republican rather than monarchic. Denial of monarchy and the true Church were, to the Spanish, dreadful sins indeed.
- Even worse, Dutch economic prosperity in this period

KEY TERMS

Neapolitan Refers to people from Naples.

Nemesis In Greek mythology, Nemesis was the goddess who dispensed fearful justice on the proud and the lawbreakers. In this context, it means that the Dutch Revolt represented divine punishment of Spain. Year after year, for some 80 years in total, the Dutch conflict had cost Spain huge amounts in men and treasure. As early as the 1570s, Philip II had been advised by his commander in the field to abandon the unequal struggle but he and successive regimes decided to continue the fight whatever the cost. Such was the price of Spain's *reputación*.

KEY THEME

Dutch independence A clear sign of Spanish misgivings was the fact that negotiations for peace had started in 1644 but took four years to conclude! The Dutch had the upper hand and were holding out for higher terms but the Spanish managed to convince them that the French had a plan to take control of the Spanish Netherlands as a straight swap for the return of Catalonia (still in French hands at this point) to Spain. The Dutch always feared France as a next-door neighbour rather more than they feared Spain.

seemed, in Spanish eyes, to rest on piracy and robbery from the Spanish and Portuguese empires.

- Furthermore, successive Spanish rulers were concerned that if the Dutch were allowed to break away from the empire, who would be next? Given the non-unified nature of the entire monarchy, inside and outside the Iberian peninsula, the threat of political collapse, if the Dutch were granted their independence, seemed very real to the rulers of Spain.
- Only a Spanish monarch with a well-developed sense of pragmatism and an ingrained sense of **anticlericalism** might have been able to settle with the Dutch earlier.

By the Treaty of Munster (part of the Treaty of Westphalia, which ended the Thirty Years War in 1648), the Spanish delegation finally and with considerable misgivings let the Dutch go.

Recovery of Catalonia, 1652

Success in ending the war in the Low Countries was followed by success in Spain. French rule in Catalonia, headed by a French viceroy proved, if anything, harsher and less popular than Spanish rule had been. Meanwhile, the French had little luck in reintroducing law and order into their **anarchic** acquisition. The death of the rebel leader Claris and the movement of many of the aristocracy into neighbouring Aragon left Catalonia in disarray.

With the French distracted by the revolts in Italy and by its own outburst of anarchy known as the Frondes between 1648 and 1652, Spain was able to turn the war in Catalonia in its favour. The Catalans, hostile to France and weakened by hunger and plague, offered little resistance and Barcelona itself fell in 1652 to an army led by Don Juan José.

Three months later, Philip generously offered a general pardon and agreed to observe the constitutions of Catalonia. Although this was a climb-down from the demands of Olivares, it was a sensible end to the Catalan Revolt. The province could not (and would never) be fully united with Castile; it would retain its own laws, taxes and identity but at least it would be and remain part of Spain.

The regaining of Catalonia was a major triumph for Spain after the years of defeat and despair.

Relationship with England and France

While peace was made with the Dutch in 1648, war with France and indeed England went on in a rather half-hearted fashion. In England, Civil War (1642–5) had led to the execution of Charles I (1649) and the coming to power of Oliver Cromwell as Lord Protector (1653–8).

- As a fierce Protestant brought up on a diet of Spain as the natural enemy of England, Cromwell sent an expedition to the West Indies, which captured the Spanish island of Jamaica.
- Worse still for Spain, Cromwell's admiral, Robert Blake, captured the two silver fleets of 1656 that caused those of 1657 and 1658 not to sail. Spain's ability to raise money was therefore undermined, which left the Spanish army in the Netherlands very much under-funded.
- The English then allied with the French. Together they went on to defeat the great Don Juan José at the Battle of the Dunes, then to capture Dunkirk, Ypres and Gravelines.
- Luckily for Spain, France was also close to exhaustion, so the resulting **Peace of the Pyrenees** (1659), negotiated between Haro and the French minister **Cardinal Mazarin** on the Island of Pheasants in mountains on the Spanish/French border, was not too one-sided.

The peace between Spain and France was crowned by a marriage between Philip IV's daughter, Maria Teresa, and the young Louis XIV. It was all rather amicable and the terms did Spain little harm. After the later successes of Louis XIV in European warfare, it has been too easy to overestimate Spanish losses at the Treaty of the Pyrenees. In reality, Spain made peace on equal terms with France. Holland had already gone but the rest of the empire apart from Portugal was intact. The Peace of the Pyrenees gave Spain genuine hope that it could now have that respite from war needed to put its own house in order.

War against Portugal, 1559–68

Despite the peace made with France, both Philip IV and

KEY TREATY

Peace of the Pyrenees (1659) Spain lost little territory. Cerdagne, Roussillon and parts of Catalonia north of the Pyrenees went to France, which created a more easily defended border between the two countries in the future. Elsewhere, Spain lost a little territory in Hainault and Luxemburg in the Spanish Netherlands. In recompense, France recognised Spanish control of the rest of the Spanish Netherlands as well as control of Franche Comté on France's eastern border. In addition, Italy was to remain a Spanish area of control and France agreed not to ally with the Portuguese or English.

KEY PERSON

Cardinal Mazarin (1602–61) An Italian Cardinal, whose real name was Giulio Mazzarini. He succeeded Cardinal Richelieu as first minister during the minority of Louis XIV 1643–61.

Haro seemed intent on counter-acting **Portuguese nationalism** and regaining Portugal for the Spanish Crown.

- Between 1660 and 1665, Philip spent 5 million *ducats* a year in a vain attempt to take back the kingdom lost so suddenly and completely in 1640.
- John IV's death in 1656 and the advent of a regency government made it look as though Portugal would be ripe for the taking.
- However, in 1661 the Portuguese were already allied with the Dutch and now allied themselves with the English as well. In that year, the newly restored English monarch, Charles II, agreed to marry the Portuguese princess, Catherine of Braganza. Undeterred by these events, the Spanish somehow contrived to raise three armies to reoccupy the kingdom but these came to grief at the Battles of Ameixalin in 1663 and Vilaviciosa in 1665.
- In 1668, Spain finally and formally recognised Portugal's independence.

However, the loss of Portugal was not a devastating blow to Spanish power. It had its own empire to defend and would not pose a threat to Castilian domination of the peninsula.

Death of Philip IV, 1665
Philip IV died in 1665, before the official loss of Portugal had been announced. He was probably little mourned by his subjects. This would have been in line with his assessment of his own limitations and unworthiness. His reign had seen Spain descend to new low points with:

- lost territory
- victories for the French, Dutch and Portuguese
- levels of taxation higher than ever before
- Crown finances in a worse state than ever before
- bankruptcies declared in 1627, 1647, 1653, 1662 and 1666 (the year after Philip's death).

It was a terrible indictment of the government that it lived on borrowed money as well as borrowed time. Yet, as a

Portuguese nationalism
While Portuguese independence was a considerable blow, it should be remembered that Portugal had only been acquired in 1580 and was always going to be hard to hang on to. With their own sense of national identity and their own empire, the Portuguese were always likely to break away.

great power, there were always creditors willing to offer money for the right rate of interest. It is not surprising that Philip and his ministers continued to exploit their apparent generosity. While Philip's legacy was bleak indeed, the peace measures of the previous seventeen years at least represented a huge decrease in military expenditure as the new regime began its work. Unfortunately, the accumulated debt by that time was so great (around 220 million *ducats*) and the Spanish economy so poor that the next half century was spent servicing the debt, with little prospect of genuine financial recovery for the monarchy.

SOCIAL AND ECONOMIC PROBLEMS, 1598–1665

The political and foreign policy problems of the reigns of Philip III and Philip IV were clearly quite severe. The enormous expenditure on war throughout the period put tremendous strain on an economy and society that found it hard to adapt itself to Spain's imperial pretensions. However, it is easy to exaggerate the scale of the social and economic problems by the time of Philip IV's death and to lay all the blame for those difficulties on the Spanish government.

Crown finances and their economic impact

Expenditure. Crown finances were already heavily mortgaged at the time of Philip III's accession, thanks to his father's heroic efforts to defend his empire. This meant that even the outbreak of peace after 1598 did little to improve the overall state of debt and meant that a discouragingly high percentage of annual royal income was being spent paying the interest payments on loans to the government, especially the bonds or *juros* which had become so popular. Whereas the interest payments on *juros* had reached 2 million *ducats* by 1574, they had soared to 4.6 million in 1621 and had risen by a further 2 million *ducats* by 1637. At the same time, when war began in earnest after 1621, the government was often spending more than 90 per cent of its income on war. Not surprisingly, the Crown relied increasingly on foreign bankers to prop it up and declared periodic bankruptcies in order to rearrange and reschedule its debts.

New taxes. Increasing indebtedness meant that the Crown had recourse to the introduction of new taxes on a population that was already seriously burdened.

- After 1624, the government brought in periodic *donativos* (free gifts), which were levied on wealthier Spaniards.
- The wealthy were also made to pay for offices, which they received and, after 1631, office holders were taxed on the income from their positions via the new *anata* tax.
- Additionally, the aristocracy were taxed heavily in terms of their direct military contribution to the Crown's wars. Since medieval times they had been expected to raise and equip troops according to the size of their income and prestige. For lesser nobles that contribution could now be changed into an equivalent cash payment known as the *lanzas* (lances tax).
- As well as that, the Church found itself paying higher taxes, and more indirect or sales taxes were brought in to boost income further. Paper and playing cards were just two of the items subjected to new taxes. Even more significant in terms of money raised was the new tax on income from *juros*. During the 1620s and 1630s this would account for 9 per cent of Crown income. Although the tax burden was therefore increased, it is crucial to notice that most of the new taxes affected the better off – nobles, *juros* holders, the Church – rather than the luckless peasants.

So the impact of these taxes in terms of social and economic problems was muted. The financial problems of those who had money were offset by the sale of royal villages. During Philip IV's reign, the *Cortes* authorised the sale of some 200,000 villagers out of royal jurisdiction. The new taxes in Spain were not unusual. Similar taxes were being introduced in countries such as France and England, where the same financial difficulties were being experienced by equally hard-pressed governments.

Debasing the coinage. Where the government can be blamed for seriously undermining the economy and adding to the poverty of the nation was in its manipulation of the

KEY TERM

Debasement of the coinage The value of a certain coin is reduced by reducing the content of precious metal in the coin. This was often done by clipping the coin. It was also done by restamping copper coins and giving them a higher face value which was an easy solution for the government's economic problems. The process was highly profitable and easy to effect. However, the policy led to inflation and those at or below the poverty line were hardest hit. Government-inspired inflation certainly did increase poverty and economic uncertainty.

coinage. The introduction and then serious **debasements** of the copper or *vellón* coinage led to serious price inflation as the copper coins became worth less and less. The government appreciated the corrosive nature of the problem when it agreed with the *Cortes* in 1608 to stop debasements. Unfortunately this was one promise the government could not keep. The problem was serious enough under Philip III, but it got worse under Philip IV as the financial crisis deepened. Between 1621 and 1626 alone, the Crown minted nearly 20 million *ducats*' worth of *vellón* coins. In 1650, the government expanded *vellón* output to pay for the campaign in Catalonia. Since Spain's payments abroad had to be made in silver, which had held its value, this meant that silver coins virtually disappeared in Spain. It was highly ironic that the European country that imported so much silver from the New World had no silver in circulation.

Overview of royal finances. Despite helping to generate inflation, the government's fiscal failings should not be exaggerated and it is rather too easy to condemn the government's indebtedness and extravagance.

- Of course, servicing the royal debt did consume a large proportion of income but we should not expect to find any government of the day able to balance its expenditure and income.
- Governments always had debts, as financiers were always keen to lend to such powerful institutions.
- In addition, by far the greatest proportion of Spain's expenditure, often 70 per cent of it, went on necessary defence of the empire from its enemies, not on extravagant schemes of aggrandisement.
- The royal court of Philip IV was not especially extravagant. In the 1630s and 1640s, the royal household consumed only about 5 per cent of overall income. There were complaints about the huge festivities and banquets held at court in 1637 in honour of a French Bourbon princess. However, like the great hunts when Prince Charles of England turned up unexpectedly in 1623, these festivities had a political purpose. In both cases the governments of potentially hostile powers had to be convinced of Spain's great wealth and largesse.

- Olivares was a great reformer and did find further sources of revenue for the Crown. In 1634, the English ambassador to Madrid estimated that the Count-Duke had doubled the government's income in the previous four years. As well as this, Olivares did take steps to improve the state of the currency. Measures undertaken in 1628, for example, caused a sharp deflation, which penalised those holding reserves of *vellón* coinage but alleviated the inflation that hit both the poor and the government's financial calculations.

- It is also worth remembering that the tax burden falling on the Crown of Aragon and on Portugal was proportionately much less than that falling on Castile. While Catalonia suffered great economic hardship that helped lead to revolt, this was not caused by the government's tax levels. Meanwhile in Castile, which was rather more hard pressed, the people as a whole were able to pay. Compared to France in the same period, the amount of popular unrest sparked off by high taxes and high inflation was remarkably limited in seventeenth-century Castile.

- Despite occasional interruptions and serious variations in the amount arriving in Spain, **the flow of silver** from South America remained high, and allowed the government to borrow and spend as demand arose throughout the reigns of Philip III and Philip IV.

Overall then, the Crown's financial demands and the economic impact of those demands should not be exaggerated. They were serious but far from disastrous and other factors also played a major part in creating Spain's economic problems during the reigns of Philip III and Philip IV.

Economic recession?

The so-called economic recession of the seventeenth century also needs to be looked at critically, if the true extent of economic problems is to be gauged. It would be too easy to create a model of economic stagnation and decline in the seventeenth century to contrast with the economic progress of the so-called Golden Age of the previous century. The reality was that both periods suffered with economic difficulties associated with natural causes.

KEY THEME

Historians' calculations of the silver supply
Hamilton's figures, which appeared in the 1930s, indicated that silver imports tailed off sharply after 1630. More recent estimates by Michel Morineau in 1985 (see below) suggest that returns throughout the century remained healthy.

American treasure returns in million pesos

1580–9	91.2
1590–9	108.8
1600–9	107.3
1610–19	90.5
1620–9	92.2
1630–9	108.6
1640–9	81.8
1650–9	90.6
1660–9	126.3

- On the one hand, Spain possessed a largely agrarian and primitive economy.
- On the other hand, it shouldered the burdens and suffered the economic dislocation caused by the possession of an overseas empire.

Decline of population. During the sixteenth century the population of Spain was rising. After 1580, it seems to have stagnated or fallen. Available raw data of birth and death rates is fairly limited, but from the study of baptisms in several parishes in three key cities (Cordoba, Gerona and Medina del Campo), it is thought that the birth rate increased after the 1530s, declined gradually after 1580 before recovering after 1650.

- Contemporaries ascribed the falling population to military service abroad and emigration to the empire. Often their estimates now seem exaggerated. One of the *arbitristas*, Navarette, claimed that Spain lost 40,000 men a year to the empire. The true figure seems to be closer to 5000. By such means, men who would have married and had children were lost to Spain.
- Perhaps more important in explaining the falling population were the occasional **harvest failures and major outbreaks of disease**, which could decimate the population in any country reliant on an agrarian economy and subsistence agriculture. A major subsistence crisis hit Spain in 1561–2 and was followed in the next century by others in 1605–7, 1615–16 and 1630–1. Added to this were outbreaks of the plague, and the government's policy of expelling the *Moriscos* after 1609. In total it is thought that the population of Spain may have declined from 8 million to 6.5 million during the first half of the seventeenth century, a loss of nearly 20 per cent.

KEY THEME

Harvest failures and major outbreaks of disease The 1647 harvest failure in Andalusia, one of the main areas of wheat production, was the worst of the century. Additionally, serious outbreaks of the plague struck the same region in 1582, Catalonia in 1589–92 and the whole of Spain 1596–1602. The last was a huge demographic catastrophe claiming as many as 600,000 victims, mainly in the towns of Castile. It was not long until the next mortality crisis, that of 1647–52, which may have carried off half a million of the population. The great city of Seville, home of New World trade, lost half its people.

Problems in agriculture. Writing in 1659, the Duke of Medina de las Torres believed that the decline in population had a devastating impact. 'Over half the surface of these realms is uncultivated,' he claimed, 'because of the depopulation.' Even allowing for the exaggeration, it is clear that the decline in population did have grave economic and social consequences. There is a great deal of evidence, for example, regarding deserted villages. The region around Arevalo saw 30 out of 83 towns described as depopulated, while around Medina del Campo the equivalent figure was 19 out of 39. However, the loss of population may have eased the food supply problems that had existed when the population of Spain was rising.

In addition, the problems reflected not the new burdens of warfare and empire but the perennial **weaknesses of Spanish agriculture**. Because of these weaknesses, **food production** in Spain fell during this period.

Also, as numbers in villages diminished, problems increased for those who remained, since taxes were levied on the village as a whole, regardless of its population. Faced with difficulties, many peasants borrowed money to pay off debts or to increase production. Very often this money could not be repaid, encouraging yet more families to abandon the land in favour of the towns.

Overall, though, the scale of the problems in agriculture should not be exaggerated. Food shortages were not endemic in Spain at this time. Rather they were periodic and linked to specific, often localised, factors.

Trade and industry. What was true of agriculture was also true of trade and industry. Both went into decline because of Spain's failure to adapt to changing conditions.

- In northern Castile the great trade fairs at Burgos and Medina were in trouble by 1600. Foreign merchants dominated the transportation of goods, as Spanish shipbuilding declined and many Spanish merchants preferred the steady returns from government bonds to the uncertainties of trade, which could so easily be interrupted by war or pirates.
- Elsewhere, manufacturers who produced goods for the home market found that, because of inflation, their prices could be undercut by cheaper foreign imports. It is believed that foreign merchants and traders would buy up Spanish wool, make it into cloth, sell it back to Spain and still make a profit.
- Meanwhile most of the peace treaties of the period

Weaknesses of Spanish agriculture These were caused by arid land, lack of water, a largely landless peasantry and primitive farming methods.

Food production Tithe returns to the Church indicate that wheat production probably peaked around the 1580s but then fell back to reach a low ebb in the 1640s. What was true of grain production also held good for livestock. The increase in sheep and cattle during the sixteenth century was replaced by stagnation or decline in numbers in the seventeenth. One modern estimate from Henry Kamen suggests that the number of sheep may have fallen by a third between 1500 and 1650.

included clauses allowing foreign merchants, French, Dutch or English, to trade on more favourable terms with Spain. Even when the government tried to ban trade as an economic weapon in times of war, this usually failed as the government was too reliant on import taxes and so allowed its ban to be easily broken.

- At the same time, Spain found it impossible to maintain its monopoly of trade with the New World. Thus a great deal of trading profit, often Spanish silver, was finding its way into the hands of foreign merchants.

- It is easy to claim that difficulties of this type reflected a deep malaise in Spanish society that failed to produce the entrepreneurs who could stimulate economic growth. The *arbitristas* referred to the problem as *empleomania*.

- As with agriculture, the other economic difficulties of the seventeenth century tend to reflect long-term, structural problems in the Spanish economy rather than the moral decline of the Spanish people.

KEY TERM

Empleomania A situation where too many Spaniards acquired a smattering of education and abandoned agriculture or industry in favour of administration.

SUMMARY QUESTIONS

1 To what extent was Philip IV more successful than Philip III as ruler of Spain?

2 To what extent did Spain become less powerful during the reigns of Philip III and Philip IV?

3 How serious were the internal problems faced by Spain in the first half of the seventeenth century?

4 To what extent can Olivares' policies be blamed for Spain's difficulties by the end of Philip IV's reign?

CHAPTER 5

1665–1700: Nemesis? The reign of Charles II

KEY POINTS

- Philip IV's only surviving son was Charles II, who was thought to be unfit to rule. Although he played a limited part in government, Spain remained stable and powerful.
- There were a number of chief ministers and favourites (*validos*) and a great deal of faction fighting during the unexpectedly long reign. Much of this centred around Charles' mother, his wife and his half-brother.
- Charles II produced no heir. This allowed the other great powers of Europe to carve up Spain's European possessions among themselves when he died in 1700.
- Claims that Spain under Charles II was chaotic and ungoverned are rather exaggerated.

Overview

By a most cruel twist of fate, Philip IV's death in 1665 left Spain with a ruler unable to bear the burdens of government. **Charles II** was only four years old, which would mean a ten-year regency period until he came of age. The regency would mean that the government of Spain would now pass into the hands of his mother, **Queen Mariana**, who was Austrian. Charles' lack of ability meant that the government of Spain would now be in the hands of foreigners. For long periods there was faction rivalry between:

- Charles' first wife (who was French) and his mother (who was Austrian)
- his mother and his second wife (who was German).

In the 1690s, the crisis grew worse as it became clear that Charles would have no children and that his demise was to be expected fairly soon. Now Spain was faced with the prospect of having a foreign king. The result was civil war in Spain after which Spain lost its European empire. At the

Charles II (reigned 1665–1700) When Charles did come of age it was clear that he was mentally and physically sub-normal and incapable of taking up the burdens of government. He suffered severely from rickets when very young.

Queen Mariana (1634–96) Philip IV's niece and second wife. She bore him two sickly sons, the elder of which died before his father. Philip's son by his first wife, Baltasar Carlos, had died in 1646.

The end of the Spanish empire in Europe.

The dates show loss of territories by treaty

Spanish territories

German Habsburg Lands

Spanish corridors to Flanders

same time, the government of Charles II, wracked with faction fighting and foreign wars, lost control of the provinces. As central government grew weaker, the governments of the provinces outside Castile became more independent and less responsive to Madrid.

Affairs without direction

In 1694, the British ambassador to Madrid, Stanhope, gave his verdict on the Spanish government. 'This country,' he declared, 'is in a most miserable condition: no head to govern, and every man in office does what he pleases, without fear of being called to account.'

Faction fighting (1665–79)

Even with a weak and incapacitated ruler, Spain might have enjoyed some measure of stability, if it had produced a worthwhile first minister like Olivares. Unfortunately this did not occur. Charles' docile and feeble personality meant that his reign saw a series of favourites rise to prominence and, all too often, the favourites were accompanied by faction fighting, which led to a kind of absence of government. **Affairs were left without direction** as nobles and officials fought to enhance their own power and prestige at the expense of others.

Queen Mariana. At the start of the reign, Charles' mother Mariana, sister of the Austrian Emperor Leopold I, assumed power as president of a five-man *Junta de Gobierno* (Regency Council). A woman of little ability who was always suspicious of the power and hostility of the Spanish grandees, Mariana soon sidelined the *Junta*. From 1666, she looked to her Austrian Jesuit confessor, **Juan Everard Nithard**, and gave him high office, including the position of Inquisitor General.

Don Juan José. The Castilian grandees tended to fall out among themselves but one of their number, Don Juan José, now attempted to rid Spain of its foreign governors. Don Juan was an illegitimate son of Philip IV and had proved himself a proficient military commander in the previous reign. Politically, however, he was not so skilled an operator. He fell out of favour with Philip IV when he appeared to suggest that that the king should allow him to marry his own half-sister. In this way he hoped that his illegitimate birth might be set aside and that he would become Philip's heir. The king was horrified and refused to see him ever again, even on his deathbed.

Mariana ousts Don Juan. After Philip's death, Don Juan José hoped for better days, only to see himself ousted by the queen mother and her Austrian confessor. His first attempt to get rid of Nithard, in 1668, failed miserably. His ally, Malladas, was arrested, charged with the attempted assassination of Nithard and **garrotted** three hours later at the express command of the queen, without any form of trial. Troops were also sent to arrest Don Juan but he fled to Catalonia before their arrival. He left an outraged letter for the queen, denouncing Nithard and begging her 'not to heed the perverse advice of that poisonous **basilisk**'.

Don Juan becomes viceroy of Aragon. The next year (1669) Don Juan was more successful. He marched on Madrid with a small force. He sent a note to the queen saying of Nithard that, 'If he does not leave by the door, I will come myself and throw him out of the window.' Just as it seemed that Castile might be plunged into civil war, Queen Mariana finally backed down and Nithard was duly

KEY PERSON

Juan Everard Nithard (1607–81) Queen Mariana's Jesuit confessor and key adviser.

KEY TERMS

Garrotte To kill someone by strangulation through using a wire or length or cord.

Basilisk A mythical hideous reptile whose gaze or breath was fatal.

KEY PEOPLE

Fernando de Valenzuela (1636–89) The son of an army captain. He became popular in Madrid by providing the people with cheap bread and bullfights.

The Duke of Medinaceli (d. 1691) Juan Francisco Tomás de la Cerda, Chief Minister 1679–85. His appointment highlighted the lack of talent among the aristocracy during this period.

expelled from Spain in February 1669. However, Don Juan's nerve failed him and, instead of assuming full power, he agreed to leave Madrid for Saragossa to take up the position of Viceroy of Aragon. This merely allowed Mariana to bring in another unacceptable favourite, **Fernando de Valenzuela**, a minor nobleman, who at least was Spanish. His handsome appearance and pleasant manner won him favour at court and the hand in marriage of Queen Mariana's favourite maid. After that he was showered with honours. When he was made 'Master of the Horse', one nobleman complained that Valenzuela was not of high enough rank to be given this prestigious position. The queen retaliated by instantly making her favourite a Marquis.

Don Juan finally assumes power. In 1675, Charles officially came of age and he summoned Don Juan back to Madrid only to send him away again empty-handed. Meanwhile aristocratic opposition to the new favourite reached a peak in January 1677. They won over the king and, in order to separate Charles from his mother, they persuaded him to leave court with all his nobles but with a note to his mother ordering her to stay where she was. The nobles then demanded and got Valenzuela's dismissal. Don Juan returned once more at the head of a large army and finally assumed power in 1677. Queen Mariana was exiled to Toledo, while Valenzuela was sent to the Philippines. Having taken so long to achieve power, it was perhaps inevitable that Don Juan's tenure would be brief. In 1679, just 30 months after his successful *coup*, he died and with him, it seemed, all hopes of political direction and stability in Spanish central government. Don Juan was perhaps the last great man of the Spanish House of Habsburg.

Medinaceli and Oroposa (1679–91)

With Don Juan's demise, the **Duke of Medinaceli** then became *Valido*. During his period of office Castilian government reached a new low ebb. Medinaceli was wholly without ability or useful experience. He relied on the Council of State made up of 24 men of rank like the Duke of Medina de las Torres who had, according to one contemporary, spent his life in complete idleness, dividing his time between eating and sleeping. Medinaceli was eventually forced out of office by palace intrigues in 1685. His government, not surprisingly, achieved little but it was succeeded by that of 'the ablest man in Spain' – the **Count of Oropesa**. Here at last was a worthy successor to Olivares. Oropesa tried desperately to reform Spain's finances.

- He abolished many superfluous offices in the army, the law courts and in the civil service.
- He then cut the pay of many other office holders and trimmed back the enormous expenditure of Charles' court.

In these ways he reduced expenditure and taxation, and made himself many enemies. Sadly, Charles II's second wife, Mariana von Neuburg, daughter of the Elector Palatine in Germany, forced him out of office after just six years. Thereafter the government of Spain descended into chaos.

Charles' personal rule (1691–1700)

- Charles claimed that he would now take charge and have no *Valido*.
- As he was quite incapable of governing, this was a recipe for disaster.
- Meanwhile, Spain itself was divided into three parts, each one governed by a different grandee.
- At the same time, at court, there was constant rivalry and faction fighting between the two queen Marianas – Charles' wife and his mother.
- Even after his mother's death in 1696, conflict continued over who should succeed the childless king. His wife and her German *clique* who dominated the court, favoured an Austrian candidate, while many grandees, led by **Cardinal Portocarrero**, demanded a French successor who would destroy the German *clique* and bring friendship rather than hostility with Louis XIV of France.

Charles himself declined markedly in these years. He was afflicted by convulsive fits and was thought to be possessed by the devil. To the intrigues of Spanish courtiers was now added the voices of exorcists and visionary nuns. It was a fitting and sad end for Spain's most unfortunate monarch.

KEY PEOPLE

Count of Oropesa (d. 1707) Manuel Joaquin Álvarez de Toledo y Portugal. He served as first minister from 1685 to 1691.

Cardinal Luiz Fernández de Portocarrero (1635–1709) Archbishop of Toledo (1678–1709) and one of Charles' leading counsellors in the 1690s. At first he supported Prince Joseph Ferdinand of Bavaria, great grandson of Philip IV, as possible heir to the Spanish throne. With his sudden death in 1699, Portocarrero switched his support to Philip of Anjou, the French candidate.

KEY TERM

Clique A small group of people with shared (political) interests. The group does not readily allow others to join it.

As he lay dying, his German wife, who had always terrified him, attempted to persuade him to change his will in favour of an Austrian successor. But, for once, Charles held firm, leaving his ailing country to Louis XIV's grandson who was proclaimed **Philip V of Spain**. Just as in 1516, Spain was to be ruled by an alien dynasty.

Foreign policy and warfare

Despite, or perhaps because of, Spain's declining power during Charles II's reign, it continued to be involved in warfare on many fronts.

- The key feature of international relations during Charles' reign was the renewed aggression of France under Louis XIV. The so-called *Roi Soleil* (the Sun King) came of age after a long minority in 1661, just four years before Charles' accession.
- His foreign policy aims were to extend French territory in general and to grab territory on France's eastern border in particular.
- Given the apparent weakness of Spanish government in the reign of Charles II, this meant that the remaining Spanish provinces in the Low Countries looked vulnerable to French attack. However, Spain held on to its territories outside the Spanish peninsula rather longer than expected. This was partly because France's territorial ambitions under Louis XIV worried other nations – the English, Dutch and the Austrians – so that Spain was able to find allies against the French onslaught.
- At the end of the reign, the Low Countries and Italian lands were lost, not through defeat and annexation but through the need to satisfy the other powers that France would not be in a position to dominate Europe completely. If the French candidate, Philip V, had been allowed to inherit all Spanish lands then France might enjoy long-term supremacy in Europe.
- The continual fighting and alliances, as well as the debate about the succession, meant that the Crown continued to experience the familiar range of financial difficulties during Charles' reign. Periodically, steps were taken to alleviate these problems but they enjoyed only limited success, especially as the continuous faction

fighting militated against the successful pursuit of policies of retrenchment.

Portugal. At the beginning of the reign, there was still hope that Portugal might be recovered. Since it was Philip IV's dearest wish to see Iberia reunited, the regime that succeeded him decided to act. Led by Philip's widow, Queen Mariana, 4.5 million *ducats* were spent on the army on the Portuguese front in 1666 and the number of troops was increased the next year from 20,000 to 25,000. The year 1667 seemed opportune to renew the attack, as the vicious young king of Portugal, Alfonso VI, was ousted from power by his wife and his brother after a dramatic palace revolution. However, Spanish campaigns achieved little and Louis XIV effectively put an end to hopes of regaining Portugal in 1667 when he attacked the Spanish Netherlands. Faced with this new and very serious threat, the government realised that it could not hope to carry on two wars at the same time and meekly agreed to recognise Portuguese independence in 1668.

The Spanish Netherlands and the wars against France 1667–97

1667–8. In 1667, Louis XIV, out of his minority since 1661, launched a major offensive against the Spanish Netherlands with an army of some 85,000 men. His pretext for this attack was an ingenious one as it involved the claim that his wife, Maria Teresa (Philip IV's daughter by his first wife), had more right to the Spanish Netherlands than Charles II, since he was a child of Philip's second wife. The Spanish response to the French attack proved ineffective. The Spanish military commander, with much inferior forces, fell back as French troops occupied a number of towns.

Back in Spain, matters were not helped by Don Juan José's refusal to take command until peace was made with Portugal. When this was done, he refused again on the rather unconvincing grounds of ill health. In reality he was unwilling to leave Spain under the control of his enemies.

However, Spain was now given help from an unlikely quarter. The Dutch, for so long Spain's enemy, were determined that Louis should not acquire the Spanish Netherlands because that would then bring France right up to the Dutch frontier. For them it was vital to retain the Spanish Netherlands as a buffer state between the new republic and French aggression. So when Louis XIV demanded that Spain hand over Franche-Comté (on France's eastern border) or twelve towns in the Spanish Netherlands, Queen Mariana agreed to the latter, knowing that the Dutch would refuse to accept this reallocation of territory. They, with their English allies, now signed an agreement to maintain the new borders of Flanders in the future. Thus Spain's northern territories were saved by its former enemies at the Peace of Aix-la-Chapelle in 1668.

1672–8. But this was not the end of Louis XIV's aggression. He invaded the Spanish Netherlands again in 1672 in a war that lasted on and off for six years. This time his army was 100,000 strong. Now the Habsburg Emperor of Austria, Leopold I abandoned his neutral stance and made a Grand Alliance with Spain and the Dutch to oppose French ambition. Spain raised money to send to its allies and without them the outcome would have been much worse. When peace was made again at Nijmegen in September 1678, Spain lost the province of Artois, the cities of Ypres and Cambrai (in the Spanish Netherlands) and the province of Franche-Comté (further south on France's eastern flank).

1683–4. The next Franco–Spanish war was declared by Spain in 1683, after Louis XIV laid claim to yet more Spanish territory on the basis that these areas had once belonged to France. The Spanish declaration of war provoked a French invasion of Catalonia and the loss of the duchy of Luxembourg at the Peace of Ratisbon (also known as Regensburg) in 1684. This was to prove the end of Spain's territorial losses during Charles II's reign.

1689–97. Despite taking part in the Nine Years War (1689–97), Spain only lost the Caribbean island of Haiti. The war saw Spain defend itself vigorously against France in Catalonia though the French still took Barcelona. At this crisis, Charles II threatened to go to Catalonia himself. In the Spanish Netherlands, which was also under attack, Spain, after 1690, left it to the Dutch to defend its interests. The Dutch sovereign, **William of Orange**, was

KEY PERSON

William of Orange (1650–1702) Son of William II, Prince of Orange, he became ruler of the Dutch Republic in the revolution of 1672. He became King of England in 1688 after the so-called Glorious Revolution when the Catholic King James II was expelled and replaced by William and his wife Mary (who was James' daughter). The couple were both Protestants and ruled jointly as William and Mary.

now also King of England, which boosted his power considerably. In Milan it was the same story. The Austrians, who wished to defend their southern flank, supplied most of the troops defending the city and its hinterland.

Despite Louis' successes in the Nine Years War, his terms at the Treaty of Ryswick (1697) were generous to Spain. The county of Flanders along with Luxembourg and Catalonia were restored to Spain. This generosity probably came from Louis' conviction that Charles was about to die. The French king therefore needed to build up a pro-French party in Spain, so that they would agree to a French take-over. Therefore, by the end of the reign Spain had lost some but by no means most of its territories outside the peninsula. Despite the great power and huge armies of Louis XIV, Spain had not been destroyed. Indeed, despite the losses one could still claim that, in European terms, Spain was a great power.

Financial difficulties and reforms

Don Juan did attempt some financial reforms during his period of office (1677–9).

- He sent out to all *corregidors* in 1678 for reports on the state of the economy and later held a survey of depopulated villages.
- In 1679, a drastic reform of the coinage caused serious short-term problems but did help bring inflation under control.
- Also in 1679, Don Juan introduced a committee for trade designed to stimulate Spain's flagging economy. Its success led to the setting-up of further such committees in Granada, Seville, Valencia and Barcelona.
- At the same time the Spanish government finally agreed to allow all Spaniards, and not just Castilians, to partake in trade with America. While trade in the ports of Seville and Cadiz continued to be dominated by foreign merchants, other ports showed revival at the hands of natives.

While these reforms were fuelled with good intentions and may have boosted economic activity, they did little to revive the **Crown's financial fortunes**. At the start of the reign interest payments on government bonds (*juros*) alone swallowed up 75 per cent of annual revenue. Inflation continued to undermine the economy and in 1678 inflation reached its peak. In 1680, deflationary measures were adopted accompanied by price fixing of basic commodities. These measures led to the coinage being abandoned in some areas with peasants reduced to bartering for basic goods.

- In 1681, the Duke of Medinaceli sent out officials to create a new tax census. Three years in the making, this did help to reduce the burden of government taxation by some 15 per cent.
- In 1686, under Oropesa, came a further devaluation of the silver coinage. Silver came into circulation and prices recovered. Interest rates were reduced from 5 per cent to 4 per cent, thereby bringing down government repayments.
- In 1688, a new budgetary arrangement allowed the government to set aside 4.7 million *ducats* annually for basic expenses. If Oropesa could do little to increase income (though he did get papal permission to levy further taxes on the Church), he was successful in pruning expenditure.
- In 1687, Oropesa forbade the purchase of offices and in 1691 reduced membership of the administrative and executive councils. He also cut back on pensions and *mercedes* (royal rewards).

Although nearly all the Spanish silver immediately left Spain to pay off debts, it is important to realise that the value of shipments remained high throughout the reign, helping to prop up the ailing financial position of the monarchy. However in the 1690s, with Oropesa removed from office and Spain going to war again, the situation deteriorated. In this period the government seemed to exist in a state of permanent bankruptcy.

Social and economic problems
Meanwhile Charles' reign saw the usual variety of social and economic crises, which have helped to create a picture of unrelieved gloom.

- The Portuguese wars led to a depopulation of the province of Estremadura.
- There were successive harvest failures in the years 1676–9, floods in 1680 and 1681, and droughts 1682 and 1683.
- Famine struck the land in 1684 and a plague of locusts hit Catalonia in 1687, leading to peasant unrest. The rebels, called *barretines* (after their peasant caps), even laid siege to Barcelona and received the usual help from the French.
- A major plague struck the south over a six-year period (1676–82) with an epidemic of typhus (1683–5). All in all, perhaps half a million people may have died.
- By 1699, food shortages led to serious bread riots in the capital, Madrid.

Despite all the gloom there is evidence that the birth rate was increasing after mid-century and that population growth helped to increase agricultural production. Certainly wool production went up around Segovia. The output of wool there quadrupled in the half-century between 1650 and 1700. Although not many contemporaries realised it, the likelihood is that, for Spain, the worst of the economic crisis was over by the end of Philip IV's reign.

The succession crisis

Charles II defied contemporary medical opinion by living far longer than most people had expected. By the late 1690s, although it was not clear that his demise was at hand, it was clear that he would have no children. Two wives had produced no hint of a pregnancy. As the king had no children and no brothers or sisters, it followed logically that Spain would have to look abroad for its next monarch. In the late 1690s the government was, not surprisingly, split on the issue.

- Charles' German queen, Mariana of Neuburg, favoured an Austrian Habsburg prince, the Archduke Charles.
- The increasingly influential Cardinal Portocarrero, favoured a French candidate.

Both sides were determined that Spain and its empire

should not be divided as a result of the succession and that the new ruler should not rule any other kingdoms. In the end, Portocarrero's arguments won over most of the grandees and Charles himself. They decided that Philip, Duke of Anjou, should be the next king. He was a grandson of Louis XIV and also a great-grandson of Philip IV of Spain. The hope was that a French succession would neutralise French hostility towards Spain and bolster Spain's position in the world. This would be backed up by a clause stating that Philip of Anjou would have to give up his claim to the French throne to ensure that the two kingdoms were never united.

Charles' death and the War of the Spanish Succession

Charles died in November 1700 but the accession of Philip, while accepted in Spain, led to a general European war known as the War of the Spanish Succession (1702–13). England, Austria and the Dutch saw the accession of Philip V as a French takeover of Spain and fought hard to put Charles Habsburg on the throne instead. There was prolonged civil war in Spain as a result but in the end Philip's claim to the throne of Spain was

Simplified family tree showing the links between the Spanish, French and Austrian royal families. Not all descendants are shown.

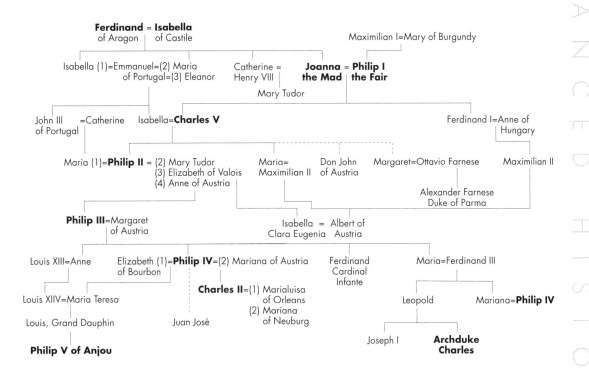

agreed upon by the warring powers at the Treaty of Utrecht (1713). There and at the Treaty of Rastatt (1714), Philip was confirmed as king but Spain lost its European empire. The Austrians took the Italian possessions (Naples, Sardinia and Milan) and the Spanish Netherlands, while Savoy got Sicily and England acquired Menorca and Gibraltar. With everyone gaining at Spain's expense, it looked as though Spanish fortunes had reached their nadir (lowest point). In fact, Spain still had its overseas empire and Philip V had used the civil wars to make himself powerful in Aragon, Catalonia and Valencia. Without the liability of its European possessions, Spain could look forward to a more secure future. The great days of empire and European hegemony were gone, but the road to recovery lay ahead.

SUMMARY QUESTIONS

1 To what extent did Spain become 'ungovernable and ungoverned' during the reign of Charles II?

2 Examine the view that, despite the personal shortcomings of Charles II, the Spanish monarchy remained strong in the second half of the seventeenth century.

3 To what extent, if at all, did Spain remain a great power in Europe during the reign of Charles II?

AS ASSESSMENT: THE RISE AND FALL OF SPAIN, 1474–1700

At present, questions on Early Modern Spain in AS exam papers and in AS coursework are essay based rather than sources based. To answer these essay questions effectively it is necessary to absorb and understand the material in the previous five chapters of this book and to develop your essay-writing skills.

ESSAY WRITING SKILLS

Reading the instructions
Make sure you understand the demands of the question. Look at the instruction words – usually at the beginning of the question. There are basically two types of question.

1 Why questions. These are asking you to explain a series of inter-related reasons for something. Such questions may start with the words 'Why ...?', 'Assess the reasons for ...' or 'Account for ...'.

Examples
Why did Ferdinand and Isabella decide to make war on Granada?

Account for the deep-seated political instability in Spain 1516–22.

2 Judgement questions. Nearly all other questions ask you to make a judgement of some sort. These questions start with such phrases as 'To what extent ...?', 'Assess the importance of ...' or 'How valid is the view that ...?'.

Examples
To what extent was Philip II's foreign policy motivated by religious considerations?

'Far from being in decline, Spain was stronger at the death of Philip III than at his accession.' How valid is this viewpoint?

Here you are being asked to construct a line of argument running throughout the essay, in which you often evaluate the relative importance of various factors.

3 Reasons and judgement questions. Just occasionally, you might be asked a question that combines the two types outlined above – asking for reasons *and* a judgement.

These questions start with: 'To what extent and for what reasons … .'

Here you need to combine the approaches of the first two types and it is best to deal with each part separately. Explain the reasons first, then answer the 'To what extent …' part.

Notice that exam questions never ask you to *describe* or *narrate the events*, so if you find yourself doing this in your essay, then you are unlikely to gain very much credit. Your essay will always be rewarded in terms of *how well you answer the question set* not in terms of *how much you know about the topic*.

Planning your essay

You cannot answer an essay question effectively unless you *plan* carefully beforehand. A plan should ensure that every part of your answer is directly relevant to the question set and should thus be structured around a series of *relevant ideas*, not around *facts* and *events*. The proper and detailed planning part of the essay-writing process may take longer than the actual writing-up of the essay, since planning involves reviewing your ideas and information and thinking hard about how the ideas and information you have can be *applied* to the question set. Remember, however, that you will be able to write your answer more quickly, more fluently and more directly if you have planned properly!

Write the question at the top of a blank piece of paper. Read through your notes, relevant chapter(s) in the book and any other relevant material you possess. As you read, think about the question and try to write down some ideas which answer the question. These should be fairly broad and you should then be able to use your notes to add in relevant information or examples, which back up or substantiate your ideas.

When you have worked carefully through all your material, review your plan and think how you might organise the ideas you have found.
- If you are answering a **why**-type question, you might think about putting your reasons *in order of their importance*, so that in the finished essay you will evaluate the relative importance of each reason as you come to it.
- If you are answering a **judgement**-type question, you will need to organise your ideas into two groups – those that support the contention in the question and those that oppose the contention. When this has been done you need to weigh up the arguments on each side and decide which side looks the stronger. This is the stage where you have to think very carefully in order to evaluate the relative importance of each idea.
- With **reasons and judgement**-type questions, follow the procedures for each part as outlined above.
- In both cases, as you start writing your essay, you must be clear in your own mind about your *overall line of argument*.

Writing your answer: the first paragraph

It is vital to get your essay off to a good start, so the first paragraph must start the argument. You should not think of the first paragraph as an introduction to the question or the topic. It should not set the scene for the essay or merely define some of the key words in the question. Nor should it be used to tell the examiner how you are going to set about the answer – for example, 'First I will look at … , then I will consider … .' Above all, you should not include further questions at this stage; you must start the answer. If you have thought carefully and planned thoroughly, your answer to the question should be uppermost in your mind as you start writing.

- In **why** questions, you should start by explaining your first reason and its relative importance. You should not give a list of all your reasons, as this will lead to unnecessary repetition later on.
- In **judgement** questions, you should outline your overall argument in clear and reasonably bold terms in order to catch the examiner's attention. The basic answer, agreeing or disagreeing with the viewpoint in the question, should be stated in the first sentence. You should be fairly decisive in the first paragraph and avoid too balanced an argument, which will make you look uncertain. You must show that you basically agree or basically disagree with the contention in the question. Don't go down the middle of the road and collect the cats-eyes! After all, you can add in reservations later on when you are arguing in detail. Try to finish the paragraph with another sentence, which clearly answers the question. If this sounds as though your opening paragraph is a concluding paragraph, it is meant to. You are not writing a detective novel, trying to keep the examiner in suspense until the last moment; you are writing a history essay where the answer must be clear from first to last.

One exciting refinement might be to look at a specific detail or episode and/or give a brief contemporary quotation (better than a historian usually!), which helps to illustrate your answer, then explain how this example/quotation answers the question and clarifies the line of argument you will be pursuing in the body of your essay.

The body of the essay: starting each paragraph

Every paragraph of your essay should start with a relevant idea, *which directly answers the question*. If possible you should also try to include a link back to the previous point, as this will add to your control of the argument. Once you have established the basic idea for each paragraph, you should explain and expand it, then add in facts and figures to back up your idea. Evidence and information therefore come later in the paragraph, *not* at the beginning. Only mention those pieces of information that clearly back up the main idea of the paragraph. In a **why** question each paragraph will deal with a separate reason.

Agreeing and disagreeing. Consider the following question.

To what extent can Olivares be blamed for the crisis of 1640?

In a **judgement** question of this type, you need to consider both sides of the argument. At the planning stage you will have thought out ideas that support the contention, and ideas that seem to contradict it. To avoid writing two parts of an essay that just contradict each other, you can adopt the following strategy.

If you basically *disagree* with the contention, start the second paragraph by discussing those factors that *agree* with the title, but as you consider them, play down their importance. A favourite device is to start with the phrase: 'At first glance, it is easy to see why Olivares might be blamed for the problems of 1640 ... .' After briefly putting forward ideas and evidence to support this view, you then put forward the arguments that disagree with the assertion in the question. This section of the essay, where you come on to the most important points, might start with a sentence such as: 'Although it is easy to blame the chief minister for Spain's problems in 1640, the reality is that Spain's difficulties in 1640 were too deeply rooted to be solved by Olivares.' You then write most of the essay in support of this line and therefore end with a clear line of argument.

The last couple of paragraphs

These can be used to summarise your argument, but this may be a little repetitious since your reasons or line of argument should be clearly stated as the essay unfolds. Rather better is to see if you can use this part of your essay to question the question. Sometimes question-setters add in key words that need to be challenged in a good essay. Consider the following question.

Why did Ferdinand and Isabella conquer Granada so easily?

Here a good essay will give the reasons for Ferdinand and Isabella's success, then discuss directly how easy the process was. This in itself might involve a structure similar to the illustration above – that is, *'It looked easy because ... . In fact it was very long-drawn-out and difficult because ... .'*

Similar demands are made by the following example.

Why were the Crown's financial problems so serious in the period 1580–1640?

Again the words 'so serious' will need to be addressed directly, probably towards the end of the essay, so that you have given a clear indication of how serious the financial problems were. This may involve considering whether the problems were more or less serious than before or after the period specified. In this way, you can see that a good essay might consider quite relevantly material from outside the period specified in the question. In the same way, your essay would be readily enhanced if you could add depth to your argument by comparing the financial problems in Spain with those in other European powers in the same period. In these ways, then, the last few paragraphs can really widen the scope and depth of your argument.

Other essay writing tips

Defining key words/terms. You will need to define and explain key terms or words such as 'revolution', 'decline', 'aggressive foreign policy', 'rebellion' and so on. However, you should do this within the framework of your argument, not as an isolated paragraph unlinked to the main ideas.

Historiography. Historiography is knowledge of different historians' viewpoints on the central topic. It can be very helpful and add depth to your answer, but only if used analytically rather than descriptively. Do not write about different views *for the sake of it* (in other words, to show what you know). Rather, make historiography part of your argument – for example, 'Elliott backs up this point clearly when he says/writes/argues …', 'Although Henry Kamen plays down the power of the Inquisition in the sixteenth century, the Holy Office was often allowed to go its own way.'

Contemporary quotations. These are very much appreciated by examiners, but again they must support a relevant idea, rather than being brought in descriptively – for example, 'Philip II's oft-repeated remark, "It is as well to think of everything" illustrates some of the weaknesses of his government.'

Other refinements. One extra refinement that you might consider in **judgement** questions is the idea of change over time – that is, the answer to the question changes during the period under review. Consider the following question.

How powerful was Spanish government 1479–1525?

Rather than giving an overall assessment saying that Spanish government was basically weak *or* basically strong, you might take the view that it was weak at first, became stronger (especially after the conquest of Granada), but was then weakened during the early years of Charles I.

WRITING ESSAYS: AS QUESTIONS IN THE STYLE OF OCR

Spain 1504–56
You will need to read Chapter 2 to answer the two questions below.

a How secure was Charles I as King of Spain in the period 1516 to 1522?
(30 marks)

b How far do you agree that Spain, during the reign of Charles I, suffered from a stagnant economy?
(60 marks)

Although this appears to be a two-part structured question, it should be treated as two essays. Notice that question b is worth twice as many marks as question a, and should therefore be allocated two-thirds of the total time available.

Guidance to answering part a of the question. The examiners' marking guide will say that this question targets the candidate's knowledge and understanding of the main features of Charles' accession and early rule. This is a judgement question, since it starts with the key words 'How secure …', and the mark Band (and thus mark) awarded will depend on how well those words are addressed.

Supporting the idea that Charles was not very secure would include consideration of the general problems in governing Spain and the fact that Charles was a foreigner. Also he made mistakes when he first visited Spain and helped to spark off rebellions (Comuneros and Germania).

On the other hand, this view should not be exaggerated. There were no challengers to Charles' rule. Rebellions were put down and orderly government reasserted.

For Band A (24–30 marks), the examiner will want to see that you have explained the key issues in the question convincingly and relevantly. The answer will present a clear line of argument from first to last, supported by a range of details, and will evaluate clearly the level of security in this period. The best answers might well consider the possibility that the security of Charles' rule varied during the period.

For Band C (18–20 marks), the answer will be well informed and make reference to the key issues but will tend to be descriptive with only limited analysis.

For Band E (12–14 marks), the answer will have one or two relevant ideas simply stated but the approach will be mainly descriptive and will only cover one or two areas.

Guidance to answering part b of the question. The examiners' marking guide will state that this question targets the state of the Spanish economy. Candidates will be expected to look at a range of areas, including royal finances, to reach the top band. Spain's domestic economy remained backward and rather provincial in this period, while income from the New World was used to pay off debts rather than stimulate the Spanish economy. Trade and industry remained undeveloped.

The examiners may well divide the mark out of 60 between a mark out of 15 for 'perspective' and a mark out of 45 for 'evaluation'.

- For perspective, the examiner is looking for your ability to place the question about the economy in the appropriate context – that is, to what extent would one expect to see the Spanish economy booming during this period of greater international prestige?

- For evaluation, the examiner will be looking for your ability to place your factual knowledge securely within the framework of a relevant and purposeful argument. At the top band, one might expect candidates to offer some balance to the idea of stagnation or to explain why political and international prominence need not be accompanied by economic success. In this way the key words, 'To what extent ...' will be directly addressed and evaluated.

The problems of Spain 1598–1659
You will need to read Chapter 4 before you answer these next two questions.

> a Assess the influence of Lerma and Olivares in Spanish government in this period. (30 marks)
> b To what extent had Spain declined as a major power by the mid-seventeenth century? (60 marks)

Guidance to answering part a of the question. This question is asking you to demonstrate knowledge and understanding of the power and significance of two Spanish ministers. It may be that candidates will be better informed on Olivares than Lerma and equality of treatment will not be expected. Success in dealing with Lerma may be a key factor in deciding to award the higher mark bands.

For Band A (24–30), candidates will be expected to demonstrate a high level of factual recall, covering a wide range of issues. In addition, good answers will look at the outcome of policies as well as their intentions in order to produce a well-rounded answer, which will consider the strengths and limitations of each minister. Answers that consider the general problems in governing Spain as well as the specific shortcomings of each minister might well reach this band. As a final flourish, one might also expect some direct attempt to compare the influence of the two men. Candidates who challenge effectively the old stereotypes of Lerma as dissolute and Olivares as the great reformer might also do well. In terms of structure, it would be best to deal with the two men separately and add the comparative section as your last paragraph.

So the opening sentences of the main sections of your essay might run as follows.

*Traditionally Lerma has been seen as enjoying only limited influence and success. ....
However, in reality he steered Spanish foreign policy with great assurance and success and his domestic policies were sound and sensible, though Spain's long-term weaknesses meant that little serious reform was instituted ... .*

While Lerma thus enjoyed a great deal of influence in Spanish government, Olivares was actually less influential and less successful. Since Olivares embarked on a course of rash and radical reforms, he actually failed to implement them and his hopes in domestic and foreign policy were dashed ... .

Given the inherent weakness of Spanish government, the continuing strength of the Church, the nobility and regional sentiment, neither minister could hope or be expected to achieve a great deal … .

This, of course, is only one line of argument and candidates are free to construct an argument that takes an opposite viewpoint to the one above. The key thing is that *your plan* addresses directly the key issues demanded by the question and that it is your plan. You will always find the task of essay writing more rewarding if you are putting forward your own arguments rather than those learnt from a teacher or textbook.

Guidance to answering part b of the question. This question calls for an assessment of Spain's international position in the period 1598–*c*. 1650. While internal matters may well be relevant here, the main focus will be an assessment of Spain's international strength and standing during this period.

The marks for these answers may well be broken down between a mark out of 15 for overall perspective in the answer and a mark out of 45 for the quality of the evaluation in the answer.

For the top Band in each case, candidates will need to construct a clear line of argument. Since it is traditionally argued that Spain declined quite seriously in this period, a good response might show that decline was limited. After all, it would be hard to deny that Spain was still a 'major power' by the middle of the century, even if it was not as dominant in European affairs as it appeared to be during the reign of Philip II.

Certainly a good answer will directly and systematically argue about the extent of decline in this period. Since this question involves quite a long time span, it might be appropriate to consider the idea of change over time. Perhaps there was little decline before 1640 but serious decline thereafter.

Overall there will need to be direct consideration of what changes, separately or collectively, constitute decline, as opposed to the usual fluctuations in the relative standing of major powers. Could one argue that Spain's problems had little to do with Spain itself and more to do with the increasing power of France? Good answers will also incorporate internal difficulties, relating them clearly to the concept of major power status and have a clear idea of Spain's standing at the beginning as well as at the end of this period.

A2 SECTION: TRIUMPH AND DESPAIR – THE IMPACT OF EMPIRE, 1474–1700

Introduction

In this part of the book, four key themes in Spanish history will be explored across wider time spans than was possible in the AS section of the book. The text is more analytical than in the AS section, there are fewer explanatory boxes and familiarity with the information in the first part of the book is assumed.

Section 1 – 1474–1556: In what ways and to what extent did the character of the Spanish Church change in this period? This chapter explores a key question in Spanish history, looking at the ways in which the Spanish Church adapted to the changing circumstances of the period. In particular, it looks at how Spain responded to the challenges of the *Reconquista*, the acquisition of empire, and the Protestant and Catholic Reformations.

Section 2 – 1474–1598: Did this period witness the Golden Age of Spain? This chapter explores the concept of Golden Age, from Ferdinand and Isabella to Philip II. It will explore the differing interpretations of the period by contemporaries and historians, as well as considering different interpretations of the idea of Golden Age. In this way it will provide an overview of this crucial century, not only politically and diplomatically but also culturally.

Section 3 – 1556–1609: Why did Spain fail to crush the Dutch Revolt? This chapter takes a more in-depth look at the Dutch Revolt and Spain's efforts to overcome the rebels. Spain's problems and difficulties elsewhere in Europe are examined carefully to put Spain's failure into its proper historical context. Perhaps the failure was not as grave or serious as contemporaries thought.

Section 4 – 1598–1700: To what extent did this period witness the 'Decline of Spain'? This theme has been much debated by historians and partially depends on one's conclusions about a Golden Age under Philip II. In this chapter, Spain's problems at home and abroad are set against the country's enduring strengths and compared to the problems facing its great rival, France, in the same period.

SECTION 1

1474–1556: In what ways and to what extent did the character of the Spanish Church change in this period?

INTRODUCTION

The tasks facing the Spanish Church from mid-fifteenth to mid-sixteenth centuries were immense. One Jesuit, writing as late as 1615, wondered why his fellow Jesuits went all over the world seeking new converts to Christianity when so many Spaniards were still ignorant of the faith. 'I don't know why the fathers of the company go to Japan and the Philippines [named after Philip II] to look for lost souls,' he said, 'when we have so many here in the same condition who do not know whether they believe in God.'

Such sentiment was not unusual. The mystic St Teresa of Avila listened to a monk preach about the Franciscan mission to the Indies, then heard a celestial voice declare that 'there is another Indies waiting to be evangelised here in Spain'. In 1603, a Dominican prior complained that the local Spaniards 'know little of faith and are the victims of a thousand superstitions'. This would be one problem the Spanish Church would do little to resolve.

THE CATHOLIC CHURCH IN THE NEW WORLD

The challenge to the Church

The discovery and colonising of parts of Central and South America by Spanish *conquistadors* presented the Church with an enormous challenge. It was assumed from the start that as land was conquered, the native Indians – the indigenous population – would be converted from paganism to Christianity. This aim was rooted in a number of considerations.

Conversion would ensure that the natives remained loyal to the Spanish colonial government by being taught the Christian virtue of obedience. Hence there would be less chance of rebellion and revolt. It was always part of the thinking and theology of the Catholic Church that one of its purposes was to spread the Christian version of the Word of God to those dark corners of the world where it had yet to be heard. Evangelism was seen as crucial to the health of the Church to avoid the corruption attendant on inactivity and settled habits. This evangelism was directed at pagans and also at those who followed non-Christian faiths such as Islam or Judaism.

Spain was particularly well placed to direct such conversion operations; the reigns of Ferdinand and Isabella had witnessed attacks on the *Conversos* and *Moriscos* and the conquest of Granada.

Royal authority over the Church

Under these circumstances, it was natural that the Spanish Crown directed the Christian mission to the New World. The Church outside Spain, like the Church within it, was **erastian**. The papacy theoretically took charge of organising missions to the heathen, but had neither the men nor the money to undertake them. As always Popes relied on putting moral pressure on temporal rulers in order to make a reality of their hopes. So in the famous Papal Bull of 1493, *Inter Caetera*, the rulers of Spain were invited to send 'virtuous and God-fearing men endowed with training, experience and skill, to instruct the natives and to imbue them with … Christian faith and sound morals.'

So it was that Christopher Columbus (1451–1506) transported a small group of friars with him on his second journey. These friars were chosen and paid for by the Crown. Furthermore, in the Bull *Eximiae Devotionis* of 1501, the papacy granted the Crown the right to collect tithes in the New World to support the Church, which was in its infancy. Nicolás Ovando, governor of Hispaniola from 1502–1509, was given detailed instructions by the sovereigns about the organisation of parishes, payment of clergy and other specific details about Church organisation. However, the Spanish Crown's complete authority over the Church in the New World was not immediately granted by the papacy.

After the conquest of Granada in 1492, the Pope had made a specific grant detailing royal authority in the newly conquered region. Ferdinand and Isabella seem to have assumed they would be given the same powers in the New World. At first they were thwarted by a Bull of 1504 in which Julius II refused to acknowledge royal authority in setting up new bishoprics. It was not until 1508, when the Pope needed Ferdinand's help against Louis XII of France, that the Crown officially received full authority over the Church in the New World.

Also in 1508, the Papal Bull *Universalis ecclesiae regimini* allowed the rulers of Spain to found and organise new Churches, and to choose all the clergy who would serve in them. This grant was made in perpetuity (for ever), and covered all lands conquered by the rulers of Castile now and in the future. It gave the Crown *Patronato*, or total control, over the Church in the Indies. Seville was made the centre for the Archbishopric for the New World Churches. The day-to-day running of affairs was in the hands first of a committee from the Council of Castile and then devolved to the Council of the Indies in 1524. In addition, the Crown controlled all movement to the Indies, forbade the spread of unlicensed ecclesiastical documents there and decided all spiritual matters within the Church without recourse to Rome.

There is no doubt that the Crown took very seriously its **evangelising** mission in the New World. **Zumárraga**, the first Bishop of Mexico, took drastic measures to protect native Mexicans from misrule, including the excommunication of a number of royal officials in 1530. The Crown backed the bishop, even though the Pope had not yet formally appointed him to his office.

Later on, when involved in border disputes with the Bishop of Michoacán, Zumárraga took the matter to the king, not the Pope. In order to carry out missionary activity, the Crown selected groups of clerics and sent them into action. Though relatively small in terms of numbers, these men achieved a great deal.

The work of the friars

Among the first to arrive in the New World were Franciscan friars, who appeared in Mexico in 1523. They were followed by Dominicans after 1526 and Augustinians some seven years later.

After Cardinal Cisneros' reforms of the **Mendicant orders**, especially the Franciscans, these orders of friars contained many eminent men, dedicated to religious reform and the evangelical mission. For them, spreading the Word of God to supposedly 'uneducated savages' was among the highest ideals of the Christian clergyman.

Vasco de Quiroga, Bishop of Michoacán, attempted with some success to found self-supporting communities of Indians based on the plan of **Thomas More's** *Utopia* on the shores of Lake Pátzcuaro. On the whole they found the natives receptive to Christian ideas and were determined to protect them from the more brutal aspects of the conquest. They organised them into villages, building churches and missions and imposing a new civilisation on their new charges. This was achieved because the natives, with the destruction of their old idols and rituals, were often prepared to accept the ceremonies and rituals of the Catholic Church. However, it may be that native acceptance of Christianity was superficial. It is notable that the natives failed to produce their own clergy and the new churches continued to be dependent on Spanish missionaries.

Largely, the friars took a genuine interest in their native charges. One of the greatest of these men was the Franciscan Bernadino de Sahagún. He developed a genuine interest in Indian culture and way of life, and

KEY PERSON

Juan de Zumárraga (1468–1548) A dedicated Franciscan, who led an exemplary life deeply imbued with the ideals of Christian humanism. Having read in some depth the works of Erasmus and Thomas More, he and others saw in the New World the perfect opportunity to create Utopian societies among the native Indians who were untouched by the corruption endemic in Europe. Here they could carve out primitive but pure Christian communities based on Christ's teaching. Zumárraga became the first Bishop of Mexico in 1527, although his appointment was not made official until 1533.

KEY TERMS

Evangelising To spread the Word.

Mendicant orders Orders of clergymen, usually friars, that relied entirely on charity from the population to survive.

recorded much for posterity before it was swept away. The Dominican Antonio de Montesinos was more concerned with the rights of the Indians. 'Are these Indians not men?' he demanded. 'Do they not have rational souls? Are you not obliged to love them as you love yourselves?'

These views did not sit well with colonists and *conquistadors*, who felt that the natives were a more primitive and therefore lesser form of humanity to be exploited by their Spanish betters. For the colonists, economic priorities were more significant than religious ones. In their view, God had guided them to the New World so they might enhance their own interests. For the friars, this was not consistent with the conversion of the natives to Christianity. The native Indians were being converted because they had the makings of rational, Christian souls who were the equal of other men.

The most famous apologist for the natives was Bartolomé de las Casas. He spent years defending the natives in the New World and the old. He argued that the Indians were subjects of the Spanish Crown and should be treated as such. In particular, their willingness to be instructed in the Catholic faith meant that they should be treated as other Christian men. The colonists should exploit the natural resources of South and Central America but should not enslave their fellow men in the process.

The arguments about this issue raged throughout Charles V's reign in the first half of the sixteenth century. This indicates that Spanish intellectuals were no strangers to debate. In 1530, a royal decree forbade the future enslavement of native Indians. This law was repeated in the famous 'New Laws' of 1542. However, this apparent victory for churchmen in the New World was accompanied by the increasing importation of black slaves from Africa. The enslavement of black Africans seems to have provoked a much more muted response from the Church.

The activity of the Church

One further problem for the Church in the New World was the relatively small numbers of clergy who were attempting to convert and look after the growing number of natives. By 1559, there were only some 800 Mendicant friars in Mexico and some 500 normal clergy – hardly sufficient for the great task the Church had set itself of converting the natives. Indeed, the shortfall of clergy mirrors the problems back in Spain where the conversion of Moors and Jews could not be fully realised for lack of a properly staffed ecclesiastical mission. The Augustinians certainly built some fine churches in **New Spain** but little is known about the effectiveness of their work.

Initially, the friars set out in small groups of two or three, founding churches as they went and travelling constantly to new areas. The friars founded some 270 churches in New Spain, most before 1576. These

missionary churches, often in urban areas and on the sites of Indian temples, were then bases for the wholesale conversion of natives to Christianity. Huge numbers were converted, often after very limited instruction in the essentials of the Christian faith. It was estimated at the time that the Franciscans alone had converted more than a million natives before 1531 and sometimes converted 1500 in a single day.

The reasons for such success were related to the destruction by the Spanish of the temples and idols the natives were accustomed to and their replacement with missionary churches. Zumárraga claimed to have destroyed some 500 temples and 20,000 idols by 1531. At the same time, new Christian churches were often built on the site of the old temples on pagan temple mounds. In this way the churches were acceptable to the natives because they were associated with ancient religious sites.

In the same way, the Catholic Church developed and expanded its religious ceremonial to make it similar to the ritualistic religion being destroyed. While some gods (such as the war gods) were perhaps easily abandoned because of their failure to protect the natives from the onslaught of the *conquistadors*, others (such as the native gods of earth mother and corn goddess) became subsumed into the **cult of the Virgin Mary**.

While missionary activity continued with great speed and fervour in Mexico, the same cannot be said of the work in Peru. Peru was more distant and less accessible than Mexico. It was conquered a decade after Mexico in the 1520s by Francisco Pizarro when the Crown needed to focus on the war in Europe against France, which lasted from 1521–9.

Perhaps by the 1520s, the Spanish Church had lost some of its reforming and missionary vigour. Furthermore, there were always fewer friars prepared to travel to Peru because it was a quite inhospitable land. The result was that traditional religion continued there, often in secret, and Christianity was seen as a secondary and separate ritual. For over 200 years the authorities in Peru would send out *visitadores de idolatria*, which attempted to suppress pagan worship. In Peru, pagan and Christian religions continued and still continue to coexist.

Colonial conflict

The natives of New Spain were defeated with relative ease and decimated by **European diseases**. Thus they offered very little resistance to the conquerors. Instead, the missionary friars found themselves in conflict with fellow Spaniards from the secular Church and from the laymen who administered the colonies. In particular, many friars were opposed to the way in which the *encomenderos*, or new landowners, used the natives as little more than slaves.

KEY TERMS

Missionary churches were founded specifically to convert pagans to Christianity. They aimed to instruct native Indians in the basics of Catholic Christian belief and to make them Christians through the ceremony of baptism.

Cult of the Virgin Mary As the mother of Christ, the Virgin Mary is especially important to Catholics.

European diseases The natives of New Spain did not have experience or immunity to European diseases such as the common cold. Neither had they experienced many of the sexually transmitted diseases brought with them by the Spanish conquerors. Exposure to these diseases led to death on a large scale.

Inspired by their Utopian vision, many of the friars wished to see the Indians involved in **communal agriculture** to support themselves, their communities and the Church. The great landlords however wished to see greater profits for themselves. In 1530, the friars' unpopularity with the landlords increased when the Crown decreed that *encomienda* grants to the landlords from the Crown should be reduced. Some landlords also strenuously opposed the friars' drive to educate the natives. They feared that a literate and educated population would be less subdued and cowed by colonial authority.

While a few friars like de las Casas were opposed in principle to the *encomienda* system, others took a more moderate view. They argued that the *encomiendas* were a vital means of organising the natives and keeping them subdued, thus allowing missionary work to take place. At the same time, many of the new landlords saw the benefits of the friars' work. If the natives were prosperous and happy, they would produce more tribute (taxes). So when the controversy over the Crown's New Laws of 1542 erupted, missionaries and landlords were on the same side in opposition.

Another area of conflict was the relationship between the friars or regular clergy and their secular counterparts who staffed the new bishoprics. The friars were often scathing about the earliest parish priests claiming they were ignorant as well as indolent. More specifically, the friars complained at the natives being forced to pay Church taxes, or tithes, as parishes became established within the new bishoprics.

On this issue and on the issue of whether they had to obey the local bishop, the friars eventually lost out. The Crown and papacy decided by 1574 that all clergy, regular and secular, should be subject to Episcopal jurisdiction. At the same time, the friars naturally lost much of their missionary zeal by the middle of the sixteenth century when the colonies were becoming more clearly established.

By 1560, the Mendicant missions had outlived their original purpose. Just as *conquistadors* gave way to bureaucrat administrators, so wandering missionary friars gave way to settled parish priests.

Conclusion

The friars who carried the Christian message to the native peoples of Central and South America achieved a great deal. They were part of a Spanish Church that had rediscovered one of its central purposes – spreading the Word of God to pagans and primitive peoples. It was a Church imbued with fervour and sympathy in equal measure, usually trying to alleviate the plight of the native peoples. At the same time, that Church enjoyed a two-edged relationship with the Crown.

In an erastian sense, it served the Crown and did its bidding in an age when the power of the king over the Church had been enhanced. However, it also reminded the Crown of its moral obligations to the conquered people in terms of providing them with a Christian mission and a settled Christian Church, and argued with it over the harsh treatment inflicted on the natives.

The Church was ultimately unsuccessful in realising its best hopes and aspirations, largely because there were too few friars to cover the vast tracts of conquered territory; there were too many powerful competing interest groups and there were not enough men of high quality.

THE SPANISH INQUISITION

Reasons for its establishment

The Spanish Inquisition was set up by Pope Sixtus IV in 1478 at the request of Queen Isabella. This Bull allowed her to appoint and dismiss two or three priests over the age of 40 years to act as Inquisitors in her realm of Castile. Nothing happened for two years. Despite such calm beginnings, the Spanish Inquisition grew to become a most feared instrument of religious persecution.

The Crown's reason for the setting up of the Inquisition was increasing concern about Jews who had been converted to Christianity (the *Conversos*, or new Christians), but who secretly practised their old faith and maintained links with unconverted Jews. Ferdinand and Isabella were slow to appreciate the apparent danger. While there had been occasional outbreaks of anti-Semitism, such as the Toledo riots of 1449, Spanish monarchs generally operated a policy of *convivencia* (living together). Ferdinand and Isabella were no different.

During their first years in power, the Catholic Kings (as Ferdinand and Isabella were known) and the Court maintained their traditional tolerance towards Jews. Not only did the Court circle include a number of *Conversos* (for example, Isabella's secretary Hernando del Pulgar), but also several practising Jews (such as Abraham Senior, the treasurer of the *Hermandad*). Both monarchs had Jewish physicians and doctors. While there was anti-Semitism in some of the towns and cities, Ferdinand and Isabella seemed keen to defend the Jews. In 1477, Isabella declared, 'All the Jews in my realms are mine and under my care and protection and it belongs to me to defend and aid them and to keep justice.' In 1475, the city of Bilbao was ordered to revoke commercial restrictions placed on the Jews by local laws.

However, the tide of **popular anti-Semitism** seemed to be growing in Spain. This pushed Ferdinand and Isabella into their petition to the Pope

KEY TERM

Popular anti-Semitism
Hostility towards Jews and the Jewish race felt by a wide cross-section of the lower orders.

to set up the Spanish Inquisition. In 1478, Alonso de Hojeda, a Dominican prior in Seville, warned Isabella in rousing sermons that many *Conversos* in the city were practising Jews. An investigation by Hojeda and the Archbishop of Seville seemed to confirm this view. It claimed that all across Andalusia and Castile, *Conversos* were secretly practising Jewish rites.

As a result of this report, Isabella sought and received papal authority to set up an Inquisition in Castile. Nonetheless, it is interesting that no Inquisitors were actually appointed until 1480. It is likely that Isabella still had her doubts about the extent of the problem and also listened to Cardinal Mendoza and Bishop Talavera who, fearful that an Inquisition would undermine their episcopal authority, urged her not to introduce it.

However, such moderation had less of an impact on the Catholic Kings than the more powerful popular anti-Semitism. In 1480, the *Cortes* of Toledo represented the views of many Castilian towns when it demanded that Jews and *Conversos* should be strictly separated, with Jews restricted to *aljamas*, or Jewish ghettos. This may have acted as the final spur to Isabella, who appointed two Dominicans – Juan de St Martin and Miguel de Morillo – as the first Spanish Inquisitors. She probably had little idea how momentous this decision would be.

In 1483, the Inquisition spread to the kingdom of Aragon. Sixtus IV gave his approval to the appointment of Thomas de Torquemada as Inquisitor General of Aragon, Valencia and Catalonia. As he was already Inquisitor General in Castile, the two Inquisitions were united under one head and the Inquisition became the only institution whose authority ran throughout Spain.

Impact of the Inquisition

The scale of persecution carried out by the Spanish Inquisition has often been exaggerated, especially by anti-Spanish Protestant writers such as J.L. Motley.

The prime target of the Inquisition in its early years was the converted Jews. In Barcelona, between 1488 and 1505, the Inquisition tried some 1200 people. All but eight were *Conversos*. The numbers arrested and condemned in those years were considerable and on a scale that makes the Spanish Inquisition the most oppressive and bloodthirsty tribunal in the history of Western Europe. A contemporary, Hernando del Pulgar, estimated that in its first decade (1480–90), the Inquisition burnt some 2000 people and reconciled 15,000 others to the Catholic Church under 'edicts of grace'. In Seville alone, one contemporary claimed that 700 were burnt in the first eight years.

Individual *autos de fé* could account for many victims. In Cordoba, 107 were burnt in a single *auto de fé* in 1504. In Ciudad Real, 30 people were burnt alive and 40 in effigy (they weren't burned, but models of them were) on one day in 1484. In Valladolid, on 5 January 1492, 32 perished in a great public spectacle.

In all, tens of thousands of Christians were executed, imprisoned, tortured, ruined or driven into exile.

Not only were absolute numbers very high in the first decade or so, but so also was the percentage executed of those arrested. In the two cities of Valencia and Avila, some 40 per cent of those arrested were executed in the first two decades of the Inquisition's existence. When the Inquisition started on its brutal work, the main targets were clearly *Conversos*, but this soon had an impact on the Jews, too. The Inquisition recommended that Jews should be physically separated from the *Conversos* in an attempt to stop reconversion to Judaism.

At the end of 1482, the Inquisition ordered a partial expulsion of the Jews from Andalusia. By 1484, the Jews had been driven out of Seville as the Crown backed the Inquisition's demands. In this way the Inquisition began to change royal policy towards the Jews, which would result in the final expulsion of the Jews from Spain in 1492.

Neither Ferdinand nor Isabella was anti-Semitic, but the setting up of the Inquisition and the scale of the early persecutions made them change their minds. By the mid-1480s, Jews as well as *Conversos* were under attack. Also adding to the huge number of cases against *Conversos* in the first years of the Spanish Inquisition was the large number of Jews who were prepared to testify against the *Conversos* who they saw as heretics and traitors.

Dreadful though the scale of persecution was, especially when one considers that most of the victims were innocent, it is clear that the levels of persecution were subject to regional variations and that the overall level of persecution fell dramatically after 1500. After the expulsion of the Jews in 1492, the death of so many *Conversos* and the fleeing of many more, the problem of the false converts had apparently been overcome. In Valencia, 80 per cent of the Inquisition's death penalties before 1592 were issued before 1530.

After the deaths of Ferdinand and Isabella, there were increasing calls for the Inquisition to be abolished, or for its procedures to be reformed to ensure that those suspected of heresy were fairly treated. Like Ferdinand, Charles I refused to accept proposals for serious reform, claiming that heresy still had to be destroyed. There was increased persecution of *Conversos* at the time of the Comuneros Revolt in 1520–1, when several were discovered among the rebels.

However, as political stability was restored and Charles became fully accepted by the Castilian ruling class, the scale of persecution by the Inquisition decreased. This was largely because after the accession of Charles I in 1516, the Spanish people did not feel themselves under threat from alien minorities. The perceived Jewish problem had been dealt with at the time of Isabella and the *Moriscos* were not yet seen as a serious threat. Most of the victims of the Inquisition in Charles' reign were **Old Christians**, not new ones. In Toledo, the percentage of those accused by the Inquisition who were *Conversos* fell rapidly after 1530. Before this date the figure averaged 77 per cent. In the last 20 years of Charles' reign, only some 2 per cent of those accused in Spain were **Judaisers** and 14 per cent were Muslims, leaving some 84 per cent as Old Christians. This also meant, in practice, that there were fewer accusations and that the accusations were usually of a less serious nature.

In the period 1540–59, the last 20 years of Charles' reign, over half the cases involved 'propositions' where the accused spoke words deemed to be against faith and morals. Furthermore, after 1500 the Inquisition burnt relatively few of its victims. Most were fined, did penance or were in some way reconciled to the Church. In his *Inquisition and Society in Spain* (1985), historian Henry Kamen claims that during the sixteenth and seventeenth centuries, the Inquisition burnt on average only three people a year or around 2 per cent of those accused.

Although the spread of Protestantism in northern Europe from the 1520s heightened fears among Catholics in Spain that their religion was under threat, the persecution of the Inquisition never approached the scale or severity of its early years.

From the 1540s to 1600, there was a gradual increase in the number of those persecuted. However, most of the victims in the period 1580–1600 were *Moriscos* who were relatively free from persecution under Charles I. Furthermore, the men appointed as Inquisitors were more serious-minded and restrained than their predecessors, and the *Suprema*, a royal council founded in 1483, showed that it was prepared to investigate individual charges of corruption among its Inquisitors. Overall the Inquisition under Charles and Philip became firmly established but also more moderate.

In another way, too, the Inquisition under Charles was clearly less aggressive than at its inception. The conquest of Granada in 1492 and the conversion of the Moors to Christianity had created another huge category of new Christians who might easily have become the basis for a further round of persecution by the Inquisition. Instead, there were very few cases where the Inquisition executed *Moriscos*.

In 1526, when it became officially illegal to be a Muslim in Spain,

KEY TERMS

Old Christian refers to those Christians who had always been Christian as opposed to those New Christians who were converts from Judaism or Islam.

Judaisers refers to those who spread Judaism and more specifically those who secretly held onto their Jewish faith while officially a Jewish convert to Christianity.

Suprema A royal council, founded in 1483. *Suprema* was another term for the Inquisition, officially the Supreme Council which directed its operations and enquiries. It was called the Consejo de la Suprema y General Inquisición.

Charles V and the Inquisitor General signed an agreement with the leaders of Valencia that the Inquisition would not prosecute the *Morisco* community for 40 years on the basis that it would take at least a generation for the Muslims to be properly converted to Spanish and Christian ways.

Although this level of tolerance was not extended to the rest of Spain, it is clear that until the early years of Philip II's reign, the efforts of the Inquisition to keep the *Moriscos* to their nominal Christianity were little more than a gesture. In this way the Inquisition's earlier aggression and unfair persecution had been moderated.

Opposition to the Inquisition

In Aragon especially, there was a great deal of opposition to the new tribunal. In some regions, such opposition stemmed from the fact that there were already Papal Inquisitions in some of the cities. Barcelona had one from 1461 and so refused to ratify the new one, since it was run by the Spanish king and dominated by Castilians. In Aragon, there were always deep suspicions that Ferdinand was using the Inquisition to increase his power at the expense of the local *fueros*. In May 1484, the Catalans claimed that the appointment of Thomas de Torquemada as Inquisitor General and the attempt to suspend the Papal Inquisition in Barcelona were 'against the liberties, constitutions and agreements solemnly sworn by Your Majesty'.

Such opposition ultimately proved fruitless. The Pope agreed to suspend all Papal Inquisitors in the Crown of Aragon and Torquemada appointed a Castilian, Alonso de Espina, to Barcelona. He entered the city in 1487 to find his work already done. Fearful of the Spanish Inquisition's approach, hundreds of *Conversos* fled the city. Most of those subsequently prosecuted were tried in their absence since they had fled.

It was a similar tale in Valencia and Aragon. Existing Papal Inquisitors, who did little, were removed. New Inquisitors were appointed, and protests at the scale and injustice of the proceedings began to grow. The town of Teruel refused to admit Inquisitors and had to be reduced to obedience by force. In 1485, the Inquisitor Pedro Arbues was assassinated while kneeling in prayer before the high altar of Saragossa Cathedral. This murder backfired on the desperate group of *Conversos* who had hired the assassins. Old Christians were shocked at the attack in such a holy place and many were now convinced that stories about *Conversos* conspiracies were true. Arbues was declared a saint and people were still being punished for involvement in the crime seven years later. The murder legitimised the severity of the Inquisition's practices.

There was also serious opposition to the Inquisition's brutality in intellectual circles. Luis de Paramo, himself an Inquisitor, wrote that many intellectuals opposed the persecution. Some pointed out that since many conversions of Jews to Christianity were forced and unaccompanied by proper education and instruction, they were invalid and so the victims were Jews not Christians. In this way they were outside the Inquisition's jurisdiction, since it could only concern itself with heresy – that is, with Christians who strayed from the Faith. Others disagreed with the anti-Semitism of the expulsion of the Jews in 1492, since this seemed to be an invitation for Christians to destroy the Jews, which was contrary to Scripture.

Friar José de Sigüenza, a sixteenth-century historian, condemned 'the evil custom prevalent in Spain of treating members of sects worse after their conversion than before it'. Archbishop Talavera, who adopted a humane approach to the *Moriscos*, took a similar line with the *Conversos*. He reasoned that 'heresies need to be corrected not only with punishment and lashes, but even more with Catholic reasoning'. The failure of such views is indicated by the fact that the tract containing these opinions was later placed on the Index of forbidden books. At the age of 80, Talavera and his entire household were arrested by the Inquisition. After torture, relatives and servants confirmed the lie that he maintained a synagogue in his palace. Although Talavera was exonerated by the papacy, this verdict might well have been questioned by the Inquisition had he not died a few days after his release. The papacy itself soon had doubts about the Inquisition's harsh attitude. Both Pope Sixtus IV and Pope Innocent VIII issued Bulls calling for mercy, leniency and reconciliation, but their words fell on deaf ears.

Procedure

The Inquisition's ability to spread fear and consternation came about largely through its procedures, which allowed a relatively small number of Inquisitors to unearth rather a lot of heresy. Most importantly, the Inquisition relied on informers to hunt out their victims.

KEY TERM

Edict of grace was read out in church by the Inquisitors. It recited a list of heresies and invited the congregation to confess if they believed in any of them. The Inquisitors also invited denunciations of other people suspected of heresy.

Inquisitors based in major cities such as Madrid or Valencia, or periodically travelling to more rural areas, would first read out an **edict of grace**. This listed a number of heresies, and invited men and women to come forward to confess their own guilt or to lay charges against others. In the early years it is astonishing how many people did confess to heresy. In Toledo, for example, there were 2400 penitents in the city in 1486. For many this was because, if they came forward voluntarily, they would usually be reconciled to the Church without serious penalties. Those denounced by others were unlikely to be so fortunate. The Inquisition's Holy Office relied heavily on informers to denounce those guilty of religious crimes and protected their informers by refusing to name them. This was justified by the need to prevent reprisals against the accuser. However, it also meant that all sorts of petty disputes and arguments might lead to charges being brought. Even if the accused was cleared, action would rarely be taken against the accuser.

Other areas of the Holy Office's procedure were even more sinister. The accused were arrested and imprisoned, often for long periods, while awaiting trial. At first, they were not told the nature of the charges. Instead, they were told to examine their consciences and confess their sins. This could lead to extra charges being laid. The accused were presumed guilty until they could prove their innocence and were denied access to the sacraments. For Archbishop Carranza, this meant eighteen years deprived of spiritual comfort. Similarly, those accused had to defend themselves and did not have the right to call on lawyers or solicitors. Finally, judgement was made by the Inquisition itself. It investigated the charges and pronounced its verdict.

The Inquisition, in line with other European courts of the period, was permitted to use **torture** to extract confessions, which has added to the tribunal's black name. The rules said that torture could only be used once. However, this restriction could be avoided by claiming that torture was merely suspended periodically and could be started again if the accused refused to confess freely.

Three main types of torture were inflicted on unfortunate victims.

The *garrucha* (a type of pulley). This involved being hung from the ceiling by ropes tied around the wrists lifted above the head. The accused was then raised slowly and allowed to fall quickly. This meant that arms and shoulders could be dislocated. To add to the efficiency of the dreadful machine, weights were often attached to the feet.

The *toca*. This was a form of water torture in which victims were tied down on their back and had jugfulls of water forced down their throats.

The *potro* (the rack). This was the most common form of torture. Cords were wound around the naked body of the victim. These could then be tightened by the torturer, which allowed the ropes to bite deeper and deeper into the flesh.

There is no avoiding the fact that the Inquisition inflicted enormous suffering on people who were often guilty of minor misdemeanours, if that.

KEY THEME

Torture

Sometimes, victims of torture were ignorant of the crimes they were being accused of. This resulted in scenes such as the one below, recorded by the Inquisition in 1568. (The Inquisition was expected to keep written records of torture sessions.)

She was ordered to be placed on the potro. She said, 'Senores, why will you not tell me what I have to say? Senor, put me on the ground – have I not said that I did it all? I have said that I did all that the witnesses say ... These people are killing me ... For God's sake let me go.'

The charges against the woman were that she refused to eat pork and changed her linen on Saturdays.

The Inquisition and popular culture

The Inquisition clearly had a huge impact on Spanish society. However, that does not mean that Spain or the Spanish Church were intolerant or racist. While popular anti-Semitism helped in the formation of the tribunal and was no doubt whipped up by the early persecution, the real causes of the persecution lay in the hands of individual Inquisitors, rather than in the popular mood or royal will. In many ways, Ferdinand and Isabella created a monster they could not fully control. They allowed individual Inquisitors a free hand to use every underhand means to pursue and convict their victims.

One of the worst cases of Inquisitors running out of control, but not untypical, was Diego Rodríguez Lucero, Inquisitor of Córdoba from 1499. He claimed to believe that there was a widespread Jewish conspiracy to destroy Spain. He arrested many leading citizens on false charges in order to confiscate their property, then used torture to force victims to name their accomplices in the supposed conspiracy. One contemporary noted that this process 'resulted in the denunciation of so many people, both *Conversos* and Old Christians, that the city was scandalised and almost burst into rioting'.

When Lucero was finally exposed, he had executed some 200 innocent people and another 400 were in the cells. An independent enquiry found that the evidence against his victims was 'all fabricated'. Eventually, Lucero was arrested, but remained unpunished for his crimes.

Since individual fanatics who were allowed too much power by a compliant monarchy perpetrated the worst excesses of the Inquisition in its early years, the impact of the Inquisition on popular culture was limited. The Inquisition had little impact on rural areas. Some 80 per cent of Spaniards lived outside the big towns, so most would only have come across the Inquisition occasionally, as Inquisitors made sporadic tours over difficult terrain. Permanent tribunals of the Inquisition were established in only thirteen cities across the peninsula, leaving huge areas unsupervised. Similarly, rural communities were more impervious to the Holy Office and often closed ranks in the face of its representatives.

Local superstitions and religious practices often went undetected and unchanged by the Inquisition. One area where the Inquisition actually played an enlightened role was the crime of witchcraft, nearly always a rural crime. Though most cases were dealt with by secular courts, the Inquisition assisted a wide-ranging investigation of witchcraft claims in the 1520s. Its report, published in 1526, played down the significance of witchcraft. Indeed, the future Inquisitor General, Valdés took the view that most claims about witches were false, as were most of their supposed crimes. Thus the Inquisition played an important part in keeping Spain free of the major increase in witchcraft persecution that affected other parts of Europe between 1550 and 1650.

Although enlightened on witchcraft, the Inquisition did little to advance the **reforms of the Spanish Church**, which were so badly needed. Indeed, the Inquisition acted as a punishing body rather than an educating one, and the local bishop or abbot who saw it as an alien body often challenged its jurisdiction. Furthermore, by punishing Old Christians for petty or imaginary errors, the Inquisition helped to stifle academic debate among leading churchmen and intellectuals, which alone could produce a serious reform programme. It is not surprising that some reforms brought in during the reign of Philip II were not Spanish but **Tridentine reforms** worked out by the Pope and leading churchmen at the Council of Trent and enforced by the royal mandate. The Inquisition stifled any meaningful debate on the Iberian Church within the Iberian peninsula. Most leading intellectuals and reformers preferred to remain silent on Church matters or went abroad.

It is often said that the Inquisition helped to ensure that the destructive forces of the Protestant Reformation did not reach Spain. While the Inquisition did have some influence in this direction, it is important to remember that very few of its cases concerned Protestant heresy. Instead, Spain's imperviousness to Protestant heresy might be attributed to a number of other factors. The increasing extent of royal power over the Church was one such crucial factor. Nowhere in Europe was Protestantism firmly established for a long period without the assent of the local king, duke or prince. Spain's rulers such as Charles I and Philip II were all unwavering Catholics who enjoyed relatively good relations with the papacy. In addition, Spain was not predominantly an urban society. This was important because Protestantism flourished in the towns and cities of Europe. Nor were there many printing presses in Spain, relative to its population, and this also inhibited the spread of new ideas. Furthermore, Spain was a long way from the storm centres of Reformation in northern Europe. It was sheltered physically and intellectually by the Pyrenees.

Although the Inquisition did help to destroy Judaism and Islam within Spain, it was not the main cause of the Reformation's failure to capture the hearts and minds of ordinary Spaniards.

Historians and the Inquisition

The operation and persecutions of the Spanish Inquisition have inevitably been the subject of debate among writers – both contemporaries and later historians. For Protestant propagandists such as the Englishman John Foxe (1516–87) the Inquisition was 'this dreadful engine of tyranny' that 'may at any time be introduced into a country where the Catholics have

Reforms of the Spanish Church Many Spaniards, including clerics, were concerned about the fact that the Church in Spain was too wealthy and that many parish priests were ignorant and idle.

Tridentine reforms Reforms of the Catholic Church passed at one of the three sessions of the General Council of the Catholic Church, called by the Pope to the Italian city of Trent. The three sessions were held in 1545–8, 1551–2 and 1562–3.

the ascendancy'. For Foxe, as for many of his co-religionists, the Inquisition was a Catholic institution designed to crush civil as well as religious liberty. Foxe's most famous work was his *Book of Martyrs*, written at the time of Protestant Queen Elizabeth. The text described in grisly detail the burning of Protestants under the **Marian regime**.

> ### KEY TERM
>
> **Marian regime**
> The government of Mary I of England. Mary ruled from 1553 until her death in 1558. As the daughter of Henry VIII and Catherine of Aragon, Mary remained a strong Catholic and reintroduced Catholic worship and practice, including the Papal headship of the English Church after the early death of her Protestant step-brother Edward VI in 1553. She married her cousin, the future Philip II of Spain, in 1554.

In *The Rise of the Dutch Republic* (1856), John Motley spoke in similar vein about the Holy Office. It taught, he wrote, 'the savages of India and America to shudder at the name of Christianity'. It was staffed by 'a bench of monks having its familiars in every house, diving into the secrets of every fireside, judging and executing its horrible decrees without responsibility'. William of Orange went further, seeing the Inquisition as an entirely natural, if bloodthirsty, product of a Spanish ruling class who, according to him, were 'of the blood of the Moors and Jews'.

For the Spaniards at the time, the Inquisition aroused contradictory sentiments. As we have seen, the Inquisition did arouse some hostility and it may be that this opposition helped to limit its operations in the reign of Charles I. On the other hand, the Holy Office was always supported by the Crown and other orthodox sections of Spanish society who saw it as a necessary defence against the heresy that seemed to exist both within and outside of Spanish society.

The Reformation failed to establish a serious foothold in Spain and this allowed Spain to see itself as the great guardian of Christian orthodoxy in a world divided and disfigured by heresy. God had sent down the challenge and the Spanish had answered the call. More neutral opinion in Spain may have accepted the existence of the Inquisition because it had little (if any) contact with it. At its peak in the late fifteenth century there were still only 50 Inquisitors in Spain with limited funding and a very small bureaucracy.

Later on, in the nineteenth century, Spanish liberals were quick to condemn the Inquisition as the cause of Spain's decline from great power status in general and its cultural sterility in particular. These claims were clearly exaggerated as the Inquisition and the Index had little impact on popular literature. The Index of 1559 attacked religious works of piety that might encourage heresy; it did not condemn the chivalric romances, the histories of Spanish imperialism or the many other themes such as mathematics and botany covered by contemporary Spanish literature.

B. Netanyahu's account of *The Origins of the Inquisition in Fifteenth Century Spain* (1995) is similarly partisan in its explanation of the Inquisition's early years. Admittedly this was when the Inquisition was at its most savage and racist. However, Netanyahu goes rather further than the evidence allows when he claims that Ferdinand deliberately manipulated popular opinion against the Jews and *Conversos* in order to steal their wealth. Ferdinand, he claims, invented a story of a Jewish conspiracy to take over Spain. Likewise, the argument appears exaggerated because of the author's clear hostility to the *Conversos* as men and women who had abandoned their true faith.

The most recent, detailed and balanced analysis of the Inquisition and its impact comes in Henry Kamen's *Inquisition and Society in Spain* (1985). Kamen demonstrates that the Inquisition was certainly responsible for some terrible persecution. However, he sees its impact as limited and largely approved of by Spanish government and society. In the end, the Spanish Inquisition was not as dreadful as we would like it to have been.

REFORM AND CHANGE IN THE SPANISH CHURCH, 1450–1556

Reform

In the period up to the accession of Philip II in 1556, reform of the Catholic Church in Spain (in terms of tending to the spiritual needs of the masses) remained limited. It is clear that in most Spanish parishes, reform did not gain momentum until the reign of Philip II, with the publication of the Tridentine Decrees in 1564.

Before 1550, only 37 per cent of those questioned by the Toledo Inquisition were able to recite the **four main prayers**. Yet by the 1580s and 1590s, this figure had reached 68 per cent and in the first half of the seventeenth century it had reached 82 per cent. Even allowing for regional variations and the possible peculiarities of those interviewed by the Toledan Inquisition, the trend is clearly upward and impressive. Whereas only 40 per cent knew the Ten Commandments between 1565 and 1584, by 1650 this figure too had increased to 77 per cent.

Outlying regions do not seem to have done as well as Castile, the heartland of Catholic piety and zeal. However, the overall impression remains that it was only after 1550 that the Spanish Church managed to increase measurably the spiritual knowledge and understanding of the Spanish people.

In the same way, the figures for the production of religious literature in Spain tell the same story. More than half the books published in Spain in the period 1550–1650 were on religious themes. By contrast, in Venice (the main centre of Italian printing) the percentage of books on religion rose from just 16 per cent in the 1550s to some 35 per cent in the early seventeenth century.

Spain was a deeply religious society, but Spanish Catholicism showed its most impressive signs of growth of influence and development after 1550.

> ### KEY TERM
>
> **Four main prayers (Pater, Ave, Credo and Salve)** The four main prayers as recited or sung during the mass or spoken in the rosary were the Pater (Our Father), Ave (Hail Mary), Credo (I believe) and the Salve Regina (Hail the Queen).

Before this date, many critics continued to lament the poor performance of the Spanish Church. They noted the irony of the fact that a Church that was attempting, with some success, to spread Christianity to pagans in the New World was apparently powerless to minister to its own flock in Spain.

This is not to say that the earlier period was without reforms (such as those brought in by Cisneros in the reigns of Ferdinand and Isabella), but these tended to affect a minority in holy orders and a minority of intellectuals who sought religious instruction beyond the basics. In addition, the whole notion of reform became entwined with the Protestant Reformation and heresy and so lost much of its appeal to Spaniards. In Spain, the reforming ideas of Erasmus, the most popular of Christian humanists in the early sixteenth century, were initially as popular as elsewhere in Europe. Francisco Jiménez de Cisneros himself was a supporter and in 1516 requested Erasmus' aid in the production of a **polyglot Bible**.

However, after 1520, as heresy spread in Germany and Switzerland apparently encouraged by Erasmus' ideas, his appeal in Spain began to wane. Although Erasmus himself was never officially condemned and remained a staunch Catholic, his supporters in Spain began to fall foul of the ecclesiastical authorities.

Furthermore, Erasmian-style reform was associated with the worrying growth of the mystical movement known as the _alumbrados_, or 'illumined ones'. Just when the alien religions (Islam and Judaism) seemed to be under control, the _alumbrados_ set off a reaction within the Church much more powerful than their numbers merited. Once again, a Church apparently certain of its own identity greeted ideas of Church reform with scepticism and hostility.

Monastic reform

Some of the earliest Church reforms concerned Spain's monastic communities. After 1400, the Crown of Castile had taken an interest in Monastic Observance, a movement that aimed to reinvigorate the monastic orders with their original purpose and order. At the Ecclesiastical Council held in Seville in 1478, Ferdinand and Isabella gave this movement added impetus.

After eleven years of papal obstruction and some hostility, Pope Innocent VIII gave his permission for the reform of the Spanish Benedictines, Cistercians and Augustinians. However, by this stage the Catholic Kings erastian plans had become more ambitious. They demanded and received from the Pope not only the right to send out commissioners to reform monastic houses but also the abolition of the monastic houses' right to appeal their case to Rome.

In keeping with his unduly compliant attitude to his fellow Spaniards, these sweeping powers were granted to Ferdinand and Isabella by the Borgia Pope Alexander VI in 1493. The Franciscan Cisneros and the Dominican Diego Deza were put in charge of the operation. They were so successful that by the time of Cisneros' death in 1517, nearly all the Franciscan Conventual Houses (which were opposed to reform) had become Observant (that is, they became members of a branch of the Franciscan Order that followed strict rules).

Under Charles I, the programme of monastic reform moved into more remote parts of Castile – namely Galicia and the Asturias, from where it was brought into Navarre and Aragon. However, the programme for reform then stalled after 1548 when the Pope vigorously opposed Charles' plans to break the opposition of Catalan nuns by putting the Inquisition in charge of the drive for observance.

Equally significant was the work of the arch-reformer Cisneros, which also produced other initiatives of reform designed to reinvigorate the Spanish Church. Cisneros encouraged the study of theology and, partly thanks to his influence, some fifteen new schools of theology were founded in the period 1500–50. He patronised the new university of Alcala and sponsored there a great multilingual Bible called the *Complutensian Polyglot*, which appeared in six volumes in 1522. Here scholars could study the Bible in Latin, Greek and Hebrew, together with helpful commentary and footnotes. It was one of the greatest monuments to Spanish humanism, but also one of the last.

CHURCH RELATIONS WITH THE CROWN

During this period, the Church in Spain became more clearly erastian, being increasingly subject, as it was, to the will of the Crown. Playing on papal approval for *Reconquista* and papal fear of France, Ferdinand and Isabella won full control over the Church in Granada (even before the conquest was complete) via the so-called *Granada Patronato*. This was granted by a grateful Pope, Innocent VIII, in 1486. By 1493, the Papal Bull *Inter Caetera* gave them control over all evangelical missions to the New World. All New World tithes then came their way in 1501. This process of royal control climaxed with the 1508 grant by Pope Julius II of universal *Patronato* over the entire New World Church (which included the right to present to all benefices).

By 1523, in the reign of Charles I, the Crown also controlled the **three great military religious orders** and was officially empowered by a Papal Grant to nominate to all sees, abbeys and other benefices in Spain.

Along with increasing rights to nominate came the right to a share of the

KEY TERM

Three great military religious orders These were the orders of Santiago, Calatrava and Alcantara. They were very wealthy and powerful and had originally been set up in medieval times to carry on the Reconquista or war against the Moorish kingdoms in Spain.

Church's wealth. Ferdinand and Isabella had acquired the right to *cruzada*, or crusade tax to fight the Moors. The tax was extended ε after the conquest of Granada was completed in 1492. Charles I l: made it permanent.

The Catholic Kings also gained the right to take for Crown use one-third of all the tithes paid by the laity to the clergy – the so-called *tercias reales*, or royal third. Charles I restored the *subsidio* tax on clerical incomes in 1519 and extended it to Aragon in 1534. Additionally, he gained the right to collect the income from vacant sees. Since he also nominated new bishops it was worth his while spending some time in his deliberations. Overall, it is clear that the Spanish Church's contribution to royal finances increased markedly in the first half of the sixteenth century and continued to increase thereafter.

Royal control over the Church was further buttressed by the advent of the Inquisition. The Crown appointed all its leading officials and it was run by the *Suprema*. At first, the papacy reserved for itself all cases of suspected heresy brought against bishops and other members of the higher clergy. However, this right was effectively given up by Leo X and his successor as Pope, Adrian VI, who was Charles I's former tutor. Thus, while Crown power over the Church rose, the authority of the papacy naturally decreased.

Despite this, the papacy did still have some rights over parts of the Spanish Church. It continued to appoint some bishops, had the power to hear appeals and could still dispense with the decrees of canon law in certain cases.

KEY EVENT

The Carranza case Carranza was the Dominican Archbishop of Toledo from 1557. In 1559 he was charged with heresy by the Inquisition after the publication of his *Commentaries on the Christian Catechism*. He was imprisoned by the Inquisition for seven years before being summoned to Rome where he died in 1576.

The picture of the increasing authority of the Crown and decreasing power of the papacy over the Spanish Church was mirrored in terms of the relations between the Crown and the papacy. In 1527, Charles I's troops unexpectedly sacked the city of Rome and effectively made Pope Clement VII a captive. Charles put pressure on him not to allow Henry VIII to divorce his aunt (Catherine of Aragon). At the same time, the growing power of the Habsburgs in Italy meant that, with the notable exception of Pope Paul IV in the 1550s, the papacy remained subservient to the will of the Spanish Crown. When a great dispute arose between papacy and Inquisition in Philip's reign – the notorious **Carranza case** (1559–76) – the Crown effectively won the day, establishing its right to ignore the demands of the Pope.

Indeed, Charles I's leading role in the struggle against Protestantism and the Ottomans gave him, as leader of the Spanish Church, added prestige and power over his Church, which would continue under his successors. Furthermore, it is clear that moves to reform the Spanish Church came from the Crown. Isabella was particularly keen to improve the condition of the clergy and the example they set to their flock.

The scale of achievement should not be exaggerated, but the Crown's control over nomination to bishoprics meant that the Spanish bench of bishops improved markedly in quality in the 80 years before 1556. Rather fewer were aristocrats, rather more were scholars and teachers like Cisneros who led exemplary lives. Even when an aristocrat was appointed, such as Cardinal Gonzalez de Mendoza (appointed to the see of Toledo in 1482), they tended to set a rather better example than before. Whatever the failings of his private life, Mendoza was a major patron of the **New Learning** in Spain. He founded the College of Santa Cruz in Valladolid and encouraged other schemes to improve the quality of the Castilian clergy. Isabella was also a major patron of Cisneros who did so much to improve the spirituality of Franciscan and other orders of monks.

The experience of the Spanish humanist **Juan Luis Vives** tells one a significant amount about developments in the Spanish Church during the reigns of Ferdinand, Isabella and Charles. Vives was born of *Converso* parents who continued to practise their faith in secret. He worked in Paris and the Low Countries, and turned down an invitation to go to the university of Alcala in 1522, perhaps fearing the long arm of the Inquisition. In 1520, his father had been arrested and was burnt alive in 1524 by the Inquisition as a Judaiser. Four years after this, the bones of his long-dead mother were dug up and burnt. No wonder he could write to his good friend Erasmus in 1534 that 'we are going through times when we can neither speak nor be silent without danger'. His tale says much about the less attractive side of the 'reformed' Spanish Church.

CONCLUSION

It is clear that the Church's power in Spain increased after the accession of Ferdinand and Isabella. Instead of being a land of three religions – Christianity, Islam and Judaism – Spain became an entirely Christian land. The expulsion of the Jews, persecution of *Conversos* and the marginalisation of Muslims before their expulsion in 1609 left the Spanish Church triumphant and powerful. The Church also became an imperial Church, spreading Christianity to areas where paganism and unbelief still flourished, and it was party to the great challenge laid down to both the Ottoman Sultans and to the Protestant Reformers by the Catholic Church, which would bring partial victory under Philip II.

In the context of the great changes inside Spain and beyond, the Spanish Church in terms of its identity and pretensions was changed immeasurably. At the same time, the advent and development of the Spanish Inquisition did much to bolster the renewed confidence and power of the Church. The result of all these changes was to create a Church that was both militant and extremely nationalist. Spanish

Christianity and Spanish identity were one and the same thing. Purity of blood was underpinned by purity of faith.

While aristocratic influence over the Spanish Church was downgraded and some attempts at improving men and morals were initiated, the concerns of the moderate humanists were not really addressed. Instead, as the Church grew increasingly subservient to the state, it became intellectually narrow, conservative and deadly. The Inquisition may not have been as brutal as tradition alleges, but it clearly spread fear and stifled debate.

On the other hand, the reformed Spanish Church became a department of state and buttressed royal power in difficult times. It ensured that Protestant-style Reformation would not cause division and discord in Spain in the way it did in much of the rest of central and western Europe. While France, the Low Countries, England and much of Germany experienced the horrors of religious civil war, Spain was spared such distress and the Spanish Church should take much of the credit for that success. The Spanish Church stood united and strong in the face of challenges from heretics, Ottomans and New World pagans.

SECTION 2

1474–1598: Did this period witness the Golden Age of Spain?

INTRODUCTION

The period in question has been judged a 'Golden Age' in Spain. Not only did Spain dominate Europe politically, but also it was home to an artistic flowering that would make it the cultural centre of the continent. The extent to which this period can be seen as Spain's Golden Age is the key theme of this section.

CONTEMPORARY VIEWPOINTS

Before making a judgement regarding the scale of the Golden Age, it is important to look at the attitudes of contemporaries. Few were more perceptive than the writers **Torquato Tasso** and Miguel de Cervantes Saavedra.

Torquato Tasso – 'The Golden Age'

O lovely age of gold! Not that the rivers rolled
With milk, or that the woods wept honeydew;
Not that the ready ground
Produced without a wound,
Or the mild serpent had no tooth that slew;
Not that a cloudless blue
Forever was in sight,
Or that the heaven, which burns
And now is cold by turns,
Looked out in glad and everlasting light;
No, nor that even the insolent ships from far
Brought war to no new lands nor riches worse than war:
But solely that that vain
And breath-invented pain,
That idol of mistake, that worshipped cheat,
That Honour – since so called
By vulgar minds appalled –
Played not the tyrant with our nature yet.
(Source: from Aminta by Torquato Tasso, 1573.)

Renaissance scholars often donned their rose-tinted spectacles when reviewing the world of the ancient Greeks, seeing in that period a Golden Age of poetry, philosophy and mathematics. In his poem 'The Golden Age', Tasso appears to dismiss such idealised concepts. Human society has always been about suffering, he claims. He makes reference to the 'tooth that slew', to the changing fortunes of men and mankind mirrored by a heaven 'which burns / And now is cold by turns'. He also comments on 'war' and 'riches worse than war'. All these things serve to make life less than ideal.

However, Tasso cannot abandon entirely the idea that once, in the distant past, human society was rather more pleasant. Therefore he claims the once-Golden Age was golden because men had not found 'Honour'. Later in the poem he explains that Honour is the root of evil, the 'masterer' of Love and Nature. So he bids Honour depart from the world:

> We here, a lowly race,
> Can live without thy grace,
> After the use of mild antiquity.
> Go, let us love; since years
> No truce allow, and life soon disappears;
> Go, let us love, the daylight dies, is born;
> But unto us the light
> Dies once for all; and sleep brings on eternal night.

Ultimately, Tasso is true to his vision of 'mild antiquity' and, like other scholars of the period, offers us a romantic view of ancient times when men and women dwelt happily together. Clearly he did not believe that his own age was particularly golden!

Miguel de Cervantes Saavedra

Cervantes (1547–1616) is the most famous Spanish writer of the period. His view of a Golden Age was similar to Tasso's and his hero, Don Quixote, offers an even more idealised picture of human happiness.

> Happy the age and happy those centuries to which the ancients gave the name of golden, and not because gold, which is so esteemed in this iron age of ours, was then to be had without toil, but because those who lived in that time did not know the meaning of the words 'thine' and 'mine'. In that blessed era all things were held in common, and to gain his daily sustenance no labour was required of any man, save to reach forth his hand and take it from the sturdy oaks … All then was peace, all was concord and friendship … .
> (Source: *Don Quixote* by Miguel de Cervantes Saavedra, 1605.)

The tale of Don Quixote, immortalised in print.

Other definitions of a Golden Age

Both Tasso and Cervantes thought their own age one of 'iron'. Their views remind us that few contemporaries thought that they were living through a Golden Age; they were too aware of human suffering and misery for that. Nonetheless, it is vital to remember that they were measuring their own age against an idealised, ancient and wholly mythical past.

If we take a more realistic definition of the Golden Age as one that is rather better than what comes before and after, then Spain in the period 1500–90 actually fares rather well. Tasso's and Cervantes' contribution is not to give us a yardstick with which to measure Golden Age but to remind us of how art and literature flourished in the sixteenth century – surely a major aspect of any supposed Golden Age.

The term 'Golden Age' suggests a clear comparison with periods before and after, which, by definition, are deemed unworthy of the name. Before 1474, Spain did not exist; Iberian society was characterised by conquest and reconquest, civil war and religious struggle. After 1600, it has been argued that Spain entered an extended period of decline, characterised by defeats at home and abroad, less effective monarchs, and economic and financial difficulties. The historian R. Trevor Davies held such a view but put the turning point rather later. His first volume on Spanish history, entitled *The Golden Century of Spain 1501–1621* (1937), was followed by *Spain in Decline 1621–1700* (1957).

Other historians have described triumph turning into disaster and optimism into despair. In *Imperial Spain 1469–1716* (1963), J.H. Elliott painted a broadly similar picture of rise and decline. 'The Spanish achievement of the sixteenth century,' he claimed, 'was essentially the work of Castile, but so also was the Spanish disaster of the seventeenth.' However he placed decline after 1650 and his analysis of the period before 1600 is too balanced to allow him to see that period as a Golden Age.

The Spanish philosopher José Ortega y Gasset (1883–1955) expressed the paradox of Spain most clearly when he wrote what may serve as an epitaph on the Spain under the Habsburgs: 'Castile has made Spain, and Castile has destroyed it.' However, if one argues that Spain experienced a Golden Age not only in the sixteenth century but also in the seventeenth, there is no need to find reasons for self-destruction.

Henry Kamen was one of the first historians to question the idea of the decline of Spain in the seventeenth century in his important article the 'The Decline of Spain: a historical myth?' (1979). Having undermined the notion of decline he was then in a position to argue in *Golden Age of Spain* (1988) that there was indeed a Golden Age and that it lasted from the end of the reign of Henry IV to the early years of Philip V, or 1474–1714.

It will be argued here that such a view is entirely appropriate. The power of Spain and the Spanish monarchy were probably at their height during the age of Philip II. However, neither were seriously undermined afterwards or before. Picking out specific dates for the Golden Age is a rather arbitrary process. It is clear that while the whole of the period 1492–1700 can be seen as Spain's Golden Age, the high point of that age, politically at least, lay between 1492 and 1600. These dates serve to remind us that a Golden Age, like decline, need not coincide exactly with the death of a sovereign.

SPAIN AS A GREAT POWER, 1492–1600

The historian W.H. Prescott, in *History of the Reign of Ferdinand and Isabella* (1838) wrote 'the nation, emerging from the sloth and licence of a barbarous age, seemed to prepare like a giant to run its course'. Prescott echoed Spanish contemporaries of the Catholic monarchs such as Andrés Bernáldez. Bernáldez believed that during the reigns of Ferdinand and Isabella, Spain had been called by God to take charge of the world by dominating Europe, defeating the forces of Islam and spreading His Word around the world.

Bernáldez was especially critical of Henry IV (ruled 1454–74) and

Spanish society during his reign. 'At this juncture,' he said, 'envy and covetousness were awakened and avarice nourished; justice became moribund and force ruled; greed ruled and decadent sensuality spread, and the cruel temptation of sovereignty overcame the humble persuasion of obedience; the customs were mostly dissolute and corrupt.'

By contrast, all these evils, according to Bernáldez, were wiped out under Ferdinand and Isabella. Another contemporary, Hernando del Pulgar, claimed that, 'as soon as they began to rule, they administered justice and these acts which they carried out made the citizens and farmers and all common people very happy'.

Such judgements need to be treated with caution. Yet there is no doubt that the reign of the Catholic monarchs seemed to usher in a new age. To contemporaries, the speed with which Spain was united and became the equal or superior of France was an indication of divine providence. In just 40 years, Spain changed from a warring group of states divided politically and religiously into a nation at the forefront of European politics.

Political achievements of Ferdinand and Isabella

While the advent of Ferdinand and Isabella did not transform Spanish fortunes overnight, their reign laid the foundations for Spain's future greatness. They brought a much greater sense of unity by joining Castile and Aragon in their personal monarchies, thereby putting an end to civil war in the peninsula. Their direct style of government, combined with a willingness to travel around the peninsula dispensing justice, helped to curb the power of the nobility and the towns, and to boost the power of the monarchy. In this way, the *Cortes* was reduced to quiet obedience and royal revenue increased.

The Catholic Kings also ensured that the power of the Church increasingly buttressed royal power rather than acting as a challenge to it. Good relations with the papacy combined with the *Reconquista* and forays into North Africa and the New World made the Spanish Church more clearly erastian and subject to royal control. Despite its anti-Semitic excesses, especially in its first decade, the Spanish Inquisition further enhanced the Crown's religious powers and sense of divine mission.

The new-found unity of Castile and Aragon also allowed Ferdinand and Isabella to undertake the conquest of Granada, which was completed by 1492. More than any other, this success laid the foundations for future greatness. The enemies within Spanish society, whether *Conversos* or *Moriscos*, were being dealt with to produce a more united realm.

While the racial price to be paid for this policy of *limpieza de sangre* (purity of blood) was high, politically it allowed future monarchs to rule over a united and internally relatively untroubled series of kingdoms. After the acquisition of Granada came Cerdagne and Roussillon (1493), Navarre (1515) and Portugal (1580), which allowed Castile to dominate the peninsula in a way it had never done before. The acquisition of territory and a willingness to rule each kingdom according to its own laws and customs brought internal peace, a boost to royal finances and growing international prestige. In addition, it meant that future Spanish monarchs had a solid financial basis for establishing Spain as a great power.

After Columbus' epic voyage of 1492, Spain acquired yet more wealth and prestige as ruler of the New World. The conquest was not carried out by the Crown but by *conquistadors* such as Cortez and Pizarro. This saved the monarchy further expense, but allowed it to claim its share of the spoils. Over the next century, that empire would bring in increasing quantities of money and materials to Spain and the Crown.

While the cost of defending that empire would increase alarmingly in the seventeenth century, the empire always represented a very valuable asset in the sixteenth century. Ferdinand and Isabella could hardly have forecast just how valuable the New World would become, but it gave Spain claims to be an imperial power and further bolstered its claims to be the most Christian of European nations.

Ferdinand and Isabella also boosted the power of the Crown, especially in Castile. The monarchy found a more secure financial footing, with extra taxes being collected. The independence of the towns was somewhat curbed by the activities of the Catholic Kings and the *Santa Hermandad*. The independence of the nobility was curbed not only by the actions of more dynamic monarchs but also by a common goal and increased royal patronage through the ten-year campaign and conquest of Granada. At the same time, Ferdinand and Isabella pursued policies against the Moors and the Jews that were broadly popular and contributed to the sense of unity.

While they may not have united the kingdoms of Spain, this was still an impressive achievement. Formal unity under a unified legal code with a common currency could not have been achieved and, had it been attempted, would have led to serious problems such as internal revolts. Such revolts broke out in Aragon and Catalonia in the seventeenth century because Olivares attempted to unify the systems of taxation and military contributions to shift more of the burden away from Castile. Attempts to create a more unified Spain, such as the proposed Union of Arms of 1624, led to failure and rebellion.

The great strength of Ferdinand and Isabella and other sixteenth-century rulers of Spain was that they were monarchs of each territory separately.

In fact, they ruled over a confederation of states. This loose and personal confederation was still very powerful, with the resulting *monarquia* (monarchies) being rather stronger than the sum of their constituent parts. As soon as they came to power, the Catholic kings could marshal resources in terms of money and men, which earlier rulers of Castile or Aragon could never dream of. The **confederation system** was to be at the heart of Spain's success and strength.

In the same way, Ferdinand and Isabella's reigns also saw Spain become a great power in Europe. After centuries of relative obscurity on the European scene, Spain now laid the foundations for future greatness in Europe. Partly this was the result of an accident of birth. Ferdinand's family had ruled Naples but with the extinction of the direct male line the kingdom of Naples, controlling much of southern Italy as well as the island of Sicily, reverted to Ferdinand himself in 1504.

After defeating the French, Ferdinand's control of Naples was confirmed by a treaty in 1504. Success against France further north added the Duchy of Milan to his territories in 1513. Although this would be briefly lost again to France two years later, in the long term it paved the way for Spain's rulers to control most of the Italian peninsula. Since these territories were acquired more by inheritance than conquest, Spain's long-term control was assured. There would be no Italian revolts against Spanish rule until 1647.

The end of the marriage with Isabella's death in 1504 threatened to destroy Spain's newfound power all too quickly. There was a crisis because Ferdinand and Isabella had no surviving son. Thus the succession to the Crown of Castile passed to a mentally unbalanced princess (Joanna) and her infant son. Nonetheless, this new disunity between Castile and Aragon proved to be temporary and so Ferdinand and Isabella had, as it turned out, laid secure foundations for Spain's future greatness in Europe and the world.

Achievements of Charles I

Spain's pretensions to greatness were confirmed in the reign of Charles I. His personal empire of **inherited states** was the greatest power in Europe and, increasingly, at the heart of that empire was Spain. Once the internal revolts of the Comuneros and the Germania were over by 1523, Spain impressed as the greatest power in Europe. The confederation of powers ruled by the King of Spain was the dominant force in European politics and Charles' efforts to defend his territories were largely successful.

Charles' empire was to include Austria, the Holy Roman empire, northern Italy and the Low Countries. Spanish troops fought alongside Germans and **Flemings** as Charles decisively defeated France in the

KEY TERMS

Confederation system Where a series of states, ruled over by the same monarch or (in this case) monarchs, have no single central government. So in Spain throughout this period, each province (Castile, Aragon, Valencia etc.) continued to have their own separate government and laws.

Flemings People from the southern provinces of the Low Countries.

KEY THEME

Charles I's inherited states included Spain, Spain's empires in the New World and southern Italy, Austria and the Low Countries. For good measure Charles was elected Holy Roman Emperor in 1519 on the death of his paternal grandfather Maximilian.

Italian Wars of the 1520s. Charles' dominance of Italy and of the Pope was demonstrated by the unpremeditated sack of Rome in 1527 in which the Pope was captured. With his power over Germany severely weakened by the Reformation, it was no surprise that Charles' personal empire was increasingly seen as Spain's empire.

The internal government of Spain under Charles was also successful. The extension of **conciliar government** was probably the only way to cope with the increasing demands of Charles' imperialism. Meanwhile, the long ministry of Los Cobos, from 1529–47, and the expansion of the *letrados* class of government officials helped to ensure a level of domestic content and absence of revolt unequalled in other European states.

At the same time Spain (unlike France and England) governed and exploited an expanding overseas empire. Indeed, Charles' rule saw increasing tax burdens on the Spanish, especially the Castilians, and this led to complaints and criticisms of Charles' wars and foreign policy as un-Spanish. Nonetheless, there was no serious challenge to Charles' fiscal policy after 1523. The nobility, towns, Church and *Cortes* remained quiescent and calm, enjoying Spain's new dominance in European affairs.

At the same time, the Spanish could flourish in their role as the only true defenders of Christendom from the internal threat of Reformation heresy. They also defended Christendom from the external threat posed by Suleiman the Magnificent (ruler of the Ottoman empire from 1520 to 1566) while Francis I, *rex christianissimus* (the most Christian King), signed a peace treaty with him! Although Charles failed to halt Suleiman's advance (he reached the gates of Vienna itself in 1529), he did devote time and resources to campaigning against the **Arabs of North Africa**.

Although Charles ultimately lost his battle to root out Protestant heresy from Germany and the Low Countries, Spain itself saw no such heretical invasion. So while this period might not be described as a Golden Age for Habsburg imperialism, it can still be seen as part of a Golden Age for Spain.

The high point: Philip II
Under Philip II, Spain's Golden Age reached its height as Spain had a Spanish ruler who spent his working life in Spain. He ruled over Italy and the Low Countries as well as Spain, and those territories were seen as Spanish rather than Habsburg.

During Philip's reign, French power was decisively eclipsed by that of Spain. After 1559, the accidental death of the French King Henry II (in a jousting accident) plunged France into the chaos of repeated Wars of Religion. England, always a lesser power than France, was also at the mercy of contending religious factions and internal rebellion. In this way, Spain stood supreme in European politics for nearly 50 years. The great Armada of 1588 sent to conquer England and the simultaneous intervention in French affairs on the side of the Catholic League symbolised this dominance, even if both failed to bring about decisive victory.

More armadas were built after 1588, and France's recovery was delayed by assassination and further internal unrest. The death of the Ottoman emperor Suleiman the Magnificent in 1566 and the naval victory over the **Ottoman Empire** at the Battle of Lepanto in 1571 gave Spain a claim to be the greatest power not just in Europe but also in the world.

Throughout Philip's reign, Spain's empire in the New World continued to grow, and receipts of silver and gold from South America filled the royal coffers. However, Spanish involvement in war meant that royal debt also grew apace – but not to the extent of paralysing Spain's policy or fighting potential. Revolt broke out in the Low Countries in 1566, but this only allowed Spain to demonstrate its tremendous ability to raise troops and control armies a long way from Spain. Lack of success in the long term showed up the latent power of the rebels and their allies rather than Spain's weakness. A weaker power, one less great than Spain under Philip II, would have caved in long before Spain did. By the end of Philip's reign, no one realised that the northern provinces would be lost forever. Above all, it is the judgement of Spain's enemies that Spain was still the most powerful state in Europe by 1600 that makes Spain's claims to greatness in this period so powerful.

Philip's reign was also successful in terms of maintaining political and social stability in Spain. Apart from the early Revolt of the Alpujarras (1568–70), which was partly engineered by a government concerned about a **Moorish fifth column**, Spain remained internally at peace. The Aragonese problem in 1591 over Antonio Pérez highlighted the need for the government to tread carefully in matters of internal sovereignty, which it did. On the other hand, in 1580 Philip acquired Portugal and its overseas empire after a bloodless *coup*, and Spain was to hold on to this difficult and rather touchy country until 1640 – in itself something of an achievement.

Under Philip II, royal power, still circumscribed by regional variations, was at its height. The nobility remained loyal and devoted to Spain's imperial calling. The Church was more clearly under royal control than ever before, staffed at the upper echelons with effective and efficient high churchmen. It had repelled the threat from heresy as well as the threat from Rome, and was united in its desire to act as the leader of the Counter-Reformation in Europe and of missionary movements in the

New World. At grass-roots level there was only limited reform of the Church, it is true, but as far as Philip was concerned the Church and the Inquisition acted as key supports for Crown power.

Was Philip an absolute monarch?

The constraints of sixteenth-century bureaucracies and local laws and customs meant that Philip could not really be described as 'absolute'. His central bureaucracy was small and the implementation of decisions tended to depend on their distance from Madrid.

As well as the local laws and *fueros* in the kingdoms outside Castile, a great deal of land there and in Castile itself was still owned by the Church and the aristocracy, which meant that local government was in their hands rather than the king's.

Furthermore, Philip was determined to act within the laws. He may have allowed the odd judicial murder (for example, Escobeldo in 1578 and possibly Don Carlos in 1568), but he always tried to enforce the law fairly on his subjects. Here, he relied on the advice of his father, ever his model of the just prince. Charles told his son that a prince should administer justice 'in such a manner that the wicked find him terrible and the good find him benign'. In 1582, the Admiral of Castile was arrested for murder, found guilty and executed. It was a profound shock to the aristocracy but a true measure of their king.

While theoretically answerable only to God and therefore absolute, Philip was not in fact absolute at all. His armed forces could not adequately defend his empire, his revenue fell far short of his expenditure and his control of Spain and its empire was ineffectual. Most of all, it is clear that Philip did not aspire to change the system of government in order to make the Crown more powerful.

Philip was one of nature's most conservative creatures, without the imagination to work for serious change. Instead, he waited to acquire all the facts before making a decision and he rarely had all the facts.

Although not an absolute monarch, Philip was the most powerful monarch in Europe and the most powerful Spain had ever seen. His income continued to grow, and if debts also increased they were not yet serious enough to cause a genuine crisis. As he worked away at his papers in his wonderful new palace of El Escorial, Philip might well have reflected that this, indeed, was Spain's Golden Age.

GOLDEN AGE FOR WHOM?

Clearly, then, the period 1492–1600 can be seen as a Golden Age for Spain and for its rulers. In just three generations, it was transformed from a series of petty states at war with each other into the greatest power on earth. Spain was effectively united, endowed with a powerful monarchy and an ideology that was anti-Moor and anti-Semitic as well as fiercely Catholic. At the same time, by accident of marriage and inheritance the rulers of Spain acquired European and New World empires, which made them the envy of other European states.

Under Philip II this process reached its climax since he was Spanish and settled full time in Spain unlike his father Charles I. Under Philip, Spain, rather than the Habsburg empire, was identified as the most powerful nation in the world, easily eclipsing France and England. Furthermore, despite attacks from other European states, Spain retained its position of dominance with apparent ease.

Of course, this was not achieved without great effort. There was to be a great spilling of Spanish and allied blood in order to defend this empire from attack, but the impressive feature is that Spain was able to muster, almost continuously, the men and resources needed to do this, and the attacks were thrown back largely with ease. At the same time this empire did have a Catholic ideology, a driving sense of divine mission and a huge energy. With the eclipse of France in the second half of the sixteenth century, Spain's astonishing triumph was complete.

The Spanish monarchy

For the rulers of Spain, too, it was a Golden Age. Before Ferdinand and Isabella rulers of Castile and Aragon had enjoyed limited powers and success. The kings of Castile were theoretically but not actually absolute. They had no fixed capital city but roved around the country, their authority undermined by an over-mighty aristocracy and Church. In Aragon the monarchs' power was limited by constitutional constraints – egalitarian oaths of allegiance, powerful *Cortes* and a *Justiciar*.

Under Philip II, matters were rather different. Madrid was fixed as the capital and the Escorial Palace as Philip's main residence. Internal unrest was very limited and Philip's commands were generally obeyed, even though he taxed more heavily than previous rulers.

Clearly then this was a Golden Age for the Spanish monarchy.

The nobility, *conquistadors*, traders and industrialists

Further down the social scale, generalisations about the extent to which this was a Golden Age are harder to make. The nobility enjoyed the fruits of internal peace and imperial pretensions. Men like Don John of Austria and the Duke of Alva led the armies and navies that defeated foes at home and abroad. They played a very important part in regional government and had not yet acquired that ossifying veneer of the empty courtier, who is close to the king but has no real power.

For the *conquistadors* like Cortes, Pizarro and the men that followed them, often energetic younger sons of landowners, there was the promise of adventure and lands in the New World. The empire may thus have acted as something of a safety valve, ridding Spain of dangerous and disruptive elements.

For traders, sheep owners and industrialists this period was likewise something of a Golden Age. Empire and foreign commitments meant trade. While Spain did not have the infrastructure to cope on its own with that increased trade, many merchants did well in this period of economic boom and more widespread prosperity.

The poor and the landless

For the poor and landless, this was not such a Golden Age. High taxes pressed on them, as well as the inflation of the price of basic foodstuffs apparent under Charles and Philip. Although the population was rising, there was a drift towards the towns and away from the countryside in search of better conditions. The result was a growing class of urban poor who had little reason to celebrate Spain's new international standing. The demographic crises of the 1590s sparked off by terrible outbreaks of disease compounded the sufferings of the less fortunate in Spanish society.

WHAT WERE THE CULTURAL AND ARTISTIC ASPECTS OF THE GOLDEN AGE?

While the political dimension to Spain's Golden Age rightly receives prominence, it is also necessary to review the cultural and intellectual achievements of this period in order to reach conclusions about the scale of Spain's achievements.

By looking at painting, architecture, literature and music of the period 1490–1600, one can appreciate the size and diversity of Spanish success. Spain's output was perhaps not so prolific or spectacular as Italy's. However, it was no less distinctive and it produced work of high quality, which has often been overlooked.

Historians have frequently claimed that Spain's religious convictions meant that intellectual and cultural life was stifled as Spain under

Philip II withdrew into intellectual isolation behind the Pyrenees. Although some foreign artists declined to come to Spain, thousands of Spaniards travelled abroad in the service of their country or empire. Spanish soldiers were to be found in Greece, Bohemia, Flanders, Italy and Africa. Great noblemen serving abroad brought home works of art as souvenirs. By the time of his death in 1655, the Marquis of Leganés had collected some 1300 paintings, mostly Flemish and Italian.

The visual arts

It is in the visual arts that one can find a clear expression of a Golden Age in Spain and the Spanish empire in Europe and beyond.

Paintings. In Spanish paintings of the Golden Age, religious themes predominated, reflecting the religious fervour of Spain's ruling class and the patronage of the Spanish Church. Queen Isabella took a serious interest in the visual arts and encouraged Flemish artists such as Juan de Flandes to emigrate to Castile. With the development of the Italian Renaissance, the provincial Spanish style of artistic expression mixed with that of Italy to produce a distinctive outcome. Pedro Berruguete (active 1483–1503), a Spaniard who studied in Italy, produced many fine paintings. These combine realism with mysticism in an austere style as seen in his 'Trial by fire', a scene from the life of St Dominic, and his disturbingly realistic 'Martyrdom of St Peter'. His son Alonso proved to be a fine sculptor.

Sculpture. Religious expression was the driving force of the cultural flowering in Spain. In sculpture, Gil de Siloe executed a number of impressively solemn wooden figures such as those found praying in Burgos Cathedral. Here he was building on the native tradition of producing superbly detailed wooden *retablo* (altarpieces) behind church altars. One of the finest of these is to be found in the Church of Santa Maria la Coronada in the town of Medina Sidonia. Exquisitely executed in polychrome wood, it depicts scenes from the life of Christ and stands some 15 metres high. The *retablo* in Seville Cathedral is the finest of all. Started in 1482 as the conquest of Granada began, it took the Fleming, Peter Dancart his entire working life to complete. It is the largest and richest altarpiece in the world, and a wondrous example of Gothic woodcarving. Such dedication indicates again the religious fervour felt by many Spanish artists of the period.

Architecture. The reigns of Ferdinand and Isabella also saw a great deal of building on a grander scale than previously seen in Spain. The Church of St Juan de los Reyes in Toledo, the Infantado Palace in Guadalajara and the College of Saint Gregory in Valladolid were all constructed at this time. Enrique de Egas began the Royal Hospital in Santiago de Compostela in 1501, and oversaw the building of the Capilla Real, or

Royal Chapel, in Granada where Ferdinand and Isabella were laid to rest at the scene of their greatest triumph. Pedro de Mena carved the figures of the Catholic Kings at prayer. The construction of Granada Cathedral (begun in 1521) and Charles I's Renaissance palace (begun in 1526) in the middle of Granada's Moorish palace complex (the Alhambra), indicate that Spanish architecture was becoming more severe, as it strove to break its ties with its Moorish and highly decorative heritage. Whereas the Alhambra itself gives an unforgettable image of paradise on a human scale with brilliant and complex decoration, wonderfully ornate gardens with amazing water features, Spanish ecclesiastical and secular architecture in this period, with its huge scale, lofty ceilings and severe austerity, invoked the awesome power and majesty of God.

While the Italian Renaissance had been fascinated and impressed by the human form and saw man as 'the measure of all things', Spanish art concentrated on man's puny nature and insignificance in the sight of God. Granada Cathedral, begun in 1521 on the site of the old mosque, is a case in point. The dimensions are huge and although the interior is fairly light and airy and the high altar magnificent, the Cathedral remains disappointingly bare and unfurnished.

The Golden Age was underpinned by military might. Indeed, Spanish military triumph was echoed in architectural design, as can be seen in Seville Cathedral. After the reconquest of Seville from the Moors, the old mosque was knocked down and, in just over a century (1402–1506), the largest cathedral in the world built in its place. Art critic Norman Lewis said that the cathedral 'expresses conquest and domination in architectural terms of sheer mass'.

Under Charles I, Flemish painters and Flemish influence remained important in Castile, perhaps because Charles himself was brought up there. The Netherlands portrait painter Antonio Moro worked for the court of Spain, as did Juan de Holanda and Francisco de Amberes. Among native artists was Luis de Morales (1500–88) who produced a famous 'Ecce Homo' and a tender 'Virgin and Child' now held in Madrid's famous Prado Museum. The passionate mysticism of Morales' work earned him the nickname 'El Divino'.

Philip II and El Escorial. Perhaps the most obvious architectural manifestation of the Golden Age is El Escorial, outside Toledo. This vast palace should be judged as the heart of Spanish architecture at the time of Philip II.

Philip took an oath to build a monastery dedicated to St. Lawrence after his victory over the French at the Battle of St. Quentin on St. Lawrence's day, 1557. Designed by Juan de Herrera and Juan Bautista de Toledo, it

SCENOGRAPHIA FABRICÆ S. LAVRENTII IN ESCVRIA

A seventeenth-century painting of the general view of the Escorial.

took Spanish severity and lack of ornamentation to its limits. In this it reflected the tastes of the man who commissioned it, Philip II. He built for himself a part monastery, part palace, part mausoleum, which would reflect his own spiritual tastes. 'Simplicity in construction, severity in the whole, nobility without arrogance and majesty without ostentation' were Philip's aims for the palace, which would prove to be, like its designer, aloof, dignified and decidedly imperial.

The ground plan of the Escorial is based on a series of precisely related rectangles. Every line, every shadow, every stone cut is part of a strict proportional system. The palace complex proved to be the most geometrical and austere building of the time and it was utterly unique. Philip saw his architects nearly every day since no detail of the building, however small, could be sanctioned without his approval. It took only 21 years to build (1563–84) which was quick by sixteenth century standards but it meant that Philip only enjoyed his completed palace for the last fourteen years of his life.

Philip set out to fill the Escorial with works by the greatest painters of the day. Long before the palace was built, he had commissioned Titian, the great Venetian artist and a favourite of his father, to do some early portraits, a series of frescoes for his palace in Madrid and several other paintings. However, Titian was an old man when the Escorial was being built and would not move to Spain.

Philip subsequently commissioned the Greek artist, Domenikos Theotokopoulos, known unsurprisingly as El Greco ('the Greek'), to do a painting of St Maurice. El Greco's reputation was growing and Philip hoped that he might provide paintings for the palace. However, the painting of St Maurice did not please the king. So he rejected El Greco, who returned to Toledo.

The Italian sculptors Pompeo Leoni and Leone Leoni were more fortunate. They became favourites of the king, producing magnificent bronzes of the crucified Christ, Philip's own family kneeling in prayer and the high altar of the basilica Church of the Escorial. At the same time Philip also collected works by the Dutch painter, Hieronymus Bosch.

As well as works of art and a huge collection of relics, the Escorial was home to a great library of books. The first intake alone was of 4000 books in all languages, including those banned by the Inquisition.

The work of El Greco: symbol of the Golden Age. Perhaps above all others a symbol of the Golden Age was the painter El Greco. In the history of Spanish painting, El Greco (1541–1614) stands alone. In his work one can find a clear argument that this indeed was a Golden Age.

El Greco created no school of art, he had no important followers and he was not Spanish. Inspired by Titian, Michelangelo and Veronese, as well as by the ancient Byzantine art of his Greek homeland, El Greco's work is now seen as the greatest expression of Spanish mysticism. The elongated

'The Burial of the Count of Orgaz' by El Greco.

limbs, swirling draperies, curious perspective, anguished expressions and violent colours all make his work distinctive. He was the finest and most innovative painter of Philip II's reign and beyond.

Since the king rejected him, El Greco's many commissions remind us of that wider group of individuals and institutions who wanted their own works of art at this time. One of El Greco's most famous paintings, 'The Burial of the Count of Orgaz', is a case in point. This mighty canvas, painted in 1586, was commissioned by a parish priest using money left to his church by the Count of Orgaz, who had died as long ago as 1312.

Spain's European empire. Just as El Greco, a foreigner, came to represent the Golden Age of Spanish painting, it should not be forgotten that many Italian, Flemish and Dutch artists of the sixteenth century flourished under Spanish rule. The fact that they flourished is testament to the cultural richness of the period. Spain controlled most of Italy by 1529 and did not seriously lose control over the Dutch provinces until 1609.

Therefore, Spain could also claim to be the patron of artists such as Antonio Moro (1512–75), who lived and worked in the Low Countries. He received more commissions from Philip II than any other artist except the mighty Titian. Moro painted portraits of Philip himself and was court painter in the Netherlands from 1552.

Fleming Pieter Brueghel the Elder (1525–69) should also be included among the artists of Spain's Golden Age. He portrayed human society in all its complexity and confusion. His wonderful canvases of the 'Seasons' show man pitted against nature, lost in the vastness of the universe.

In Italy, artists living under benign Spanish rule would include the great Caravaggio (1573–1610), producer of some of the most disturbing canvases of the period.

Literature

Torquato Tasso (1544–95). The Italian Tasso's work has already been noted at the start of this chapter (see pages 204–5). His pastoral drama *Aminta* and his epic *Jerusalem Delivered* are particularly fine, establishing his reputation as one of the great poets of the age.

Miguel de Cervantes Saavedra (1547–1616). Cervantes' tale *Don Quixote* actually appeared some years after Philip's death and has established itself as the greatest work of fiction of Spain's Golden Age. It records the adventures of an errant knight, Don Quixote, and his faithful servant Sancho Panza. The book established Cervantes, a wandering soldier and minor official, as one of the great writers of the age. His own career reflects the cultural enrichment derived from Spain's imperial mission.

'The Burial of the Count of Orgaz'
Legend has it that after the Count of Orgaz' death, Saints Stephen and Augustine descended from heaven to place the Count in his tomb. El Greco conveys in full the extraordinary miracle showing the Count's burial in the lower half of the canvas and his welcome from Christ in heaven in the upper half. The religious fervour of his paintings led to many more commissions from the Church and the aristocracy. El Greco produced a marvellous series of portraits of saints, especially St Francis and St Peter, which are all dynamic and extremely moving. The saints are given living faces, perhaps of peasant stock to illustrate their humanity. Yet at the same time they have an unmistakable aura of divinity and sanctity, which makes them especially engaging to the viewer.

KEY TEXT

Don Quixote In Cervantes' novel, the Don is a dreamer, living in a world of romantic illusion 'tilting at windmills' which he mistakes for the enemy. Sancho Panza is the realist, attempting to rescue his master from his follies. In *Imperial Spain 1469–1716* (1963), J.H. Elliott argues that *Don Quixote* thus reflects the crisis of the 1590s in Spain, a decade he saw as 'separating the days of heroism from the days of *desengano* (disillusionment)'. Perhaps this view of the book is a little too neat in its analysis. *Don Quixote* is essentially timeless, dealing with the eternal paradoxes of the human condition. Cervantes makes no judgement, holding the balance between optimism and pessimism, enthusiasm and irony. His epic tale ranges over the whole of Spanish society and its problems. Its constant probing into the nature of reality and truth also makes *Don Quixote* one of the great philosophical novels.

Cervantes had travelled all over Castile and Andalusia, went to Rome and enlisted in Naples, fought at Lepanto and was enslaved (for five years) in Algiers. Cervantes had seen the world.

Francisco de Vitoria (1486–1546). De Vitoria was a Spanish Dominican theologian and jurist. He gave lectures expounding the concept of an international community and the principles of international law. In particular his *War and the Law of Nations* (1532) was a searing indictment of the Spanish conquest of the New World. He examined and dismissed all the possible justifications for making war on the Indians:

> First proposition: Difference of religion is not a just cause of war.
> Second proposition: Extension of empire is not a just cause of war.
> Third proposition: Neither the personal glory of the prince nor any other advantage to him is a just cause of war.
> Fourth proposition: There is a single and only just cause for commencing a war, namely, a wrong received.
> (Source: *War and the Law of Nations* by Francisco de Vitoria, 1532.)

Alfonso de Valdés (1500–32). By contrast, in his dialogue called *Lactantius*, Valdés defended the imperial policies of Charles I and the sacking of the city of Rome by imperial troops in 1527. He was an Erasmian humanist and Latin Secretary to Charles. His analysis of the Lutheran Revolt, which he witnessed first hand in 1521, is surprisingly even-handed:

> This evil [the Lutheran Revolt] might have been cured, with the greatest advantage to the Christian republic, had not the pontiff [the Pope] refused a general council, had he preferred the public weal to his own private interests. While he is anxious that Luther be condemned and burned at the stake, I see the whole Christian republic hurried to destruction, unless God Himself succour us.
> (Source: Letter from Alfonso de Valdés written in May 1521.)

St Teresa of Avila (1515–82). In its Golden Age, Spain produced two of the greatest mystical writers yet known. The first was St Teresa of Avila, a Spanish Carmelite nun and tireless founder of reformed convents. Her profound but practical writings on the mystical life, which got her into trouble with the Inquisition, can be seen in her *Autobiography* and the *Book of the Foundations*. In *A History of Spain and Portugal* (1960), William C. Atkinson suggests that both these works are 'masterpieces of warm humanity by any secular reckoning'.

St John of the Cross (1542–91). St Teresa was a friend of the other notable Spanish mystic of the time, St John of the Cross – also a

Carmelite and a reformer. According to Atkinson he wrote 'some of the most ethereal poetry ever written'. His most famous piece is probably the haunting poem entitled 'The dark night of the soul':

> When the first moving air
> Blew from the tower and waved His locks aside,
> His hand, with gentle care,
> Did wound me in the side,
> And in my body all my senses died.
> All things I then forgot,
> My cheek on Him who for my coming came:
> All ceased, and I was not,
> Leaving my cares and shame
> Among the lilies, and forgetting them.
>   (Source: 'The dark night of the soul' by St John of the Cross, 1578.)

Non-fiction

As well as imaginative and mystical writings, Spaniards of the Golden Age also produced more practical literature to answer some of the challenges of empire. There were pamphlets on engineering, artillery and navigation. The stimulus to intellectual development was often the New World. It brought about writing on geography, cartography, metallurgy (that is, how to use mercury to extract silver!) and natural science.

Pedro de Medina (in 1545) and Martin Cortés (in 1551) produced treatises which, between them, went through 42 editions and appeared in five languages. Nicolas Monardes made a considerable contribution to the study of plants. In 1570, Philip II himself financed an expedition to the Indies 'to study the history of living things in the Indies, sketch the plants and describe the land'. A year before, Bernardino de Sahagún had completed his great *History of the Things of New Spain*, a masterpiece of anthropological research.

As well as this, Spaniards produced a great deal of literature on medicine. Andreas Vesalius (1514–64), court physician to both Charles I and Philip II, was a Spanish subject and great anatomist. Michael Servetus (originally Miguel Serveto, 1509 or 1511–1553), from Aragon, burnt at the stake by Calvin in Geneva for denying the Trinity, was one of the first to argue for the circulation of the blood.

Since Spain's period of greatness was relatively short-lived and the country's intellectual development was somewhat arrested by the Inquisition, it has been easy to underestimate the power and originality of Spanish writers. However, it is clear that Spanish writers of the sixteenth century made a telling contribution to European literature. If it is only Cervantes who is internationally recognised, this is surely parallel to

English literature of the period, where many would be hard pressed to name a famous English writer of this period other than Shakespeare!

CONCLUSION

For many historians, writing about sixteenth-century Spain means writing about how Spain was different and isolated from the other European states of the time. In his *Structure of Spanish History* (1948), Américo Castro was one of the most forceful exponents of this view. Since Spain was unique in the coexistence of three major religions during some seven centuries, it has been argued that culture and society developed along different lines from those seen elsewhere in Europe. Spaniards of the Golden Age have thus been characterised as non-capitalist and anti-entrepreneurial as well as being narrow-minded and lazy religious zealots with exaggerated concepts of honour and a perverse pride in poverty.

Lope de Vega (1562–1635)
Spanish dramatist and poet, often regarded as the founder of Spanish drama. Considered by many as the greatest Spanish dramatist, he is believed to have written some 2000 plays, of which 500 survive. He sailed with the Spanish Armada and survived. His most famous play is called *The Sheep Well*.

Lope de Vega's plays were used to show that Spaniards were so obsessed by honour, they were unable to progress economically and were therefore doomed to decline and failure. This isolationism and peculiar Spanishness has been used to explain why the Golden Age was so brief and led to decline and decay in the seventeenth century. This theory has also led to scholarly question marks about the whole concept of Golden Age. If Spaniards always possessed these enfeebling characteristics, then surely it is questionable whether they could sustain a Golden Age in culture and international prestige.

More modern and dispassionate historians such as Henry Kamen in his *Golden Age of Spain* (1988) take a less prejudiced view. It is clear, in fact, that Spaniards were not so different from other European peoples. A Spanish middle class of merchants did develop that underpinned the country's imperial achievements, and the nobility were rather more involved in economic concerns than used to be thought. Spain provided soldiers and adventurers to expand and defend its empire, and showed that it was capable of raising sufficient funds to defend the empire throughout the seventeenth century.

Intellectually, we find that the Church and the Inquisition did not strangle Spain's development, and that Philip II did not exercise the kind of absolute power that would discourage political and scholastic progress. Instead of isolationism, we find that Spaniards were well travelled and interacted productively with other cultures in Europe and the New World. Art and literature flourished as never before as Spaniards strove to interpret their imperial mission. So it is clear that in the period 1492–1600, Spain, or more precisely Castile, did experience a truly Golden Age.

1556–1609: Why did Spain fail to crush the Dutch Revolt?

INTRODUCTION

After 1560, Spain faced serious problems in the Low Countries. By 1609 Spain had agreed to a Twelve Year Truce, admitting its inability to finally overcome these problems. Spain's failure to crush the Dutch Revolt and the eventual loss of the Northern Provinces of Spanish territory in the Low Countries by 1648 has often been seen as a great failure on Spain's part. If this is so, then the Dutch problem tends to colour one's view of the scale of Spanish achievement at this time. Surely Spain must already be a weak or declining power, if it was unable to put down revolt in a few Dutch provinces. In fact this view is largely misleading. It will be argued here that Spain's problems in the Low Countries were not of its own making and that its inability to crush the revolt should not be seen as a serious failing on Spain's part. It was inherently unlikely that Dutch Protestants would accept easily rule by Catholic Spain. The success of the Dutch war effort had more to do with Dutch strengths than Spanish weaknesses.

CONTEMPORARY AND HISTORICAL VIEWPOINTS

Owen Feltham, an English observer of the Dutch Revolt, held the Dutch in great admiration. Writing four years after the Dutch had finally secured independence from Spain in the Treaty of Westphalia of 1648, he lavished high praise on his Dutch contemporaries.

> They are in some sorte Gods … They are Gideon's Army upon the march once again. They are the Indian Rat, gnawing the bowels of the Spanish Crocodile … They are the little swordfish pricking at the bellies of the Whale. They are the wane of that empire, which increased in the time of Isabella and in the time of Charles the fifth was at full.

In the same way, the popular tale of the elephant overcome by ants has also been used to express the apparently uneven nature of the two sides. The Dutch rebels are small rats, swordfish or ants, yet they take on and defeat the mighty Spanish crocodile, whale or elephant.

This view of the contest as one between plucky David (the Dutch) and tyrannical Goliath (the Spanish) was taken up by historians of the revolt such as the American J.L. Motley in his *The Rise of the Dutch Republic* (1856). For him the revolt was a morality tale. Since the Dutch represented the forces of democracy, liberty and Protestantism, they quite naturally triumphed over the forces of tyranny and Catholicism.

In his *Revolt of the Netherlands 1555–1609* (1932), the Dutchman Pieter Geyl takes a rather different standpoint about the morality of the two sides, but still expresses the view that Dutch success was a great surprise, given that they were fighting against the greatest power on earth at that time.

In her book *William the Silent* (1944), C.V. Wedgewood added to this view by stressing the early failings and unheroic character of the Dutch leader William of Orange, whose compatriots nonetheless went on to triumph at Spain's expense.

Behind all these analyses of Spanish failure to overwhelm the Dutch lies the idea that Spain ought to have triumphed easily in this unequal contest and, therefore, something must have gone spectacularly wrong. In fact, this assumption is largely incorrect. Just as Castile found it impossible to persuade Aragon to contribute its fair share to the imperial finances, so Spain's control over the Low Countries was always precarious. As and when he was faced by revolt, which combined the nobility, merchant elites and large numbers of fortified towns, all bound together by deep-seated hostility to Spain, then Philip II was in trouble. Once the revolt had spread to encompass all the provinces by the Pacification of Ghent in 1576, even mighty Spain would struggle to recover lost ground.

After all, the Dutch provinces had a history of independence and a political organisation to match: each province had its own assembly called the States and they already had a common assembly called the States General, which could act as a focus for common grievances.

This area of Europe was also wealthy, with the economic means to carry on a war for a long period. Additionally, it was one of the most urbanised areas of Europe. This meant that the war for Spain was a slow one of sieges against fiercely independent towns and cities. The elite of this region were well educated and at the centre of new ideas emanating from humanism and the Reformation. The greatest humanist of the early sixteenth century was the Dutchman Erasmus of Rotterdam.

The Low Countries were soon to be overrun with humanism and reforming ideals. The Reformation began in Germany and Switzerland, and continued in France and England. In this way, the Low Countries could hardly avoid its full force. Given that the area was ruled after 1556 by a staunchly Catholic monarch from Spain (Philip II), it was hardly surprising that there was serious trouble. From this perspective, Spain's recovery and retention of half the provinces was something of a triumph.

In addition, one must remember the logistical difficulties faced by Spain in fighting a war so far from home. The whole business of collecting troops, then supplying them with food, weapons and pay, was tremendously complex to organise. Especially difficult for Spain was fighting a war where most of the civilian population was hostile to its troops. The difficult terrain and lack of pitched battles also presented serious problems. Once several provinces in the north had broken away, Spain could only proceed by means of sieges, slowly and painfully reducing town by town to submission.

It should also be remembered that Castile faced difficulties in ruling its other Spanish provinces. In 1640, Spain would lose Portugal forever and Catalonia temporarily. As in the Low Countries, these rebellions were aided and abetted by Spain's enemies. A serious handicap of being (or being seen as) a superpower is the inevitable attraction of powerful coalitions of enemies. Such was Spain's fate during the Dutch Revolt. By putting the revolt in the context of Spain's relations with other major powers, it can be seen that the suppression of dissent in the Low Countries was only part of Spain's military and financial commitments abroad. We should therefore not be surprised at the scale of Spanish difficulties.

SPANISH WEAKNESSES

This section looks sympathetically at the difficulties which Spain faced in dealing with opposition in the Low Countries. In particular, it will take a realistic view of the problems facing Spain's leaders in the Low Countries. These problems were political and financial as well as military. It is important also not to look at Spain's efforts in the Low Countries in isolation. Spain's wider foreign policy and the aggression it faced from other countries helped to explain its limited success in dealing with the continuing difficulties with its empire in Northern Europe.

A FAILURE OF LEADERSHIP?

Margaret of Parma and Granvelle, 1559–67
It is often thought by Protestant historians that Spain's failure to crush the revolt had much to do with the failure of Spanish leadership in the Low Countries. Margaret of Parma, the regent, is seen as feeble and vacillating in her dealings with the disgruntled grandees in the period

before the revolt of 1572, while Cardinal Granvelle was insensitive and high-handed. Certainly, Margaret was not politically astute. But then she also operated with one hand tied behind her back. She needed to wait for instructions from Philip and she had to work alongside the unpopular Cardinal Granvelle until Philip dismissed him in 1564.

In April 1566, some 200 noblemen from all over the Netherlands, led by **Hendrik van Brederode**, forcibly presented Margaret with the Petition of Compromise. They demanded that the Inquisition be dismantled and threatened armed revolt if their petition was turned down.

The roots of the conflict between the Spanish and Dutch went back a long way. They combined two very powerful and interwoven ideological themes – religious and political. On the one hand, there were growing numbers of Protestants of various types in the Low Countries for whom the repression meted out by the Inquisition was unacceptable. On the other, there were many from the ruling classes who were fearful that Philip's reforms would undermine their powers and privileges.

Many noblemen and magistrates, both Catholic and Protestant, were prepared to turn a blind eye to heresy and resented the interference by the Inquisition into affairs that were traditionally dealt with by the laity or by the fairly easygoing Catholic Church. Furthermore, there was widespread anticlericalism in this region, one of the early centres of humanism and reformation. This meant that laymen of all types resented Philip's attempts to make the Church more powerful.

Nowhere was this seen more clearly than in Philip's proposals to introduce new bishoprics into his northern European provinces. The Pope had approved the idea in 1559 and concrete plans were drawn up in 1561. Antoine Perrenot de Granvelle was made first Archbishop of Mechelen to oversee the plans, but they met with resistance on all sides.

To establish and fund the new sees, it was proposed that abbey lands be transferred. At the same time nomination to all sees would be in the hands of the Crown rather than cathedral chapters, and Philip wanted to be sure the posts would be filled by trained theologians rather than the sons of aristocrats. In addition, the number of bishops would increase from six to nineteen – a worrying development for an anticlerical ruling class.

The new scheme thus brought together fears about the increasing power of the Spanish government and its willingness to persecute heresy. At every level, it seemed that local rights and privileges were in jeopardy at the hands of an uncaring, innovative and foreign government.

KEY PERSON

Hendrik van Brederode
(1531–68) A Dutch nobleman and ally of William of Orange. He was a Protestant who introduced the Reformation into his home town of Vianen. He presented the Petition of Compromise to Margaret of Parma in 1566 but by the next year was forced to flee by government forces.

Ultimately, Margaret did not have the power to defeat such opposition, led as it was by the class of people whose co-operation was essential for the operation of any form of Spanish government in the Low Countries. Naturally enough she gave way, just as Philip II had done in 1564 by dismissing the unpopular Granvelle. The edicts against heresy (the placards) were suspended and a delegation from the States General was permitted to go to Spain to petition the king directly concerning the grievances of his loyal subject in the Low Countries.

Unfortunately for Margaret and for the noblemen who presented the Petition of Compromise, the relaxation of the heresy laws led to mass Calvinist preaching in the open air, the so-called hedge-preaching. These great gatherings, often numbering thousands of people, then unleashed a huge and dramatic wave of iconoclasm where Catholic Churches were attacked by unruly mobs intent on the destruction of images.

The Iconoclastic Fury of 1566 indicated the latent religious tensions in this region. It spread from centres in the south into the northern provinces. In Antwerp, all 42 of the city's churches were ransacked, with images, paintings and other objects being taken into the streets and smashed. These acts were overseen by large crowds. They chanted their support for those who had presented the petition to Margaret of Parma by giving voice to the catchphrase '*Vivent les Gueux*' ('Long live the beggars').

The authorities – both Margaret and the disgruntled nobility – were taken by surprise at the scale of this apparently popular uprising. Naturally enough, they clamped down and order was restored. Margaret did the best she could in a very difficult situation. Her willingness to compromise made her more likely than Philip to succeed in effecting some sort of religious and political deal that would pacify the provinces. By sending in the Duke of Alva in 1567, Philip showed that her flexible approach was not acceptable. Margaret, quite rightly, walked out.

The Duke of Alva, 1567–73
Traditionally, Dutch historians such as Geyl have cast the Duke of Alva in the role of villain in chief for the Spanish cause – the man who did more than anyone else to prevent a Spanish victory. Certainly, the rebels produced much exciting propaganda denouncing the duke and his soldiers as the embodiment of evil and wickedness. Dutch refugees in particular produced a torrent of pamphlets denouncing Alva's regime with lurid tales of cannibalism, rape and the contamination of the country with syphilis. One pamphlet claimed that 'all market places are blazing with fires in which the simple people are burnt alive; all the canals are filled with dead corpses'.

The Iconoclastic Fury in the Low Countries, 1566.

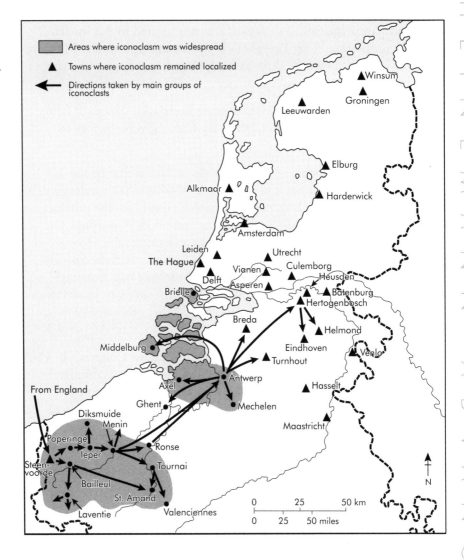

In 1572, the citizens of Ghent found the streets littered with a parody of the Lord's Prayer in honour of the duke.

> Hellish father who in Brussels doth dwell
> Cursed be thy name in heaven and hell;
> Thy kingdom, which has lasted too long, be gone,
> Thy will in heaven and earth be not done. ...
>
> Our Father, in heaven which art,
> Grant that this devil may soon depart;
> And with him his Council, false and bloody,
> Who make murder and plunder their daily study;
> And all the savage war-dogs of Spain,
> O send them all back to the Devil again. Amen.

The propaganda against Alva's regime was not limited to the written word. Flemish artist Pieter Brueghel's biblical painting entitled 'Massacre of the Innocents' shows the duke as King Herod, watching with approval as his soldiers massacre small children.

As a result of all this hostility to Alva, there is always a danger of falling into the propaganda trap and exaggerating Alva's adverse impact on Spanish fortunes.

The most significant point to remember about Alva is that he was successful in crushing the revolt. Arriving in 1567 and taking charge of an army of 70,000 men, he hastened to reimpose control on the provinces so recently the scene of aristocratic discontent and popular uprising. The execution of two prominent Dutch noblemen (Egmont and Hoorne) in 1568 was a powerful example to others who had criticised the Spanish government of the Netherlands. Egmont and Hoorne had remained loyal sons of the Catholic Church and thought that they were immune from prosecution. Their execution for treason meant that other nobles either fled or hastened to make their peace.

William of Orange's four-pronged invasion of the Low Countries in 1568 was a total shambles and his attempts to attract foreign aid completely failed. For most of the period 1567–72, the duke was in complete control. He set up the Council of Troubles to bring troublemakers to justice. The rebels renamed it the Council of Blood, but it was not as harsh as they thought.

In the coming months, some 12,000 persons of all ranks and degrees were investigated for their part in the troubles of 1566 and 1567. While 9000 lost some or all of their goods, only 1000 were executed. This may still sound a large number, but these were dangerous times and the revolt against Spain had been extensive. Showing a more benign side to his regime, the Duke of Alva passed the reforming Ordinance of the Penal Law, which standardised procedure in criminal cases and was designed to give protection in law to the innocent. Meanwhile he began a programme of building up fortifications in key towns and assigning garrison troops to them to ensure future quiescence. In all this he was successful.

However, Alva antagonised the ruling classes with his illegal collection of new taxes. In 1569, he summoned the representatives of the provinces, the States General, and asked for approval of three new taxes. The first two – the Hundredth Penny (a one-off tax of 1 per cent on assessed wealth) and the Twentieth Penny (a permanent 5 per cent tax on all future sales of landed property) – were approved. The third, the Tenth Penny, caused real trouble. This permanent 10 per cent tax on all sales (modelled on the Spanish *alcabala*) was the subject of strenuous opposition. However, a compromise was reached that allowed Alva to collect it for the next two years as a temporary tax.

The States General were worried about the levels of tax, about the fact that the taxes would be used to oppress the people and that a permanent Tenth Penny would mean that the States General would never be called again. Without such a body, resistance to the Spanish governments in Brussels and Madrid, or at least the chance to express grievances, would be impossible.

As a result, two years later, the States General refused to make the Tenth Penny permanent or to renew the temporary grant. Alva's reaction was an immediate decision to collect the tax by force. In 1572, this policy was put into action. It proved to be Alva's most serious mistake. Opposition to the tax was universal, and the second revolt began with the occupation of the two Zeeland ports of Brill and Flushing by a motley assortment of anti-Catholic Dutch pirates known as the Sea Beggars.

Alva had over-reached himself, but popular discontent in itself was not enough to defeat the Spanish in the long term. For many years, the second revolt seemed to be weak and the rebels divided among themselves. Furthermore, the rebellion in Holland and Zeeland only started and spread because Alva had withdrawn Spanish forces from the north in order to counter the perceived French threat to the southern provinces.

Alva could be forgiven for giving a higher priority to the defence of the southern provinces and for thinking that the urban rebellions in Holland and Zeeland could be speedily crushed. And for much of the rest of 1572, he seemed to be right. Attempts to raise southern towns largely failed – apart from at Mons (and that was duly recaptured). By August 1572, the massacre of Protestants in Paris on St Bartholomew's Day ended hopes of French intervention. Meanwhile, the massacres of Mechelen and Zutphen by Spanish troops allowed Alva to regain control everywhere except for the maritime provinces of Holland and Zeeland. Even here, the city of Amsterdam had remained loyal and the Prince of Orange had retreated from Alva, vowing to make that province his tomb if necessary.

Alva's failure at the eleventh hour to crush the remaining rebel towns is partly explained by his continuing harsh attitude towards the rebels. After Haarlem had been taken, the duke gave the order for 2000 of the rebels to be executed. This broke the word of his local commander, who assured the town that no one would be harmed if they surrendered. In addition, the lengths of the sieges took their toll on Spanish resolve. At Haarlem the siege lasted seven months. Other factors working against Alva were that the Spanish fleet suffered a crushing defeat at the hands of the rebels and the soldiers' pay was seriously in arrears, leading some companies to refuse to fight.

Appalled at the lack of conclusion to the revolt and urged on by those who opposed the duke in Madrid, Philip sacked Alva in 1573. This plunged the Spanish cause into further and more serious difficulties. Alva's main mistake is that he did not know how and when to try a more merciful approach to the Dutch problem. He successfully cowed those who had been involved in opposition to the Spanish government 1566–7 and might have continued to rule without serious disturbance but for his insistence on collecting the Tenth Penny without the consent of the States General.

Alva's failings can be seen clearly in a letter written to Philip II just a few months before his dismissal. 'I cannot,' he wrote, 'refrain from beseeching your Majesty to disabuse yourself of the notion that anything will ever be accomplished in these provinces by the use of clemency.' As political epitaphs go, this one clearly elucidates Alva's strengths and weaknesses.

Requesens and Don John, 1573–8

These two governors oversaw Spanish efforts at reconquest at a crucial time.

Don Luis de Requesens. Requesens succeeded Alva in 1573, but little blame can be attached to him for the continuance of the revolt. He was rather more moderate than Alva, issuing a general pardon and abolishing the hated Tenth Penny. He defeated another of Orange's invasions at Mook in 1574, but was faced with huge problems in attempting to continue the war effort.

Money shortages culminating in Philip's bankruptcy in 1575 led to a series of mutinies during 1573–4. This meant that Requesens had to start negotiating with the rebels. However, he made little headway because Philip would make no concessions on religion.

Requesens' sudden death in 1576 probably contributed more than anything he did in life to the decline in Spanish fortunes. Unpaid Spanish troops sacked Antwerp later in the year and the provinces now called their own States General, which agreed to the Pacification of Ghent. Now Holland and Zeeland had been joined by all the other provinces in an alliance against Spanish troops.

Don John. Don John, who was governor only briefly from 1576 to 1578, is rather more culpable than Requesens in terms of a failure of leadership. Admittedly, he had no money and few clear instructions from Philip. However, his reckless decision to tear up the agreement he made with the States General (the **Perpetual Edict of 1577**) and bring back Spanish troops to the Netherlands was a huge mistake.

It was clear from the outset that the rebels were divided between the more

Don Luis de Requesens (1528–76) was born in Barcelona and was a page to Philip II before he became king. He succeeded Alva in the Netherlands where his temperament and the shortage of money led him to negotiate seriously with the rebels. Always of delicate health, he died suddenly in 1576.

KEY TERM

Perpetual Edict of 1577 This was signed by Don John and the States General. Without funds or troops, Don John had to agree to withdraw all Spanish troops from the Low Countries.

hard-line provinces of Holland and Zeeland (led by Orange) and the other provinces in the States General (where the conservative Duke of Aerschot was a major player). These provinces were prepared to toe the Catholic line in religion and wished to effect some sort of political compromise with Philip. Don John only had to drive a wedge between the two groups to win back most of the provinces to their natural obedience, leaving Orange and friends in the north exposed and vulnerable.

The divisions between the provinces were already evident in 1577, when the States of Holland and Zeeland refused to sign the Perpetual Edict with Don John. By tearing up that agreement and bringing back Spanish troops to the Netherlands, Don John made a disastrous mistake. His action merely ensured that the States General would be driven back into the arms of Holland and Zeeland. This was the worst possible moment to confirm rebel suspicions about Spanish perfidy. All Requesens' efforts to erase the memories of Alva's oppression were undone at a stroke. How could Spain now persuade the rebels that they were prepared to negotiate in good faith?

In truth, Don John's failure was not unexpected. He was a reckless individual and, as the victor in 1571 over the Turks at Lepanto, it was unlikely that he would adopt the role of diplomat and peacemaker with any degree of success. His appointment was an unwise choice by Philip.

The Duke of Parma, 1578–92
The doubts about Don John's leadership are thrown into high relief when surveying the career and qualities of his successor, Alessandro (or Alexander) Farnese, Duke of Parma. Don John's finest decision came on his deathbed, when he nominated Parma for his job.

Parma combined the patience and perception of a great diplomat with the strategy and tactics of a military genius. During his tenure of power, the rebels were successfully divided into three antagonistic groups.

The Union of Arras was formed by the three most southerly provinces of Hainault, Artois and Walloon Flanders in 1579. They were prepared to accept Spanish troops and Spanish government as a means of protecting themselves from France and they naturally walked out of the States General. The Union of Utrecht was formed the same year, consisting of six northern provinces. These provinces bound themselves into a confederation to prosecute the war against Parma and to safeguard religious liberty. This left the middle provinces, still represented in the States General but with aims rather less revolutionary than the Union of Utrecht.

The conquests of Parma, 1578–89.

Operating with fewer funds than most of his predecessors, Parma succeeded in winning back provinces in the north and south to such an extent that the rebels thought total defeat was at hand. Had Philip not demanded that Parma simultaneously take on campaigns against England and France in the 1580s, Parma just might have finished the job and been hailed as the great commander he was. As it was, he died in 1592 with the task unfinished, and the threat of dismissal and arrest by an ungrateful sovereign. If there was any failure of leadership here, it was Philip's not Parma's.

Post-Parma leadership, 1592–1609

After Parma's death, Spanish leadership was rather more confused and unclear. In reality, though, the damage had been done. Even another leader of Parma's stature would have struggled for success against a confederation of rebel provinces, which was economically prosperous, enjoyed foreign assistance, and was well led both politically and militarily.

After Parma's death, Spanish leadership in Brussels was in chaos. Count Mansfelt, who had been Parma's deputy, made constant trouble for the Count of Fuentes, who had been sent in by Philip to command the armed forces. They issued contradictory orders to the same troops and appointed different men to the same post.

Meanwhile, the war reached something of a stalemate. The last loyal town in the north, Groningen, was lost by Spain in 1594. In addition, the people of the southern provinces were becoming restive as tax burdens to finance the war against the Dutch and the French continued to bite deep. Once again, lack of funds would lead to further mutinies of Spanish troops, some 37 in all in the period 1589–1607.

In 1599, Philip III appointed his sister and brother-in-law, Isabella and the Archduke Albert, as regents. However, the new royal representatives brought little change to the stalemate.

In 1604, Spain achieved its last great victory when it captured the Channel port of Ostend. The leader of the Spanish forces was Ambrogio Spinola, an unlikely commander with no military experience. Still, what he lacked in experience he made up for in personal wealth, which helped to fund Spain's flagging war effort. Although peace was made with France and England in this period, the bankruptcy of 1607 could not be avoided. This led to the ceasefire and eventually Truce of Antwerp in 1609. In the end, Spain had been defeated. Though it retained the southern provinces, this was cold comfort.

Overall, Spanish defeat cannot be explained in terms of a failure of leadership in the Low Countries. Parma was brilliant, while Margaret of Parma, Requesens and the post-Parma leadership did little wrong. Don John and Alva did make crucial errors of judgement, so some blame can be attached to them. Ultimately, some blame must also be apportioned to Philip. He was a long way from being the ruthless tyrant of black legend but it was difficult to direct operations from faraway Madrid. Perhaps his biggest mistake was in refusing to visit the Low Countries during the dispute. A little personal monarchy, operated in the style of his grandparents Ferdinand and Isabella, might have gone a long way to improving Spanish fortunes in its remote north European outpost.

Naturally, Dutch grievances went deep, and conflict between the ruling classes there and in Spain was perhaps inevitable. Could Philip have found a solution? His best chance might have been to broker a deal with the aristocracy and merchant elites, which would have guaranteed them their traditional rights in exchange for a nominal adherence to Catholicism. The traditional rights of the ruling class would have involved their independence in religious matters – in other words, the power to persecute Protestantism or to turn a blind eye as they wished. Given the divisions among the Protestants, such a *modus vivendi* might just have worked.

On the other hand, to hope that Philip would agree to even unofficial religious toleration would be to wish that Philip II were not Philip II. He wrote to Requesens, then his ambassador in Rome in 1567, in the following terms:

> To negotiate with those people is so pernicious to God's service that I have preferred to expose myself to the hazard of war rather than allow the slightest derogation from the Catholic Faith and the authority of the Holy See.

In case his attachment to the Catholic faith were still in doubt, his words to Alva six years later, as his cause in the Low Countries hung in the balance, were: 'I would rather lose the Low Countries than reign over them if they ceased to be Catholic.'

FOREIGN INTERVENTION

It is clear that the Spanish failure to quell the revolt in the Low Countries was not simply the consequence of Spain's own weaknesses or failings and it is often said that foreign aid was crucial to the success of the Dutch rebels. Yet the direct aid given by powers such as France and England had rather a limited impact on the fortunes of war. More significant in explaining Spain's inability to crush the Dutch Revolt was the indirect foreign aid the rebels received. This arose from Philip II's other commitments as leader of a European superpower. Spain could not deal with the Dutch Revolt in isolation because it had other enemies who, at times, assumed a higher priority in Philip's eyes.

At first, the king may have underestimated the scale of the Dutch problem and his first priority in the 1560s and early 1570s was the Ottoman threat, rather than the Dutch difficulties. Once he could turn his full attention to the Dutch, the situation was so serious – in terms of both rebel strength and Spain's lack of money – that little could be achieved.

The Spanish position was at its weakest in the period 1575–80. Then, in the 1580s, just as the tide seemed to be turning decisively Spain's way, England and France diverted its attention so that recovery of territory was slow and ended in stalemate. Thus, in 1609, Spain had come to accept the possibility that though the southern provinces had been recovered, the northern provinces might be lost forever.

The Turks

The first example of indirect foreign aid for the Dutch came from the Turks. The wars between France and Spain, which concluded at the Peace of Cateau-Cambresis in 1559, had left the Spanish government in the Low Countries with severe debts. During the war, much of which was fought along the border between France and the Spanish provinces of the Low Countries, Spain had sent some 22 million florins to that area, but it had not been enough. The Spanish government in Brussels was virtually bankrupt by 1559.

Furthermore, in the period 1561–7, Spain sent only some 5.7 million florins to the Low Countries, so that the Spanish government there remained in serious financial difficulties and unable to find enough money to preserve law and order, when protests at Spanish government began to grow into serious discontent. The main reason for this financial mismanagement in the 1560s was Philip's continuing obsession with the Turkish threat.

As a relatively new king who had just made peace with France, Philip II was keen to make war on the Ottoman Turks and take this opportunity to enhance Spanish control of the Mediterranean. In 1560, he launched the ill-fated expedition to Tripoli and Djerba, where the Turks destroyed much of Spain's fleet. The years 1561 and 1562 thus saw huge investment in building up a new fleet, which, in its turn, was largely destroyed by a freak storm while on manoeuvres. In 1564, Philip sent a successful expedition to the port of Penon de Velez. Through much of 1565 he was preoccupied with the blockade of the island of Malta, in the centre of the Mediterranean, by the Ottoman fleet.

As a result of Philip's war against the Turks in this period, the growing discontent in the Netherlands was both underestimated and dealt with in a conciliatory way. In 1564, Philip gave way to the demands of the discontented grandees in the Low Countries and removed his chief minister there, Cardinal Granvelle. This allowed the grandees, acting in the Council of State, to take control of affairs, at the expense of Philip's regent, his aunt, Margaret of Parma. In 1566, Philip agreed to another conciliatory move to defuse opposition in the Low Countries. He agreed, admittedly under protest, to allow Margaret to moderate the operation of the heresy laws. This action led to a serious escalation of the Dutch troubles with the Iconoclastic Fury of that year, which swept through many of the southern provinces. Yet again the reason for the concession by Philip was the Turkish menace in the Mediterranean. In 1566, the Turks sent out their fleet once more to avenge their defeat at Malta the previous year. At such a time, Philip wanted to avoid trouble in the Low Countries. Once more it was the Turks who unwittingly and indirectly fuelled the Dutch Revolt.

Preoccupation with the Turkish threat also explains Spain's later problems in the Low Countries. The death of Suleiman the Magnificent in 1566 and his successor's early difficulties meant that Spain was free of the Turkish threat in 1567–9, years that saw Alva's military success in the Low Countries. However, when the Turkish menace reappeared in 1570–6, it meant that Spain was now funding two great enterprises at the same time and could win neither.

The Turkish dimension to the problem is therefore crucial in explaining Spain's financial problems that led to the Spanish Fury and Sack of Antwerp, and then to the Pacification of Ghent in 1576. This agreement between all provinces to refuse to accept Spanish troops and to band together to defeat the mutinous army proved to be Spain's undoing. The Turkish threat had helped to make the revolt so serious that Spanish recovery would be slow and difficult.

At the same time, the Dutch rebels and the French were not slow in perceiving the link between the Turkish threat and Dutch success. In 1566, William of Orange, leader of the revolt, sent an ambassador to the Turks urging them to launch a new campaign in the Mediterranean to undermine Philip's efforts in the Low Countries. In 1574, the French ambassador in Constantinople explained how the king of France was giving money to the rebels, urging the Sultan to do the same.

France

While the Sultan refused consistently to aid the rebels directly, it was foreign aid from France and England, both direct and indirect, that would ensure Spanish failure in the Low Countries. However difficult the situation in 1576, Spain might still have recovered all the provinces, had it not been for French and English determination to keep the revolt going and Philip's willingness to fight more than one war at a time.

Despite, and at times because of, the Wars of Religion, which laid France low at the time of the Dutch Revolt, French aid to the rebels would prove invaluable. Direct French intervention did not seem promising at first sight.

**Admiral Gaspard
de Châtillon
Coligny
(1519–72)** One of
the leading French
Protestants of his
day. In 1557 he
defended St.
Quentin from the
Spaniards but was
taken prisoner.
Made Admiral of
France in 1552, he
announced his
conversion to
Protestantism in
1559. He led
Protestant forces in
several civil wars in
France before being
killed, probably on
the orders of the
Queen Mother,
Catherine de
Medici during the
famous massacre of
St. Bartholomew's
Day in 1572.

In April 1572, Charles IX of France, influenced by his Protestant favourite **Coligny**, had signed a treaty of friendship with England (the Treaty of Blois) in which the two parties recognised the Duke of Alva as a common enemy. The French thought he might use his troops to invade France, and Elizabeth I had been goaded by Alva's support for the Ridolfi plot of 1571, which had hoped to overthrow the queen and replace her with her Catholic cousin, Mary Queen of Scots.

Later in 1572, Charles IX allowed a French army of 6000 men to march into the Low Countries. Their objective was to relieve the town of Mons, which was being besieged by the Duke of Alva's forces. The French army marched into a Spanish ambush and was destroyed, both by the Spanish troops and by local peasants for whom France was still the traditional enemy. Though unsuccessful, this expedition did help the rebels. Fearful of an all-out French invasion of the Low Countries, Alva had moved troops from the provinces of Holland and Zeeland, thus allowing the rebellion, which had been started that year by the Sea Beggars at Brill and Flushing, to spread from town to town largely unhindered.

Direct French assistance for the rebels again became important in the period 1581–3. Determined to renounce Philip II's right to govern the Low Countries, the northern rebels, led by Orange and the States General, offered sovereignty over the Netherlands to the Duke of Anjou, younger brother of the French king Henry III.

In military terms, Anjou's intervention in the south with an army of 17,000 men was a failure. He became increasingly frustrated by the restrictions on his powers imposed by the States General and in a wild escapade known as the French Fury (January 1583), he failed to capture Antwerp and other towns. Disgraced and unpopular, he left the Low Countries in June 1583, never to return. His efforts did little to slow down Parma's advances in the south and at one point he left the Netherlands to woo Queen Elizabeth. Nonetheless, his intervention relieved pressure on the north, as Spain had to prepare for a French invasion once again.

Anjou's greatest contribution to the rebel cause came, paradoxically, with his death in 1584. This event meant that the heir to the French throne was now Henry of Navarre, a Protestant.

Faced with the possibility that France might become Protestant at any moment, and rightly annoyed that a Frenchman had dared to assume the sovereignty of the Netherlands, Philip turned his attention to France with disastrous consequences for his efforts to defeat the Dutch rebels.

Just as the Duke of Parma was winning back large areas of rebel territory,

Philip opened up yet another theatre of operations. At first this merely diverted much-needed money from the Low Countries. In December 1584, Philip signed the secret Treaty of Joinville with the French Catholic League, which was dedicated to the defeat of Navarre. Philip agreed to pay 50,000 crowns a month to help his new French allies. By 1587 he had paid out 1 million crowns in this way, to be followed by 2 million between 1588 and 1590, and a further 2.5 million between 1591 and 1595.

Financial aid to the League was followed by military intervention, as the Spanish continued their quest to keep Henry of Navarre from claiming the throne. The murder of Henry III and Navarre's military successes at Arques (1589) and Ivry (1590), persuaded Philip that only military intervention by Spain could now save the situation. Naturally, he redirected his troops, already well-placed in the Low Countries, to France.

Parma entered Paris in 1590 to prevent Navarre's coronation. The next year he was back, attempting to lift Navarre's siege of Rouen in Normandy. A year later he was dead. Spain's decision to send troops to France once again cost it dear. Although he changed his religion, Navarre was crowned King of France as Henry IV in 1594. Parma's considerable successes against the north were halted. Maurice of Nassau hit back in 1591 retaking the towns of Zutphen and Deventer. Over 4000 Spanish troops were involved in serious mutinies in 1594 for lack of pay and food. In 1596, overwhelmed by these commitments Spain went bankrupt again. French assistance, direct and indirect, meant that Spain could not crush the Dutch Revolt.

England

As if Turkish and French entanglements were not enough, Philip also had to deal with England.

At first English involvement was very limited, as Elizabeth had no wish to provoke war with Spain. The Treaty of Blois of 1572 was merely a declaration of dislike, accompanied by a few hundred soldiers who were soon recalled. In 1578–9, however Elizabeth secretly sent cash and goods to the value of 1 million florins. John Casimir, administrator of the Rhine Palatinate, with an army of 12,000 mercenaries, used some of this money to fund an armed intervention. This force was actually designed to undermine French influence in the southern provinces, as Elizabeth feared that France might exploit the troubles to annex further territory along the Channel coast. However, the expedition was a damp squib and Casimir withdrew after a few months. Thereafter, English assistance dried up until 1584. The deaths of Anjou and Orange that year, combined with Parma's successes in Flanders and Brabant, forced Elizabeth reluctantly into action.

At first, English aid was rejected by the States General, as they hoped for help from Henry III of France. When he turned down their desperate appeals, they settled for second best. By the Treaty of Nonsuch (1585), Elizabeth agreed to supply 4000 infantry and 400 cavalry, to pay the States General 600,000 florins a month and to provide a governor general, in this case the Earl of Leicester.

English troops arrived too late to save the city of Antwerp and had little, if any, direct impact on the balance of forces on the ground. England had no standing army, so the expeditionary force, like most English expeditionary forces, was of limited value as a fighting force. Leicester spent most of 1586 trying to persuade the rebel provinces to adopt a strong, central government rather than fighting against Parma. By 1587, the English position was even weaker. While Leicester was back in England, English troops betrayed Deventer and an important fort near Zutphen to the Spanish. As an Englishman, Thomas Wilkes, noted at the time: 'There grew a wonderful alteration in the hearts and affections of the people against the English. They uttered lewd and irreverent speeches against his Excellency (Leicester) and the whole nation.'

Worse was to follow. When Leicester returned, he upset the rebels by advising them to open negotiations with Parma. Although the English intervention seemed feeble, the Spanish were convinced that it was the main cause of continuing Dutch resistance.

A tapestry of the Armada, designed in the sixteenth century.

So it was that English intervention, like that of the French, brought about such a powerful response from Philip II that the reconquest of rebel territory was once again deferred. For most of 1587, Parma was preparing for the Armada and for much of 1588, his efforts were directed at effecting the impossible task of getting his troops across to England.

The defeat of the Armada was expensive in terms of its cost (estimated at 30 million florins) and its diversion of resources to a new theatre of war. In 1588, Parma experienced his first major setback when he failed to take the key town of Bergen-op-Zoom. In addition, the Armada's dismal failure dealt a serious psychological blow to the Spanish and gave a huge lift to the morale of the Dutch – perhaps God was on their side after all.

Furthermore, the Armada of 1588 was not the end of the story. Spain continued the war against England, attempting further nautical enterprises in 1596, 1597 and 1601 before peace was finally made in 1604 (the Treaty of London). Once again, Philip's attempts to crush the Dutch Revolt led to fighting elsewhere. Given the range of Spain's commitments at this time it is remarkable that it nearly defeated the rebels and actually retained the southern provinces.

Conclusion

Taken individually, the wars against the Turks, France and England help to explain why Spain failed to crush the revolt at particular times, and why it was unable to supply its troops and government in the Low Countries with sufficient funds to kill off the uprising. Taken together, they explain Spain's failure during the long-drawn-out conflict.

It would be easy to blame Philip for this outcome, claiming that he should have made the recovery of the Netherlands his top priority. However, this view is rather disingenuous. Only hindsight would tell the Spanish how difficult it would be to crush the revolt and, at various times, Spain seemed to have victory in its grasp. At the same time it was impossible for Philip to ignore attacks from elsewhere. The defeat of the Turks, or at least the defence of the Mediterranean against Ottoman aggression, was always likely to be one of Philip's chief concerns. As the most powerful empire in Europe, it was his God-given duty to repel Islam. Furthermore, he could not reasonably ignore the attacks on his lands, which were the reality behind French and English interference in the revolt. In that way, for Philip, the Spanish offensives against France and England were all part of one global struggle to defend his territories against aggression and his religion against heresy.

MONEY AND TROOPS, MUTINIES AND MASSACRES

While fighting on other fronts does much to explain Spanish failure, it is important to analyse the impact this had on the ground in the actual military struggle between Spain and the rebels. If we link Spanish problems at crucial times on the ground, we can see the very damaging impact of these other conflicts on Spain's attempts to crush the revolt.

Most spectacular in its negative impact was the series of mutinies that affected the Spanish forces in the Low Countries. For much of the period 1567–1609, Spain had an army of about 70,000 men, a heterogeneous collection of soldiery made up of Germans, Dutch, Walloon, Italians and Spaniards. During one particularly protracted mutiny, which began at Zichem in 1594 and involved some 3000 veterans, a total of thirteen languages were spoken! With such an exciting collection of troops, keeping order was always likely to be difficult. In addition, most of the troops were **mercenaries** who could draw on a long history of organised mutinies when their pay or supplies got too far in arrears.

So it was that the Spanish army endured five major mutinies in 1572–6 and a further 37 in 1589–1607. The most spectacular was in 1576, leading to the terrible **Sack of Antwerp**, or 'Spanish Fury' as the rebels chose to call it. The Sack of Antwerp dealt a massive blow to Spanish fortunes in the Low Countries.

It was a huge propaganda triumph for the rebels, stoking up the black legend of Spain as a bloodthirsty and oppressive nation and its king as a tyrant. Not since Alva's massacre of the people of Naarden and his sacking of Mechlen and Zutphen (all in 1572) had the rebels been given such an immense propaganda boost. Some rebel reports claimed that 18,000 had been killed by the untamed Spanish soldiers.

Antwerp was the richest city in northern Europe, a centre of civilisation and culture, and it had not been in revolt against Spain. If such cruelty and destruction could be meted out there, then nowhere was safe from Spanish depredations. As well as giving substance to the myth of Spanish cruelty, the attack on Antwerp cemented the Pacification of Ghent whereby for the first time all the provinces now came out against Spain. Before the mutinies, only Holland and Zeeland were in open revolt, and the Spanish army was gaining ground. After the mutinies, all the provinces had united against Spanish soldiery.

This unity and Spain's newfound weakness in the Low Countries were further underlined by the signing of the Perpetual Edict of 1577. Here the new governor general, Don John of Austria, shorn of troops and funds had to capitulate to rebel demands that the Spanish army should be removed from the provinces. This was a real low point in Spanish fortunes made worse by Don John's unwise attempts to reassert Spanish power in 1578 by abandoning Brussels and setting up his headquarters in Namur. This action brought new unity between the more conservative States General and the more radical States of Holland and Zeeland. These two rebel groups would always be wary of each other's intentions, but the Sack of Antwerp had driven them together.

The root cause of the mutiny was lack of pay. Early in the revolt, Spain had been relatively efficient in supplying troops and retaining discipline among a force that was likely to be together for some time. However, Philip's commitments in the Low Countries and elsewhere meant that by 1574 he was facing huge financial problems. In autumn of 1575, he announced the expected bankruptcy and pay for the troops began to dry up. Nonetheless, Requesens (governor general, 1573–6) managed to borrow more money in the Low Countries itself, but his sudden death in March 1576 paralysed all attempts to pay the troops.

The spectacular mutiny of 1576 was not the first to affect the Spanish army. There was a series of mutinies after Alva's dismissal in 1573 that were highly embarrassing to the Spanish and led to a complete change of policy. For the first time, the Spanish were prepared to negotiate with the rebels. In March 1575, even before the bankruptcy, Requesens met William of Orange at Breda. Not surprisingly, the negotiations foundered on the issue of religious toleration but they gave the rebels further breathing space at a time when the revolt seemed close to collapse. Spain could not press home its military advantage at this crucial stage because of lack of funds and consequent mutinies.

But mutinies were not confined to the 1570s. Spanish offensives in 1589, 1593 and 1600 were undermined by mutinies in the field. Mutinies among troops detailed to relieve Groningen in 1594 and Grave in 1599 led to the loss of these towns to the rebels. A major mutiny at Diest in 1607 helped to sabotage Spain's position during negotiations with the Dutch for a ceasefire, helping to delay the truce until 1609.

Finally, it is important to realise how much the campaigning in the Low Countries cost Spain. The cost of warfare is always high and in this period it was getting higher. In 1572–6, the cost of the war to Spain was running at 1.2 million florins per month. 'No treasury in the world,' wailed Requesens, 'would be equal to the cost of this war.' The table on page 245 gives a graphic indication of the long-term costs of the conflict to Spain.

The scale of the Spanish commitment was thus colossal and growing as the period went on. The irony was that Spain regained most ground in the early 1580s when funding was at its lowest. This is because so much of the

Date	Total	Annual average
1572–7	22	3.5
1580–5	15	2.5
1580–90	45	7.5
1590–5	38	6.3
1595–9	53	8.9

Cost of the Spanish war effort in the Low Countries, estimated in millions of florins.

(Source: Geoffrey Parker, *The Army of Flanders and the Spanish Road*, 1972.)

funds thereafter went towards France and England, and because as each year passed the Dutch became more securely dug in against Spanish attacks.

Spanish brutality

Another factor often cited as explaining Spain's defeat is the brutal measures undertaken by the Duke of Alva to extinguish a rebellion that had already been put down before he arrived.

In 1572, his troops took the town of Mechelen when the pro-Orange party fled from the city and the gates were thrown open. Despite its surrender, Alva decided to make an example of the town allowing his men to sack it and kill anyone they found. On this occasion the reprisal had the desired affect. Leuven, Oudenaarde and Diest, other southern towns in rebellion, hastened to submit and escaped with heavy fines. Thus the revolt in Brabant and Flanders was soon in tatters.

The same happened at Zutphen. Hundreds of citizens were massacred by Alva's troops there. Rebel towns in the northern provinces of Gelderland, Overijssel and Friesland rushed to capitulate, terrified of suffering a similar fate. However, on the third occasion, at Naarden, the trick did not work. Although most of the town was slaughtered, other towns in the province of Holland failed to capitulate. Indeed, Alva's actions only stiffened their resolve.

This exposes the differing regional responses to the revolt. In the south and north-east, provinces and towns were more likely to give up the cause and seek an accommodation with the Spanish, so they fell into line, impressed by the brutality of Alva's methods. In Holland and Zeeland, the storm centres of revolt where Calvinism was strong and the people were fired up by religious zeal and hatred of tyranny, such tactics would be counter-productive.

The nature of the fighting

Further difficulties for Spain derived from the nature of the fighting and the landscape. Primarily, this was a war against towns and thus a war of sieges. Even when well supplied and equipped, the Spanish forces found it hard to take towns that were determined to hold out. Many of the towns in the north, especially along the coast, had been fortified by Charles V, fearing that a French fleet might invade his lands. Many of the more inland towns had walls and defences, which were naturally strengthened during the revolt.

Maurice of Nassau, Orange's son, fortified border towns in the 1580s and constructed a line of forts that would complement the natural defensive barrier of the great rivers that flowed through the region. In these circumstances, sieges by Spanish forces often took months and were not always successful. The sieges at Leiden and Haarlem were particularly protracted, tying down Spanish forces for several months. It is easy to see how years could pass with Spain making very little headway.

Leiden was particularly crucial to the Spanish. Success here in 1574 might have ended the revolt. William of Orange was on the verge of despair. The Dutch broke the nearby dykes to try to flood the Spanish besiegers, but this plan failed. The Dutch were on the verge of surrender, their relief fleet unable to break through, when a fortuitous period of heavy rain improved the water level and forced the Spanish to retreat. On the other hand, Spanish forces themselves could be besieged in their turn, particularly isolated Spanish garrisons. In February 1574, the starving Spanish garrison in Middelburg was forced to surrender by the Dutch rebels after a long stand-off.

It is often thought that the boggy ground, large rivers and lakes in Holland and Zeeland in particular made life especially difficult for the king's forces, and that the Spanish could be driven off by the breaking of dykes. One English observer at the time wrote of the Dutch landscape, 'It is the buttock of the world, full of veins and blood but no bones in it.' A lot of land was admittedly below sea level and protected by man-made dykes. However, there is no indication that this landscape was a particular problem for the Spanish. Dykes were broken during the Spanish sieges of Alkmaar in 1573 and Leiden in 1574, but in neither case did this have a decisive impact on Spanish fortunes.

In *The Revolt of the Netherlands* (1932), Pieter Geyl put forward the idea that the great rivers Waal, Maas and Lek proved a great barrier to Spanish advances. This is now largely discredited. Though crossing rivers took time, they were not really a protective barrier and much of the fighting took place to the south of them. Furthermore, Maurice's construction of a line of forts to the north of them presumed that the rivers could be crossed.

Perhaps more significant than the rivers were the deep channels that made the province of Zeeland a series of islands. Reconquering this area proved impossible, especially as Spain lacked a war fleet. Its fleet was destroyed in 1572–4 by the Dutch in a series of violent engagements and was never replaced. Without a fleet to attack or blockade the ports, Spain was at a severe disadvantage against the Maritime provinces. At the same time, this meant that the rebels did control the coastline leaving them free to welcome patriotic pirates such as the Sea Beggars and to carry on trading, which was the backbone of the Dutch economy.

Problems of supply

Another subsidiary problem for the Spanish was actually getting their troops and money to the area of conflict. Although some of the troops were mercenaries hired locally, most were from outside – mainly from Spain, Austria, Germany and Italy. In *The Army of Flanders and the Spanish Road* (1972), Geoffrey Parker has done a great deal to elucidate Spain's difficulties and expenses even before the troops started fighting. Much was lost before it arrived. For example, most attempts to send troops and money from Spain to the Low Countries by sea usually ended in disaster: in 1572, a fleet with 1200 Spanish recruits was largely captured or sunk by the Sea Beggars; another expedition of 1575 was hit by mutiny and storms, so that only some 400 soldiers reached their destination, and in 1588, Spanish troops again failed to reach their destination, though this time it was England, not the Netherlands that was the target.

All this made it imperative to find an overland route (the so-called Spanish Road) from the Mediterranean to the Netherlands, which was duly done after serious negotiations with various rulers along the way. Alva and other Spanish commanders used this route, but it meant that troops took far longer to reach their destinations than by going directly by sea. Spanish troops had to undergo a voyage across the Mediterranean and a march of several hundred miles from Genoa to Brussels. Additionally, the Spanish Road was clearly vulnerable to attack.

After the Treaty of Lyon (1601), Spain was forced to expend a greater amount of money and effort in finding an alternative route, at least across the Alps, when the king of France, Henry IV, acquired territory so close to the original route that his forces could cut it at will. This they did in 1602, holding up Spinola and his troops for several months. As if this wasn't enough, the Spanish commanders faced the logistics of lodging and feeding thousands of troops for perhaps two months as they marched along the Spanish Road. Additionally, there were all the problems associated with bad weather and poor roads.

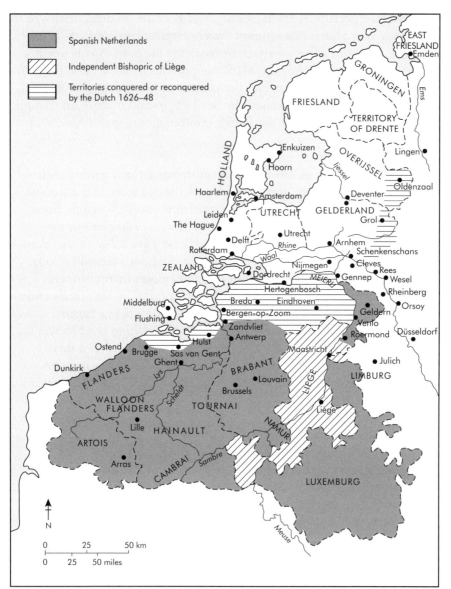

The Netherlands, 1621–48.

Legend:
- Spanish Netherlands
- Independent Bishopric of Liège
- Territories conquered or reconquered by the Dutch 1626–48

DUTCH STRENGTHS

Having analysed the difficulties and problems faced by Spain in its attempts to quell unrest in the Low Countries, it is also vital to understand the strengths of the Dutch rebels which were so crucial in ensuring final victory against the Imperial power. No country can control an empire in the long term without the willing or at least active collaboration of the ruling classes inside that empire. After the rule of Alva and the Sack of Antwerp, that collaboration was largely lost, especially in the Northern Provinces. The strength of Dutch leadership and political organization, combined with a fierce Calvinism and racial hostility to all things Spanish, meant that, in the long term, Spain was unlikely to retain control of the Northern Provinces. Perhaps it is surprising that Spain did not lose control of this area sooner.

DUTCH LEADERSHIP

William of Orange
It would be hard to exaggerate the importance of William of Orange in keeping the rebel cause afloat in the period 1566–84. He was faced with enormous difficulties in holding together the very disparate elements of opposition to Spanish rule. Many conservative aristocrats distrusted him as a populist who sought favour from the common people. Serious Calvinists were dismayed by his genuine belief in religious toleration. Even among the Catholics and Anabaptists, Orange believed that many worthy men could be found. He was also open to the charge of not taking religion seriously; he was brought up a Catholic but became a Lutheran in 1567 and a Calvinist in 1573. While his pragmatic attitude to religion was a strength in a region where so many different strands of Christianity existed, many of the leaders of the revolt and of the Spanish government were religious zealots.

Militarily, Orange had little success against Spanish forces. Going into exile in the wake of Alva's arrival, he invaded Brabant in 1568 with 3000 men but was forced to retreat without engaging the enemy. This episode also left him on the verge of bankruptcy. Another invasion organised by Orange's brothers ended in disaster at the Battle of Mook (1574).

While military success eluded him, Orange proved to be a dogged opponent of Spain. He gathered widespread support with his appeal for religious toleration combined with the restoration of the traditional rights of the aristocracy in the Council of State. He quickly realised the significance of the revolt of 1572 in Holland and Zeeland, and put himself at the head of that opposition. When it seemed that the second revolt might be crushed, he went back to Holland vowing that he would make it his tomb if necessary. Then at the time of the Spanish Fury he managed to bring these provinces into line with the States General in the Pacification of Ghent and was welcomed by rapturous crowds in Brussels.

When the States General sought to undermine Orange's standing by bringing in the Archduke Matthias, Orange countered this by being made his deputy with full powers. He oversaw the union between Holland and Zeeland in 1575 and the Union of Utrecht in 1579, co-ordinating the efforts of the rebel provinces. He saw the need to bring in outside powers but the immediate results of his efforts in this direction were limited. French help from Anjou was counter-productive and Leicester's forces made little, if any, headway.

Orange's greatest contribution was to facilitate the process whereby the revolt became internationalised. One could argue this might have happened anyway, but Orange was clear-sighted about this from the start and his international standing allowed him to set in train long-winded and tortuous diplomatic discussions. Orange's final contribution was the manner of his death. A Catholic fanatic, posing as someone seeking alms, assassinated him at his house at Delft. 'As long as he lived,' opined the historian J.L. Motley, 'he was the guiding star of a whole brave nation and when he died the little children cried in the streets.'

Certainly Orange was seen as a martyr for the cause and acted as inspiration for those who would lead the revolt thereafter. In practical terms, his death was a powerful reason for English involvement, which would do much to confound the king of Spain. Orange had shown that, against the odds, the rebels could hold out.

Maurice of Nassau and Oldenbarnevelt

After Orange's death, the leadership of the revolt was taken up by his son, Maurice of Nassau, who was made *stadtholder* (regional governor) of Holland and Zeeland in 1585, and *stadtholder* in Utrecht, Overijssel and Gelderland in 1590. Maurice was appointed commander of Dutch forces in 1587, and proved a capable and worthy opponent for the Duke of Parma. He divided his army into smaller, speedier units, which could harass Spanish troops with guerrilla-type strikes. He standardised equipment and distributed it by a system of supply depots. Maurice regained considerable territory from Spain, and built a series of forts to defend Holland and Zeeland.

Nonetheless, much of Maurice's success was actually brought about by Spanish weaknesses. Ground was regained when Parma was away in France. In 1591, Maurice led an army of 10,000 men that recaptured Zutphen and Deventer after short sieges. At the time, Parma had first left 6000 men in France and a further 2000 in the Low Countries were mutinying for lack of pay. In 1592, Parma was actually in France and Maurice captured more towns in the north-east. The doubtful loyalty of the king's forces also played a key part in Maurice's success. Much of the area north of the River Maas, which he captured between 1591 and 1594, was held by Spanish troops on the verge of mutiny. In 1594, Groningen was recaptured in this way. In 1600, some Spanish troops gave up their conquests, provided the Dutch paid their arrears!

Maurice's success derived not from his military prowess but from the failings of Spanish finances. Back in the 1570s, Requesens had forecast that the Netherlands would be lost, not by the activities of the rebels but by the action of soldiers born in Valladolid and Toledo. While Maurice provided a united military leadership, **Jan van Oldenbarnevelt** gave the rebels much-needed political cohesion.

KEY PERSON

Jan van Oldenbarnevelt (1547–1619)
One of the leaders of the Dutch Revolt. As Advocate of the States of Holland he managed to impose some political unity on the states rebelling against Spain. Later he fell foul of religious divisions within Dutch Protestantism, was arrested by Maurice of Nassau and beheaded on a charge of treason.

In *The Dutch Revolt* (1979), Geoffrey Parker claimed that Oldenbarnevelt was 'the man who did most to create a workable political system in the Republic after the death of William of Orange'. A lawyer by training, Oldenbarnevelt acted as advocate, or spokesman, for the States of Holland from 1586 until his overthrow in 1618. In this position, he was ideally placed to give some sense of direction to policy emanating from the rebel States General, where Holland was the most powerful of the provinces.

As early as 1589, Sir Thomas Bodley (an Elizabethan scholar and puritan who went on to found the Bodleian Library in Oxford) wrote from the Netherlands that 'all here is directed by Holland and Holland is carried away by Barnevelt'. Oldenbarnevelt's main problem was that, having rejected Philip II's sovereignty in 1581, the rebel provinces failed to find a substitute sovereign and were thus feeling their way towards some sort of radical republican government. This posed enormous problems for rebel leaders in terms of how and by whom power should be exercised.

So Oldenbarnevelt spent much of his time smoothing over the many disputes that arose in the States General and between rebel towns and the factions within them. In addition, he was crucial in getting Maurice chosen as *stadtholder* in three more provinces in 1590, adding to the two he already held. This was vital in concentrating power in fewer hands. In the same way, Oldenbarnevelt managed to sideline the new Council of State so that real decisions were taken by the States General, which meant, in effect, the States of Holland led by Oldenbarnevelt himself.

Despite this constitutional novelty and the many divisions among the Dutch rebels, Oldenbarnevelt was crucial in holding the rebel cause together. The dangers of the situation became apparent in 1618, when Oldenbarnevelt was overthrown by Maurice then tried and executed by the States General themselves. Peace proved fatal for Oldenbarnevelt.

Overall, then, the leadership provided by Orange, Nassau and Oldenbarnevelt played a vital part in bringing about Spain's failure to crush the revolt. This was because the whole affair was a very close-run thing.

In 1567, as Alva arrived, the revolt was apparently over. In 1575, Spain captured south Holland cutting the rebel heartlands in two. In 1585, Antwerp was recaptured by Parma, leaving Holland and Zeeland alone.

At various times, then, the revolt was close to collapse, nearly overwhelmed by Spanish pressure and internal dissensions. It was at these times that Dutch leadership proved vital. If Spain had faced lesser men, all might have been well.

ECONOMIC GROWTH AND TRADING

If the Dutch leadership was important in explaining success, so too was the increasing economic prosperity of the northern provinces in this period. Funding from outside powers was extremely helpful, but so too was the increased trade and commerce carried on by Dutch merchants. By this means the Dutch, ironically enough, were able to collect much higher levels of taxation than those envisaged by Alva in order to fund their war effort. The war effort itself did not bring about prosperity and it is clear that the Dutch people suffered a great deal in order to fund the war.

In 1610, there were riots in Amersfoort and Utrecht against the prolonged taxation. One English observer wondered 'how these men [the Dutch] can subsist of themselves'. In 1606, Oldenbarnevelt told the English agent Ralph Winwood that he had to 'seek all artifices and to use sophistries and fallacies to keep them from despair ... their wants being so great that they live from day to day'.

Even allowing for exaggeration from someone hoping for a renewal of English aid after the Peace of London in 1604, it is clear that the Dutch were faced by a sustained financial crisis. Like the Spanish they had to tax heavily and raise loans at high rates of interest (usually 10 per cent in the 1600s) in order to keep the Republic afloat. Far from decreasing during the virtual stalemate from 1596 to 1607, the cost of the war to the Dutch actually increased substantially. From an average of around 5 million florins in the 1590s, the military expenditure of the Republic rose to 10 million florins a year in 1604–6. Meanwhile, this expenditure had little impact on the military balance of power. Oldenbarnevelt complained about Maurice that the campaigns of 1600–7 had brought 'little glory and great expense'.

Given these financial problems, it is clear that increased trade and commerce was very important in sustaining the Republic, not only in terms of high taxes in general but also from loans from wealthy merchants and merchant companies. Throughout the war it was the province of Holland that led the way in trade which contributed most to the States General's war budget.

In 1586–98, Holland normally supplied some 64 per cent of the budget, peaking at 70 per cent in 1597. With the Dutch East India Company leading the way, Dutch trade with the East Indies and Africa grew in the 1590s and thereafter. Often preying on the Spanish and Portuguese seaborne empires (Portugal belonged to Spain 1580–1640), the Dutch established colonies and factories in the East and the West.

In 1598–1605, the Dutch were annually sending on average 25 ships to West Africa, 20 to Brazil, 10 to the East Indies and a massive 150 to the Caribbean. At the same time trading posts were established in the East Indies, around the Indian Ocean and even in the inhospitable islands of Japan. Furthermore, the Dutch expanded their carrying trade around Europe, regularly carrying goods from the Baltic to western and southern Europe. In 1590, Philip II even lifted the official embargo on Dutch ships and cargoes in the Iberian peninsula.

What was especially important about this increased trade in the 1590s was that much of it was now carried on in 'rich trades' such as spices, silks, dyestuffs, sugar and even American silver. This access to more valuable goods increased profits and also helped to nurture the new Dutch textile industries. While new trades were expanding, the Dutch also increased their ability to dominate the bulk carrying of the more traditional goods such as grain, timber, salt and fish. Especially important here was the development in the 1590s of the famous fluit boat, a specialised carrier of cargo designed to combine maximum loading with minimum cost.

The economy of the Republic also benefited from many of the hard-working and enterprising refugees who came to the Republic from the southern provinces. In 1611, over 50 per cent of the 320 wealthiest depositors at the Amsterdam Exchange Bank were southern refugees. Some 27 per cent of shareholders in the Amsterdam chamber of the Dutch East India Company were likewise southerners. Many of the refugees were skilled artisans in textiles – often weavers, whose ability would improve the Dutch cloth trade. The town of Leiden produced around 500 pieces of cloth annually in the 1570s, but 35,000 pieces in the following decade.

Such refugees, perhaps in the region of 100,000 from 1567 to 1609, helped to bring about a massive increase in the population of Holland in general and Amsterdam in particular. Amsterdam grew from 31,000 people in 1585 to 120,000 by 1632. Leiden saw a five-fold increase in its population between 1574 (13,000) and the 1640s (65,000).

In these circumstances, it is no wonder that some contemporaries believed the war had actually stimulated economic prosperity. The Amsterdam magistrate C.P. Hooft (1547–1626) claimed that 'whereas it is generally the nature of war to ruin the land and people, these countries on the contrary have been notably improved thereby'.

A further indication of economic improvement comes with the increasing value of land in the Republic and the new schemes to reclaim more land from the seas. The amount of land reclaimed annually in the province of

Holland rose from 128 acres in the 1580s to 580 acres between 1590 and 1614. Many lakes were drained and were now yielding crops. This process of reclamation continued throughout the seventeenth century.

THE ROLE OF CALVINISM

It is easy to suppose that the brand of reformed religion associated with the teachings of John Calvin (1509–64) provided a major strength for the Dutch rebels in their struggle for independence from Spain.

From 1575, when the Union between Holland and Zeeland was constructed, *stadtholders* were instructed to uphold 'the practice of the Reformed evangelical religion' and to prohibit 'the exercise of the Roman religion'.

Despite the aspirations of William of Orange that the Republic would become religiously tolerant (even tolerating Catholicism), the states of the provinces making up the Union of Utrecht, which eventually became known as the United Provinces, decided that Calvinism would be the official state religion, leaving only limited room for the practice of other faiths. From this it would be easy to argue that Calvinism must have been crucial to the success of the revolt. Calvinists were at the centre of the enormous **Iconoclastic Fury** of 1566, which can be seen as the start of the Dutch Revolt proper.

In the wake of the destruction, Margaret of Parma issued a decree allowing freedom of worship in those places where Protestant congregations already existed. Calvinists were quick to respond, setting up churches, buildings as well as congregations, in most cities in the Low Countries by the end of the year. Within each congregation, there were appointed pastors and lay elders to guide the community, doctors to teach the faith and deacons to supervise poor relief. This model of organisation derived from Calvin's *Ecclesiastical Ordinances* of 1541.

At the same time, Calvinism provided an ecclesiastical structure that would help to bind together the rebel churches and towns in a common confession of faith. Starting with individual congregations, ordered and organised by the consistory, made up of pastor and lay elders, each Church was then represented in a local *classis*.

By 1581, there were six of these *classes* in north Holland, one in each of the six main rebel towns – Haarlem, Amsterdam, Alkmaar, Horn, Enkhuisen and Edam. These regional *classes* met frequently and co-ordinated the churches under their care. They acted as a link between urban and rural churches and were responsible for setting up new consistories as new congregations of Calvinists came into being.

KEY TERM

Iconoclastic Fury (see map on page 229). In 1566, there was extensive destruction of Catholic churches and church property, especially in the southern provinces of the Low Countries. These violent and apparently spontaneous outbursts led to the Duke of Alva being sent to the Netherlands in 1567.

Above the regional *classes* came the provincial synods. These synods represented the churches in each of the provinces, except for Holland, which had two synods (north and south).

Finally, at the top of the structure was the National Synod, designed to meet once every three years. The first National Synod was held at Dordrecht in 1578. All of this church structure was put in place at the synod of Emden of 1571. This synod, meeting outside the Netherlands, reminds us that many determined Calvinists went into exile during Alva's regime but were determined that their Church would be set up and organised one day, in their homeland.

This surprising optimism from a group, who at that time were still relatively small in terms of numbers, indicates the unquenchable aspirations of these Calvinists. Combined with its powerful structure, Calvinism also offered powerful theological beliefs that would help to fortify the rebels in the long-drawn-out struggle with Spain. The Calvinist doctrine of **predestination** may have given the rebels inner strength and determination. Although no one could be certain of their election to salvation, it was believed that those who acted in a godly way, especially those who were prepared to suffer for their faith, might be amongst the chosen. In addition, Calvinism preached that Catholicism was really the equivalent of devil worship and the Pope in Rome really the Antichrist, spoken of in the *Book of Revelation*.

So, in a war against Catholic Spain, the Calvinists were more determined and quite immune to ideas of compromise or negotiation with Catholic forces. Surely this would help to explain the determined resistance of Dutch towns when subjected to Spanish sieges.

Furthermore, in this period Calvinism was notable for its development of theories of resistance. Faced with the huge struggle between Calvinists and Catholic rulers in countries such as France and the Netherlands, Calvinist theologians were anxious to explain how one could legitimately oppose a ruler apparently appointed by God. Calvin himself moved slowly on this issue, but his successor in Geneva, Theodore Béza, was more radical. By the time of the second Dutch Revolt of 1572, Calvinists took the view that active opposition to an ungodly ruler such as Philip II was possible, provided such resistance was led by godly magistrates.

Magistrates could be anyone properly holding and exercising temporal power, from kings to local town councillors. So resistance to the king was perfectly possible provided it was led by people who exercised temporal power. As there were many such magistrates in every Dutch town, usually known as regents, Calvinism gave the rebels a powerful justification for continuing opposition to the king of Spain.

KEY TERM

Predestination
The idea that individuals are predestined by God to heaven or hell and therefore cannot influence the outcome by the manner of their earthly lives.

Naturally, in a land with so many towns and printing presses there was a flood of persuasive pamphlets arguing that the revolt was morally and politically justified.

So it was that the Calvinist minority came to play a crucial part in spreading the revolt in Holland and Zeeland in the wake of the Sea Beggars' capture of Brill and Flushing. Seeing this as a providential sign from God, Calvinist minorities in several towns expelled Catholic priests, took control of town government and raised the flag of revolt. In the coming months and years, these Calvinists were crucial to the revolt's success. William of Orange admitted as much when he became a Calvinist in 1573 and in the same year had to accept the Calvinist demand that only Calvinism should in future be tolerated.

The revolt after 1572 established Holland and Zeeland as the centres of opposition. This meant that many Dutch Calvinist exiles returned here and were joined by many Calvinist refugees from the southern provinces as it became clear that the south would continue to be held by Spain. Thus the northern provinces acted as a magnate for Calvinists and this further consolidated the revolt.

Limitations of Calvinism's role

However, Calvinism's role in defeating the Spanish should not be exaggerated. The Calvinists must take some responsibility for the failure to create a unified state from all thirteen provinces making up the Spanish Low Countries. The destruction of the unity of 1576, when all the provinces came together in the Pacification of Ghent, was partly caused by the Calvinists. The southern provinces tended to be more Catholic, and were appalled when Calvinist minorities staged *coups* in the southern cities of Antwerp and Ghent, briefly taking charge of civic government. This happened despite the clause in the Pacification, forbidding the Calvinists from disturbing the religious peace in the southern provinces.

Furthermore, the Calvinists were and remained a relatively small proportion of the total population, often only 10 per cent or so. At the time of the Iconoclastic Fury, it was noted that much of the destruction came not from Calvinists but from people of no fixed religion who were hostile to the Church as a whole, whatever its political affiliation. In Alkmaar, there were only 156 communicant members of the Reformed Church (as the Calvinists liked to refer to themselves) as late as 1576. Even where the Reformed faith was at its strongest in towns like Delft, Dordrecht and Leiden, active membership remained around 10 per cent in the late 1570s.

Everywhere in the new republic, old Catholic churches remained boarded-up and redundant, while Reformed churches were still small in number. Fines Moryson of Utrecht noted in 1593 that in the town of Utrecht, 'there be 30 churches but only three are used for divine service'.

Even in Holland and Zeeland, the storm centres of the revolt, Calvinist ministers were disappointed to find that many town magistrates among the regents' class were determined not to lend support to a Church that was more intolerant than the Catholic Church it sought to replace.

In 1576, the regents in the states of Holland and Zeeland rejected the Calvinist *Heidelberg Catechism*, which was put forward by the Calvinist synods as the official doctrinal basis of the Reformed Church. As a class, the regents realised that Calvinism really aimed at the creation of a theocratic state where political and ecclesiastical power was in the hands of the Church. The same anticlericalism that had animated Dutch magistrates against the Spanish Inquisition would now make them opponents of the Reformed faith.

Among the common people, too, Calvinism was slow to make widespread gains. This was partly because of the elitist nature of Calvinist beliefs and the perception that Calvinism was a faith for rulers rather than ruled. The implications of predestination were that there should be a large group of doomed people in society who would act in a godless way. Just as the godly acted in a godly way, so the damned must act like the damned.

Certainly, Calvinism was a faith for the more literate among the population. It was, like most strands of Protestantism, a faith of the Word with little appeal to those who didn't enjoy sermons or catechism. In addition, the Low Countries were religiously pluralist. Large Anabaptist and Lutheran congregations flourished as well as Calvinist ones, and even the Catholic Church would make a comeback later on. Calvinism became the official religion of the United Provinces, not because it was popular but because Calvinist congregations at home and abroad had been to the fore in the revolt after 1572. They translated this into official dominance, but it still left them with many enemies.

Finally, Calvinism in the United Provinces would soon be split in a fundamental way, as some of its theologians, led by Jacobus Arminius (1560–1609), began to question the central doctrine of predestination. Appointed to the Chair of Theology at Leiden University in 1603, Arminius established a more liberal section among the Calvinists, one that had wider appeal to the lay magistrates as he played down the role of the Church in civic government. These disputes within Calvinism would plague the Republic and the Reformed Church for generations.

One of the most famous victims of the conflict was one of the greatest leaders of the Dutch Revolt – Jan van Oldenbarnevelt. He and the States of Holland were tolerant of Arminius' views and believed that predestinarian and anti-predestinarian theology could co-exist. Maurice of Nassau thought otherwise. Oldenbarnvelt was arrested and executed in

1619. This incident is a timely reminder that Calvinism was not always a unifying faith for the Dutch rebels.

A CLOSE-RUN AFFAIR

While the Spanish failure can be attributed to both Spanish weaknesses and Dutch strengths, it is important to bear in mind the scale of the Spanish failure, since this underpins our view about the strengths and weakness of Spain in this period. If Spain had been easily defeated or thrown out of all of the provinces, we might see it as a decadent nation already on the way to decline and disintegration as a world power. In fact, this chapter has shown that the Dutch revolt against Spain was an extremely close-run affair and the outcome might easily have been very different.

The Spanish managed to sustain a huge war effort in the Low Countries for some 40 years. For much of his time in office, the Duke of Alva was very successful in crushing opposition and building up the power of the Spanish government. Parma was even more successful in recovering Spanish fortunes, so that rather than losing all seventeen provinces, Spain ultimately lost only seven.

At the same time, the people of the Low Countries were very much divided in their attitudes to Spain. Many nobles, such as the Duke of Aerschot, continued to back Spain because it was the legitimate authority and because they feared French aggression or radical religious sects. Others were cowed by Spain's power into submission and acquiescence. For these reasons among others, the southern provinces, closer to the French threat and more Catholic, remained with Spain.

In the northern and central provinces there were very serious political and religious splits between those who, at one time or another, fought against Spain. It would be quite wrong therefore to see the revolt as a one-dimensional national revolt against a hated foreign government, where the north won through but the south failed.

In the end, Spain came close to complete success on a number of occasions during the revolt and its failure should not be seen in terms of moral or military decadence. Neither Philip II nor even the Duke of Alva was a tyrant. Spanish soldiery was no better or worse than that elsewhere. Taxation levels would be much greater during the revolt than before it, for both north and south. Given the problems that Spain was bound to face in ruling these disparate, faraway provinces at a time of Reformation and growing nationalism, it is surprising that it did not do worse.

1598–1700: To what extent did this period witness the 'Decline of Spain'?

HISTORIOGRAPHICAL INTRODUCTION

The idea of the 'Decline of Spain' as a received historical concept began with Spanish writers in the seventeenth century. The *arbitristas*, most notably Sancho de Moncada, analysed the ills of contemporary Spanish society in a mood of often bleak pessimism and it was another of their number, González de Cellorigo, who was one of the first contemporaries to speak of *declinación* as early as the year 1600. His view of decline, comparing the supposed Golden Age of the sixteenth century to the failings of his own time, came to be accepted as a historical reality and analysed as an essentially moral failure.

J.H. Elliott, one of the foremost English historians of Early Modern Spain, who investigated in depth the works of the *arbitristas*, had little doubt that Spain did experience serious decline in the seventeenth century. In his seminal volume *Imperial Spain 1469–1716* (1963), he concluded his survey of the period 1469–1716 in the following terms.

> There is no doubt a certain paradox in the fact that the achievement of the two most outstanding creative artists of Castile – Cervantes and Velázquez – was shot through with a deep sense of disillusionment and failure; but the paradox was itself a reflection of the paradox of sixteenth- and seventeenth-century Castile. For here was a country which had climbed to the heights and sunk to the depths; which had achieved everything and lost everything; which had conquered the world only to vanquish itself.

Writing just a little earlier in his book *Spain in Decline 1621–1700* (1957), R. Trevor Davies also thought that Spain experienced serious and sustained decline in this period: 'Spain, the Hercules of European states, whose labours had astonished the sixteenth-century world, weakened and collapsed in the seventeenth century with a suddenness that calls for careful diagnosis of the disease.'

Both writers rightly emphasised the achievements of Spain's Golden Age and therefore needed to find some dramatic explanation for the supposed decline afterwards.

Other historians more overtly hostile to Spain – for example, the American J.L. Motley in his *Rise of the Dutch Republic* (1856) – had rather less to explain since they built up the black legend of Spain in both the sixteenth and seventeenth centuries. According to that historical tradition, Spain was always a force for evil, dominated by a tyrannical monarchy and a tyrannical Church. Therefore, political eclipse was not surprising. This message was underpinned for Motley by the contrasts he found between Spain and the Dutch Republic. Spain had to represent the antithesis of the Dutch virtues of republicanism, economic enterprise and religious enlightenment. Since the 'Decline of Spain' argument came to be seen as essentially a moral one, it could not be argued with any great precision and it was left to Earl J. Hamilton to offer a famous economic justification for using the term. His article 'The Decline of Spain' written for the *Economic History Review* in 1938 became the classic statement about Spain's economic decline.

More recently, Henry Kamen and other historians have challenged the whole notion of decline by attacking first and foremost the economic data on which Hamilton based his analysis. In his aptly titled article 'The Decline of Spain: a historical myth?' (1978), Kamen claimed that Hamilton's economic data was so flawed that his conclusions should be seen as doubtful. Later, these views were expanded in his *Spain in the Later Seventeenth Century 1665–1700* (1980). By 1988, Kamen could claim that 'the concept of "decline", in effect, is no longer used by working historians as a guide to what really happened in Early Modern Spain.'

One other area of debate about decline has been over the reasons for Spain's decline as a great power during the seventeenth century. In his 1961 article *The Decline of Spain*, J.H. Elliott asked whether the loss of Spain's international standing was due to internal decadence or to the revival of France. On the whole, historians have come out in favour of the latter explanation. Spain's rise and decline were inextricably linked to the fortunes of the largest and potentially most powerful state in Europe – France.

Between 1559 and 1629, France was in eclipse and this allowed Spain to gain an unusual and, in one sense, unnatural advantage over its rival. Antonio Perez, minister to Philip II, noted this succinctly in his own day when he wrote: 'The heart of the Spanish empire is France.' In this way it might be argued that any decline of Spain was relative rather than absolute, an expression of the shifting balance of power in seventeenth-century Europe, rather than the internal disintegration of Spain.

Overall, it is clear that to talk about the 'Decline of Spain' (notice the capital D) as though this were a fixed and generally accepted historical concept is rather unhelpful, especially if it colours one's view of seventeenth century Spain as a whole. It assumes a general and continuous worsening of Spain's political, economic and moral power, which obscures more than it clarifies. If one starts with such a concept, it is easy to select and focus on the problems and failures, of which there were many, and to ignore the successes and elements of continuity, of which there were also many. In other words, everything is seen and analysed through the prism of inevitable decline. The argument of this chapter will be that there was no 'Decline of Spain' in the seventeenth century.

ECONOMIC DECLINE?

Demographic change

Traditionally, the supposed economic decline of Spain set off decline in politics and foreign affairs. As Spain became unable to finance its imperial pretensions, so it declined in a number of other areas too. Yet it is easy to exaggerate the economic decline.

To begin with, historians do not possess the raw quantitative economic data on which to make real judgements about the state of the Spanish economy as a whole. Most of what we know is about Castile, not Aragon or Valencia. Regional studies have thrown up differing conclusions. For example, in looking at patterns of demographic (population) change, some Spanish historians claim that there were serious variations between central and peripheral areas of Spain. For obvious reasons Seville and Madrid expanded more quickly than other Spanish towns.

The historian Kamen has suggested that the total population of Spain may have decreased from a high of 8 million in the late sixteenth century to around 7 million by 1700. Even if this were true, it is hard to draw firm conclusions about whether this decrease in population necessarily had seriously adverse implications for the Spanish economy as a whole. Fewer people can mean more food to go round and lower prices.

There were several periods of demographic crisis caused by disease and bad harvests, and by the expulsion of racial/religious minorities. Great epidemics occurred in 1596–1602 and 1647–54, the Jews were expelled in 1492 and the *Moriscos* in 1609–14. However, these incidents by definition were temporary and caused more hardship in some areas than others. Many historians now play down the economic impact of the expulsion of the Jews and *Moriscos*.

Bullion imports

In the same way, there is serious disagreement about the scale of bullion imports in the later seventeenth century. In his classic exposition, Earl J. Hamilton claimed that bullion imports tailed off dramatically during the reign of Philip IV, sinking from an average of 7 million pesos a year to less than 1 million pesos during the reign of Charles II. Therefore, the monarchy was shorn of funds and Spain became economically much weaker. This bullion failure, Hamilton claimed, underlay the economic decline of Spain.

By contrast, and writing later, the historians Henry Kamen, John Lynch and Michael Morineau believe that bullion imports were actually higher during Charles II's reign than earlier, reaching 12–16 million pesos each year. Hamilton missed this because much of the bullion did not enter Spain but went straight to Spain's creditors. This evidence again would cast doubt on the idea of serious economic decline during the seventeenth century.

Economic trends and weaknesses

Where one can sketch in broad economic trends, they tend to be trends common to most of western Europe and not peculiar to Spain. Like other countries, Spain witnessed economic growth in the sixteenth century and economic slow-down in the seventeenth. This slow-down was accompanied by rising prices sparked off by importing New World bullion and debasements of coinage under Philip III and (more seriously) Philip IV. At the same time it seems that agrarian production in Spain fell after the 1580s, but if this also coincided with a period of falling population, then the impact need not have been especially serious.

Henry Kamen has argued, with some justice, that ideas about economic decline need to be set against Spain's long-term, underlying economic weaknesses. If the Spanish economy remained weak and did not rise significantly in the sixteenth century, then it is wrong to speak about serious economic decline thereafter. The true picture is of a weak, pre-industrial economy struggling throughout 1500–1700 to come to terms with the challenges of imperial and great power status, and suffering the usual economic downturns caused chiefly by the vagaries of weather, harvest and disease.

Furthermore, most historians agree that the Spanish economy experienced an upturn in later decades of the seventeenth century, which would confirm our picture of the usual ups and downs of the economic cycle rather than long-term, serious decline. The last great mortality crisis of the seventeenth century occurred during 1676–86. At that time, successive bad harvests produced very high food prices and famine. Exacerbating the crisis were floods, drought and even locusts. However, this economic downturn was caused by natural factors rather than the inherent weaknesses of the economy.

This prolonged but often regional economic crises masked the fact that many of the economic indicators turned upwards again after 1660.

The birth rate, both in cities and countryside, began to rise after this date and continued to increase for the rest of the century. Monetary inflation, which had soared under Philip IV, was largely brought under control after 1686. This helped manufacturers to make reasonable profits without inflationary costs. Furthermore, committees for trade were established in Castile and in a number of cities outside Castile designed to increase trade and to show that trading as an occupation was no barrier to noble status. Increasing production, trade and population in this period also stimulated increased agricultural output.

And all this at a time when bullion shipments reached their height. So, it can be argued with some confidence that to label the whole of the seventeenth century as a period of economic decline for Spain would be seriously misleading.

How serious were the economic problems?
While historians will always argue about the scale and severity of economic decline, it is useful to bear in mind certain key ideas.

Economic problems in the seventeenth century were not serious enough to lead to starvation or mass peasant unrest. Where there was unrest, as in Catalonia and Portugal in 1640, this was more to do with political rather than economic problems. In Castile, which bore the brunt of the economic burdens of empire, high taxes, high food prices and inflation, there was no serious unrest at all. By contrast, France in the 1630s and 1640s – supposedly a period of political advance for Richelieu and the French monarchy – saw repeated peasant uprisings.

Between 1648 and 1653, at the time of the Frondes, the power of central government in France virtually collapsed under the weight of rebellion from all sections of society, including the aristocracy. At the same time, uprisings in Naples and Sicily against Spanish government look very minor by comparison! Furthermore in this period, England, Scotland and Ireland were convulsed by Civil War, which lasted on and off from 1642 to 1651, while Germany experienced the terrible traumas of the Thirty Years War.

It seems Spain's problems were not as bad as elsewhere in Europe and need not have been sparked off by an economic decline. And the same point can be made in relation to Olivares' attempts to bring in economic reform. While Olivares' schemes in the Union of Arms failed to come to fruition, he did, in the 1630s, raise more taxation and troops than ever before. His failure merely meant that Aragon and Valencia were still under-taxed relative to Castile. Here again, no signs of an economic crisis.

The *arbitristas*
R. Trevor Davies, a historian who did believe in the economic decline of Spain, claimed that decline occurred because of debasements of the

coinage and what was called *empleomania* – that is, the employment of too many men in government bureaucracy.

There may be an element of truth in the latter, but it should be borne in mind that Davies may have taken the complaints of the *arbitristas* too much at face value. This is a general problem for historians of the period. The *arbitristas* show us that there was a perceived decline – although it is questionable how reliable their view is. In addition, government bureaucracies in this period were relatively small and needed to grow if the country was to be effectively governed. Even if there were too many officials being paid too much money (a common enough complaint even today!) there is still no hard evidence that this caused serious economic problems.

POLITICAL AND FINANCIAL DECLINE OF THE MONARCHY?

Arguments in favour of political decline of the monarchy

If the supposed economic decline of Spain is thus reduced to the status of non-proven, then other aspects of decline also begin to look rather shaky.

At first glance, it would be easy to claim that politically the Spanish monarchy became weak and enervated during the seventeenth century. It might be argued that the courageous and indefatigable personal monarchy of Ferdinand, Isabella, Charles I and Philip II was replaced, in the seventeenth century by the lazy and effete sovereignty of Philip III and Philip IV and the mental incapacity of Charles II. Instead of hard-working monarchs, Spain was ruled by worthless favourites and rocked by scandal and corruption.

Meanwhile, the good advice of the *arbitristas* was ignored as the monarchy failed to implement much-needed reforms. At the same time government debt continued to rise, resulting in bankruptcy and royal poverty (see Chapter 4). Interest payments on outstanding loans swallowed up a large part of annual revenue and that revenue was usually spent years in advance. Internally, all was far from well with a major revolt in Catalonia and the successful defection of Portugal from the Spanish confederation. The French ambassador, the Count of Rébenec, summarised this viewpoint in 1689.

> If one looks closely at the government of this monarchy, one will find it in excessive disorder, but in the state it is in, it is scarcely possible to bring about change without exposing it to dangers more to be feared than the evil itself. A total revolution would be necessary before perfect order could be established in this state.

Continuing limitations on royal power

The views of the French ambassador should be taken with more than a pinch of salt. He was French, and no doubt enjoyed contrasting the inefficiency and lethargy of the Spanish government with the supposed energy and competence of its French counterpart. In addition, ambassadors are outsiders and not in a position really to appreciate the workings of an alien government.

In the same way, the views of the great painter Peter Paul Rubens, who knew Philip IV personally, need not be taken as reliable evidence. He claimed that the government and Philip were widely unpopular, though he conceded that the king himself was worthy and well intentioned. On closer inspection, then, the notion of the declining power of the Spanish monarchy can be seen as unduly gloomy, a case of making the evidence fit the theory, certainly if one is attempting to use the evidence to argue that decline was structural, serious and irreversible.

First, when looking at the limitations of royal power in the seventeenth century, one must remember the limitations on the power of earlier monarchs. They too, like their successors in the seventeenth century, ruled over a loose confederation of semi-autonomous states, which were each jealous of their local powers and privileges. None of the rulers of Early Modern Spain, not even Philip II, controlled a centralised, modern-style state, and it has already been argued that even Philip was far from being an absolute monarch. So the revolts in Catalonia in 1640 and 1697 were similar in their origins to the Germania in Valencia in 1520–2 and the Aragonese revolt of 1591.

In all these cases the Crown faced popular unrest because of hostility to Castilian government, but in all these cases the Crown retained control. The loss of Portugal after 1640 was, of course, a serious blow to the Crown's prestige. However, Portugal was always going to be hard to hold on to. Unlike Catalonia or Valencia, it had been a powerful, independent kingdom with its own empire and traditions, and it had always chafed under Castilian rule. In addition, it had help from other countries in its bid for independence.

This adds a further strand to the argument about the residual strength of the monarchy, within the peninsula and outside. Its weakness was not structural, but depended on the strength and number of its enemies – other states who were frightened of Spanish power.

Looking at the situation dispassionately, it is surely most impressive that there was no Castilian revolt during this period. As most of the burdens of empire were heaped upon Castile, it really is surprising that there was no popular or aristocratic revolt. After all, even Charles I, for all his success, did face serious unrest in Castile with the Comuneros Revolt at the start of his reign. Yet, in the seventeenth-century not even Charles II faced revolt from his Spanish heartland.

Rebellion outside Spain

At the same time, it would be unfair to say that no attempts were made to further centralise the government of seventeenth-century Spain. The great reforms of Olivares were designed to do just that, to ensure that the outlying 'Spanish' kingdoms – including Italy and the Low Countries – paid their fair share of budget and contributed their fair share of men and resources.

Olivares' failure showed the strength of these other kingdoms and their ability to resist change, rather than the weakness of the Crown. After all none of the main powers of western Europe, except perhaps England, was free of such problems in the peripheries. The Huguenot (or Protestant) side in the French wars of religion (1559–94), for example, was sustained by such forces. Much of the south of France backed the French rebels partly because there were many Huguenots there but also because of the residual hostility of the south to government from Paris. Areas such as Brittany and Normandy would continue to display such characteristics right up to the great Revolution of 1789 and beyond. In Germany, an even more extreme picture emerges. Here the independence of German states such as Saxony, Brandenburg and Bavaria continued in defiance of Habsburg imperialism and German nationalism for centuries. Though England was a more centralised state than either France or Germany, the Civil War of 1642–5 highlighted serious divisions between the three kingdoms the Stuarts ruled over in the seventeenth century – England, Scotland and Ireland.

So the failure to create a more unified Spanish state (and therefore a more absolute Spanish monarchy) should not be seen as part of a more general political failure and decline in this period. Spain's strength had always been in Castilian hegemony over a federation of European states. Any attempt to seriously alter the balance of power within the confederation would have brought disaster.

Absence of religious and aristocratic opposition

The residual strength of the Spanish monarchy is further highlighted by the absence of religious conflict in Spain. In France, England, Germany and the Low Countries, the power of princes was seriously undermined by wars of religion.

In France, these lasted off and on for 100 years and two monarchs, Henry III and Henry IV, were assassinated by religious fanatics. In England, the Civil War can be seen as England's wars of religion and resulted in the trial and execution of Charles I. In Germany, religious conflict started the so-called Thirty Years War (1618–48), which saw widespread conflict and the death in battle of the King of Sweden, Gustavus Adolphus.

Meanwhile Spain in the seventeenth century was free from such debilitating conflicts. The success of the Spanish Church and Spanish rulers in avoiding the onward march of Protestantism and the Reformation ensured that Spanish monarchs of the period slept safe in their beds.

At the same time, the absence of religious conflict meant that the Spanish aristocracy, unlike its French, German and English counterparts did not turn against the Crown. By contrast with the French aristocrats who led the Huguenot cause with such success, the attempted revolt by the Duke of Medina Sidonia in 1641 was an extremely damp squib. Even when royal power in the person of Charles II seemed to be at its weakest, Spanish aristocrats did not attempt to overthrow the king. The Venetian envoy Fredrico Cornaro reported in 1681 on the quiescence of the aristocracy. 'There is hardly a noble,' he claimed, 'who does not live off the king's treasury or who, in the absence of royal pensions, could keep himself on his own income.' In the same reign, Don Juan José, despite his royal birth and popularity, wanted to be first minister, not sovereign.

The reign of Charles II is thus a testimony to the strength of the monarchy, not its weakness. If foreign powers eventually invaded Spain and treated it as a diplomatic pawn, at least they did so after his death not before. They did it not because the monarchy as an institution was enfeebled but because there was a genuine succession crisis, provoked by the intricate intermarrying of the Spanish Habsburgs. The power of the Spanish monarchy thus survived relatively unscathed during the seventeenth century. It survived the rule of an idler (Philip III), a mentally retarded sovereign (Charles II) and a royal minority (Charles II again).

Increased power of the Crown under Philip V
Even after Charles' reign, Philip V, the new king, enjoyed wide powers, at least in theory, and the monarchy was far from doomed. In 1707, Philip issued a decree abolishing the *fueros* of Aragon and Valencia on the grounds that they had rebelled against him. In 1714, Catalonia's constitution was abolished and the laws of Castile subsequently introduced. In the same year, the customs barriers between Castile and Aragon were torn down.

So, under Philip V, Spain became politically and economically much more united than it had been under Ferdinand and Isabella, and the power of the monarchy was enhanced. As Kamen wrote in 1983 of the power of the Crown under Philip V: 'Its authority enhanced by a unified state, its treasury richer by substantial new revenue, its armed forces expanded and invigorated by the war, the Spanish Crown emerged strong and wealthy from the War of Succession.'

Velázquez

One of the less convincing lines of argument used to claim that the monarchy was becoming weaker is a judgement often made about Velázquez' paintings of the royal family.

Commonly these paintings are meant to capture a royal family stagnating in the excesses of empty court ritual. The colours and expressions supposedly capture the mood of pessimism affecting the royal court. In fact, this is a good example of evidence being manipulated to fit a prevailing theory. Royal families and royal courts exist and operate around ritual, and the Spanish Court was much admired by King Charles I of England, for example, since it enhanced the aloof withdrawal and thus divine mystery of the Spanish royal family. Looked at dispassionately, court paintings of the period could just as easily represent a confident and stylish royal family enjoying the panoply of regal powers.

The *Validos*

The *Validos*, or favourites, and first ministers of the period should not be judged too harshly either. The Duke of Lerma cut back on Spain's

Velázquez' painting 'The Maids of Honour' (*Las Meninas*) – see page 273.

foreign policy commitments. Peace with England (1604) and peace with the Dutch (1609) were not popular moves by any means but indicate Lerma's serious side. He may have been involved in financial scandals but that should not obscure his achievements.

Olivares was rather more dynamic and certainly enthusiastic about wide-ranging reforming measures. His policies failed to achieve their aims, but this was more to do with attendant circumstances and problems than Olivares' own failings. He persuaded Philip IV to take an active part in government and clearly did not use his office to enrich himself excessively. Under Charles II, Oropesa was also serious and single-minded in his approach.

There was also a wider range of favourites and foreign queens in seventeenth century Spain but the business of government did not break down. Thanks to the efforts of the *letrados* class, government at both the central and local levels continued to function.

Meanwhile, the inefficiencies of Spanish government during the so-called Golden Age should also be remembered. If Philip III did very little work, this may have been as useful as Philip II's chronic overwork. Unwilling to delegate authority to ministers, Philip II spent his life taking the business of government too seriously. Except for a large part of the 1520s, Charles I was mostly an absentee ruler. But this had little impact on the running of government, which sailed on smoothly enough in the hands of royal Councils and Francisco de los Cobos. By contrast, Philip IV was always resident in Spain and played an important part in giving support to Olivares rather than ditching him at the first sign of trouble.

Most *Validos* ended up being sacked rather than retiring. Lerma, Olivares, Nithard, Valenzuela and Oropesa all suffered this fate and it is a phenomenon not peculiar to Spain. Favourites are a crucial means of protecting the mystique of monarchy. In the face of spectacular failure, the *Valido*, not the king, can be blamed.

Limitations of the Crown's financial problems

In similar vein, it would be wrong to make too much of the financial problems faced by the Spanish monarchy in this period. The kings of this period spent much – they had occasional bankruptcies (as they had in the sixteenth century) but they continued to have quite a lot of money. In 1689, the French ambassador Rébenac claimed: 'The king of Spain gives immense sums to the lords of his court. Pensions of 30 thousand to 50 thousand pesos are common.'

Under Charles II there was actually financial reform, which staved off disaster. The currency was stabilised, inflation was largely eliminated and taxation reduced. Furthermore, bullion shipments from America reached their highest figures ever.

During Lerma's period in office, growing financial problems meant that Spain tried to cut back on military expenditure. Under Lerma this was successful; under Charles II it was more problematic given the renewed power and aggression of the French King, Louis XIV. Nonetheless, Spain still maintained large armies in the field throughout the period. They had their successes and failures, as armies often do, but the important consideration from the point of view of government finances is that these armies were continuously raised, supplied and deployed in the defence of the Spanish empire.

IMPERIAL DECLINE?

It is in the area of Spain's power in relation to its rivals in Europe that the supposed decline of Spain seems most apparent.

In 1600, Spain was the greatest power in Europe by far. France was just beginning to recover from devastating internal conflict. The success of the Dutch provinces seemed far from secured and Spain still controlled the largest seaborne empire ever seen.

By 1700, the picture had changed. The Dutch provinces were now lost to Spain and independent, France had eaten away at the southern provinces of the Low Countries and Portugal was once more an independent nation. Yet Spain's European empire, like its overseas empire, was not seriously dented in this period.

Spain's continuing military strength

As so much focus is put on the Dutch Revolt and the growing power of France, it is easy to think that Spain's power in Europe was constantly and consistently eroded. Spain's defeat at Rocroi in 1643, for example, looked bad but should not be exaggerated. It came as a result of the Spanish invasion of France, not a French invasion of the Spanish Netherlands, and did not lead to any immediate loss of territory. Much was made of it by the French and Dutch, but that was a tribute to Spain's long line of military successes beforehand. Rocroi in itself made no difference to Spain's military potential. For the next two decades, Spain would continue to fight on a broader range of fronts than any other nation was capable of.

At the same time, we must remember the capability and effectiveness of Spain's military machine during the seventeenth century.

In 1625, a year of great victories, Philip IV reported that during that year Spain had maintained, '300,000 infantry and cavalry in our pay, and over 500,000 militia under arms and the fleet, which consisted of only seven vessels at my accession, rose at one time in 1625 to 108 ships of war'.

In 1634, Philip IV's brother, the Cardinal Infante Ferdinand, inflicted a crushing defeat on Sweden at the Battle of Nördlingen. There were defeats ahead, but the main point to remember is one also made by Philip IV in 1625: 'We have had all Europe against us.' In the seventeenth century, Spain was faced by a wide range of opponents and had no reliable allies. It seemed to be a very unequal contest. Again this was a tribute to Spain's perceived strengths. Though attacked by France, the Dutch and the British both in Europe and across its widely strung-out empire, Spain's land losses by 1700 were limited. Spain was a great power at the start of the period and remained one at the end of it – still raising armies to defend its possessions.

Territorial losses after 1700

It was only after 1700 that Spain lost most of its European empire (see map on page 161). This was as a result of the long-drawn-out War of the Spanish Succession (1702–13) rather than military decline.

After many battles between the Bourbon King of Spain, Philip V (who was supported by France), and the Habsburg claimant, Charles III (who was supported by Britain, Austria and the Dutch), Spain's European empire was partitioned. Under the Treaty of Utrecht (1713), Philip V was confirmed as ruler of Spain and the Indies, but the rest of the European empire was lost. The Spanish Netherlands went to the Habsburg Emperor; Sicily went to Savoy; and Britain gobbled up Gibraltar and Menorca. A year later France agreed that the rest of Spain's Italian possessions – Naples, Sardinia and Milan – would also go to the Austrian Emperor.

Since the Spanish empire was partitioned after the death of Charles II by other European powers, it has been too easy to think that this was the result of imperial decline in the previous century. Spain, it seemed, had become so weak that it was easily dismembered by other powers. In fact, it was the disputed succession and the involvement of the other major European powers that brought about partition. The Allies (Austria, Britain and the Dutch) did not want Spain and its empire to be taken over by France in the shape of the Frenchman Philip V. France was determined that it should expand its influence and limit the power of its enemies. Thus, by accident of birth, or rather lack of it (Charles II had no children or siblings), Spain was caught up in a grand European struggle for power. If Charles II had produced a son, or even a daughter, the loss of Spain's European possessions would not have happened.

The New World

Meanwhile, apparently against all the odds, Spain did retain control of its overseas empire largely untroubled for some time to come. This would ensure that Spanish was and remains today one of the most widely spoken languages in the world.

The **disintegration of this empire** was not complete until 1898, some two centuries later, when Spain lost its final possessions – Cuba and the Philippines. Naturally enough, this led to much anxious self-examination by Spanish scholars and historians. Where had Spain gone wrong? Why had it failed in its imperial mission? In reality, Spain's retention of empire for such a long time had been a major achievement in itself and reflected once again the truth of the notion that Spain had not become weaker but its enemies had grown stronger.

Furthermore, it must be remembered that Spain could not expect successes on the scale achieved by its rulers and armies in the sixteenth century. It would be unfair to compare Spain's imperial achievements in the two centuries to validate ideas about the 'Decline of Spain'. In the sixteenth century, Spain expanded and built up an empire through inheritance (in Europe) and conquest (by the *conquistadors* in the New World). In the seventeenth century, Spain's task – to defend the empire against all comers – was very different.

So, in the seventeenth century, Spain could not, almost by definition, enjoy the successes of the previous century. Only by comparing different things have historians been able to conclude that Spain was in decline. One needs to remember also that the sixteenth century was not a period of continuous victories and expansion. It had seen spectacular military reverses such as the armadas sent to England and Ireland, and the virtual loss, by 1609, of the Dutch provinces.

CULTURAL AND INTELLECTUAL DECLINE?

One only need look at cultural and intellectual advances of the seventeenth century to appreciate that Spain was not quite the declining force that J.H. Elliott described:

> The men of the seventeenth century belonged to a society which had lost the strength that comes from dissent, and they lacked the breadth of vision and the strength of character to break with a past that could no longer serve as a reliable guide to the future. Heirs to a society which had over-invested in empire, and surrounded by the increasingly shabby remnants of a dwindling inheritance, they could not bring themselves to surrender their memories ... At a time when Europe was altering more rapidly than ever before, the country that

Disintegration of empire In 1898 Spain fought a colonial war against the United States of America, and lost. As a result it forfeited its colonies of Cuba and the Philippines.

HEINEMANN ADVANCED HISTORY

had once been its leading power proved to be lacking the essential ingredient for survival – the willingness to change.

(Source: *Imperial Spain 1469–1716* (1963))

The links between the arts and society are hard to define with any precision but if we looked dispassionately at the Spanish cultural achievements in the seventeenth century, we should see that Elliott's remarks, as well as being low on evidence, are perhaps too pessimistic. The Golden Age of Spanish culture continued well past 1600 and, indeed, it might be argued that the arts reached new heights after that date.

Spanish painting after 1600: Velázquez

In painting, Spain produced one of the greatest European painters of the century and this time, unlike El Greco, he was a native talent – Diego Rodríguez de Silva y Velázquez (1599–1660).

A disciple of Caravaggio, Velázquez was of noble birth, which may account for the reserve and formality of many of his sitters in his paintings. He depicted a great range of subject matter – religious, mythological, still life, hunting scenes, character studies and, as already noted, court portraiture. His art is great because of its simplicity, richness and sense of proportion.

Velázquez made his name in Seville before travelling to Madrid, where he was employed by Philip IV. Some of his most famous paintings are of the royal court. He painted several portraits of his royal master Philip IV that have an air of melancholy and also a painting of the Court Jester, Don Diego de Acedo. Perhaps more famous still is 'Prince Baltasar Carlos on Horseback', a striking depiction of the young prince who died before his father at the age of seventeen. There is every sign of formality in this painting along with the idea of dynamic kingship in waiting.

Also at court, Velázquez gave us a sumptuous and splendid 'The Maids of Honour' ('*Las Meninas*', see page 268), depicting the Infanta Margarita and her maids together with Velázquez himself and the Infanta's proud parents, the King and Queen, reflected in a mirror at the back. It is a wonderful composition and reflects rather more than just the formality of the court; indeed, there is an air of informality and spontaneity about the picture. Viewed dispassionately, Velázquez' court paintings cannot really be taken to reflect the supposed pessimism and introspection of Spanish government and society. They are court paintings of the highest quality painted by an artist of tremendous ability.

As well as the court, Velázquez also recorded some of Spain's triumphs of the period. His large-scale 'The Surrender of Breda' (painted in 1634/5) depicts one particularly important triumph in the Low Countries, when the Spanish general Spinola captured the town in 1625.

Velázquez was also rather more than an insular Spanish painter. He often travelled to Italy in order to absorb ideas from ancient as well as contemporary Italian artists. This was all very natural, as most of Italy was under Spanish control at this time.

Velázquez is also an important figure because he played a key role in the development of impressionism. By using freer and separate brushstrokes, he moved away from the traditional chiaroscuro (light and shade) effect and made a major contribution to western European art, which would reach its climax 250 years later. Given his contribution, it is difficult to describe this period as being one of cultural decline.

Spanish painting after 1600: other Spanish painters

It should also be pointed out that, although Velázquez should be considered the greatest painter of his age, he was not the only talented Spanish painter of the period but one of many.

Francisco Ribalta (1565–1628) is traditionally seen as the first master of Spanish Baroque painting. He was followed by the likes of José de Ribera (1591–1652), Francisco Zurbarán (1598–after 1664) and Alonso Cano (1601–67). The latter was a sculptor and architect as well as a painter. Francisco Rizi (1608–85) painted wonderful frescoes in Toledo Cathedral, while Juan Carreno de Miranda (1614–85) produced melancholy and intense pictures of Charles II and Anne of Austria. Bartolomé Esteban Murillo (1618–82) was a tremendously productive

'The Vision of St Peter Nalsco' by Francisco Zurbarán, 1629.

Spanish artist with some 500 paintings attributed to him. His greatest masterpiece, according to Murillo himself and many art critics, was his 'Charity of St Thomas at Villanueva'. He died at Seville as a result of falling off scaffolding in Cadiz.

And there were many more Spanish sculptors, painters and architects in the front rank of European art in this period. A real favourite, is the great Juan Valdés Leal (1622–90) who worked in Seville and produced some of the most intense and morbid paintings yet seen. His *Las Postrimerias de la Vida* ('The last moments of life') of 1672 still hangs in the Hospital de la Caridad (Charity Hospital) in Seville, which commissioned it. The haunting picture (see below) depicts the skeletal figure of death, complete with grim scythe, extinguishing life's flame. Above the flame is the disturbing motto *'In Ictu Oculi'* ('In the blinking of an eye'), a reference to the brevity of human life. As death stands upon a globe, some have seen this painting as a depiction of the end of the world!

This may seem deeply pessimistic, but Valdés Leal was partly reacting to the terrible outbreaks of plague that swept through Seville rather than the perceived ills of Spanish society as a whole. The painting is a summons to repentance, a familiar enough theme in Christian art and was entirely appropriate in an aristocratic confraternity, which cared for the terminally sick. Furthermore, representations of death and *momento mori* (remember death) in art are as old as art itself, since art reflects all aspects of the human condition.

A great deal of art in this period was commissioned by the Spanish Church, which continued to have the available money to afford notable

'Las Postrimerias de la Vida' by Juan Valdés Leal.

commissions. The Baroque art commissioned in this period has an exuberance and energy that belies the notion of *desengano* (disillusion).

Rubens and Van Dyck

As well as Spanish artists, the seventeenth century produced two towering figures in Flemish art, men who lived under Spanish rule in the Low Countries – Peter Paul Rubens (1577–1640) and Anthony Van Dyck (1599–1641).

Rubens was based in Antwerp, which became one of the great centres of European art while he lived there. He travelled to Madrid and London as a diplomat, where he painted for both Philip IV of Spain and Charles I of England. In Whitehall Palace, he produced the magnificent ceiling in the banqueting house, which was King Charles' tribute to his father James I. Other masterpieces included 'The Coronation of Marie de Medici', a series of 21 gigantic compositions for the Luxembourg Palace in Paris; the 'Descent from the Cross' (1612) in Antwerp Cathedral (see above); and the 'Judgement of Paris' (1638). Such is the scope and sweep of Rubens' achievement in all forms of art that one critic, Paul Fierens has called him 'one of the most complete geniuses Europe has produced'.

Very much his contemporary but painting in a rather different style was Van Dyck. He was the prince of portrait painters, travelling widely across Europe (especially to Italy) and settling in London in 1632 as court painter to Charles I. In Italy, he painted a magnificent series of portraits of the Brignole Sale, Balbi, Doria and Spinola families. In England, he developed a romantic charm in his works, which inspired a whole generation of eighteenth-century painters. Particularly famous paintings by Van Dyck include 'St Martin Dividing his Cloak' (1621), 'Charles I with Groom and Horse' (1638) and the mighty portrait of the Earl of Strafford (1639).

Spanish literature after 1600: non-fiction
Outside painting, Spanish culture in the seventeenth century produced excellent and extensive literature. The Inquisition produced no Index of Prohibited Books between 1640 and 1707, so new ideas did reach Spain – particularly from Italy.

Dr Diego Zapata, a physician who helped to found the Royal Society of Medicine in Seville in 1700, had books by the likes of Francis Bacon, Pierre Bayle and Blaise Pascal, plus many other foreign authors. The late seventeenth century saw the development of a new scientific movement led by men such as the Italian Juan Batista Juanini, who was private physician to Don Juan José. In Valencia there were literary academies like the Parnassus and the Alcázar, and a scientific academy after 1687. These intellectual trends continued under Philip V, who founded both the Royal Library and the Spanish Academy.

Political theory was also much written about and debated by Spaniards after 1600. The pamphlets of the *arbitristas* bear witness to the intellectual freedom and political ideas of the time. Major works on political theory included Quevedo's *Política de Dios* ('Divine Politics') of 1626 and Fajardo's *Political Enterprises*. Quevedo admittedly was something of a pessimist, stating: '*Los muros de la patria mía, un tiempo fuertes, ya desmoronados*' ('The walls of my fatherland, once strong, [are] now crumbling'). The point here is that while most artists have their pessimistic moments, the cultural health of Spain is demonstrated not by an unmeasurable overall mood but by the sheer volume and quality of the ideas being put forward.

Spanish literature after 1600: fiction
In the world of fictional literature, the Spanish achievement in the seventeenth century was great indeed. The magnificent prose of Cervantes and the plays of Lope de Vega have already been noted, and both produced their best work after 1600. Where Lope led, other dramatists such as Guillén de Castro, Juan Ruiz Alarcon and Tirso de Molina followed.

Castro's play about El Cid was the basis for the French playwright Pierre Corneille's more famous version and Molina's play *The Seville Seducer* became the prototype for the immortal Don Juan, who later appeared as the hero or, rather, anti-hero in Wolfgang Amadeus Mozart's wonderful but problematic opera *Don Giovanni*.

The most famous Spanish dramatist of the later seventeenth century was Calderón de la Barca (1600–81). His *autos sacramentales* (morality plays) became the central feature of Corpus Christi festivals across Spain. Outside Spain his fame rests on plays such as *Life's A Dream*, *The Prodigious Magician* and *Devotion to the Cross*. Like Lope de Vega (see page 223), Calderón produced hundreds of plays with a wonderful outburst of creative energy. Philip IV contributed directly to theatrical developments in Spain. He was a very important patron of Spanish drama and built his own private theatre. He was one of the first to introduce elaborate scenery and stage machinery to produce astonishing backdrops for the action of the play. Up to this period, theatres had no scenery and audiences were forced to imagine the essential background to the action on the stage.

While Spanish literature of this period is not terribly well-known today, this should not be taken as a sign of its insignificance or insularity but rather as a demonstration that seventeenth-century literature in general, apart from the towering later plays of William Shakespeare, is relatively neglected by scholars and students alike. In its own day Spanish writing made an important contribution in the continuing development of European literature.

CONCLUSION

While much of the artistic work produced in Spain and its European empire might be uneven in quality, and while there was much that was prosaic and mediocre, there is no doubt that the artistic Golden Age continued and even reached new heights in the seventeenth century.

The high quality of much of this artistic endeavour must argue strongly against the notion that Spain, as a nation or as a ruling class, was suffering a serious moral malaise. The artistic output shows a society capable of challenging the established order of things, and of disseminating new ideas and techniques. At the same time Spanish civilisation across Europe was still at the forefront of artistic developments in Europe as a whole. Furthermore, much of the artistic work of that time had a direct impact on the spreading of Spanish civilisation in the New World. Spanish paintings, architecture and literature were copied and imitated the length and breadth of the empire. Castilian became the most widely spoken European language after 1600. After surveying the enormous Spanish artistic achievement of this period, one can only conclude that the notion of the 'Decline of Spain' seems rather wide of the mark.

What was true of art also seems to be true of politics, the economy and the empire. In none of these spheres, individually or collectively, did

Spain suffer serious and sustained decline during the seventeenth century. The Spanish empire was not notably diminished, nor was the power of the Crown in this period. Spain's weaknesses were not new but largely those inherited from the previous century. It was weaker compared to other states in Europe but this was rather more to do with their rise rather than Spain's decline.

The notion of the 'Decline of Spain' with all its attendant baggage of moral decline, political disintegration and continuous trends should be discarded as an unhelpful presupposition in the analysis of Spanish society at this time. The impact of empire on Spain was very much more complicated and subtle than ideas about decline would suggest.

A2 ASSESSMENT: TRIUMPH AND DESPAIR – THE IMPACT OF EMPIRE, 1474–1700

INTRODUCTION

These questions make useful practice questions whichever exam board you are studying for. You might like to refer back to 'AS Assessment' to refresh your memory about essay writing technique.

QUESTIONS IN THE STYLE OF EDEXCEL

The Golden Age of Spain, 1474–1598
You will need to read and note Chapters 1, 2 and 3 and Sections 2 and 3 before you attempt to answer this question.

Study Sources A to G, then answer the questions that follow.

Source A
As soon as they had begun to reign, they administered justice to certain criminals and thieves who in the time of Don Enrique (Henry IV) had committed many crimes and evils … And it was debated many times in the towns whether they should establish some Brotherhoods … in order to remedy so many ills and violent acts that they had to suffer continually … This was because the King and Queen, in spite of the fact that they were punishing criminals as far as they were able, had no time or opportunity to carry out all the remedies that they would have desired, owing to the impediment of the war which they were waging against the King of Portugal.

> Adapted from 'The Chronicles of the Catholic Kings', written in the 1480s by Hernando del Pulgar, confidential secretary to Queen Isabella of Castile.

Source B
We neither are nor have been persuaded to undertake this war by desire to acquire greater rents nor the wish to lay up treasure, for had we wanted to increase our lordships and augment our income with far less peril, labour and expense, we should have been able to do so. But the desire which we have to serve God and our pure zeal for the holy Catholic faith has induced us to set aside our own interests and ignore the continual hardship and dangers to which this cause commits us; and thus can we hope both that the holy Catholic faith may be spread and Christendom quit of so unremitting a menace as abides here at our gates, when these infidels of the kingdom of Granada are uprooted and expelled from Spain.

> Letter explaining the invasion of Granada in 1482, written in 1485 by Isabella to Pope Alexander VI.

Source C

The Holy Office of the Inquisition, seeing how some Christians are endangered by contact and communication with the Jews, has provided that the Jews be expelled from our realms and territories, and has persuaded us to give our support and agreement to this, which we now do, because of our debts and obligations to the said Holy Office: and we do so despite the great harm to ourselves, seeking and preferring the salvation of our souls above our own profit ...

> Letter written on 31 March 1492 by King Ferdinand to the Count of Aranda.

Source D

The defeat at Villalar left Castile even more exposed to absolutism than it had been before. The Comuneros had been concerned not only with objectives but also with means; the revolt was not only a protest against Spain's involvement in the European and imperial policies of Charles V, it was also an attempt, no matter how vague or rudimentary, to defend the interests of Castile by imposing constitutional checks on royal power. These were now brushed aside and from this moment Castile lay completely at the mercy of its sovereign. Municipal government was already incapable of exercising independent authority. Local elections were far from democratic, but even the elected officers of the towns had little power when face to face with the *corregidores*, those judicial officers who since the reign of the Catholic Monarchs had also been invested with administrative powers and sent to every town in Castile where they acted as royal governors ... Owing to a decline in the standards of selection ... there were complaints that the nominees of Charles V were not university-trained jurists but ignorant favourites.

> Adapted from John Lynch, *Spain under the Habsburgs, Volume 1: Empire and Absolutism 1516–1598*, 1981 (2nd edn).

Source E

I was utterly shocked to see that the priests did not treat those people in the gentle way they should have done; I frequently witnessed the clergy turning around in the very middle of consecration, between the host and the chalice, to see if the *Moriscos* and their women were on their knees, and from that position subjecting them to such horrifying and arrogant abuse, a thing so contrary to the worship of God, that my blood ran cold; and after mass the priests would walk through the town with an attitude of menacing contempt towards the *Moriscos*.

> Report written in 1569 to Philip II's secretary Gabriel de Zayas by Frances de Alava, Spanish ambassador in Paris, after his visit to Granada.

Source F

I don't believe there is anyone in the world so blind as not to understand the responsibility thrust on me in Aragon. I understand it perfectly well and the greatest responsibility of all for me is the service of Our Lord. There is also the responsibility I have to the administration of justice in that kingdom and the punishment of those who have put both the Inquisition and justice in the condition in which they are. If for the sake of religion we have been through and done what you have seen in Flanders and then in France, the responsibility is even greater to our own people on our own doorstep.

Letter about the riots in Aragon in 1591 from Philip II to the Council.

Source G

The building of the Escorial (1563–84) is a reminder of a very important fact about Philip II, which has often led to a maze of misunderstandings, viz. that he was a devout Catholic. The religious motive moulded his whole character and coloured all his ambitions. Philip's deep religious feeling has misled many historians into supposing that his policy was completely dominated by religious considerations; that it turned upon religious bigotry rather than dynasticism, and the extirpation of heresy rather than political advantage. Such a view is a complete misunderstanding of the man and of the European situation. To Philip, no doubt, all his policy was consciously directed to the glory of God and the good of the Church; but these were things identical in his mind with the exaltation of the power of Spain. Though he was by no means conscious of the fact, his policy was a completely secular one.

It will be remembered that in England he came to the conclusion that the persecution of Protestants was inexpedient. He consequently did his utmost to restrain the persecuting zeal of Mary Tudor. In the same way Philip's relations with the papacy might well have been those of a completely non-religious statesman.

Adapted from R. Trevor Davies, *The Golden Century of Spain 1501–1621*, 1937.

Questions

1 How far do Sources A to G suggest that in the period 1474–1598, Spanish religious interests became a less important consideration in the development of royal policy? (16)

How to answer this question. In terms of the assessment criteria for this question, the official top-level descriptor (explanation of how to get good marks!) might say the following.

Interrogates the evidence from all the sources with confidence and discrimination using appropriate criteria throughout. Understands the relative importance of the different pieces of evidence and uses the evidence to establish a clearly articulated and sustained judgement, directly addressing the contention in the question.

Plan. Having read the question carefully, the first important step to achieve this top-level response is to use the sources to draw up an essay plan. On one side of the plan, select evidence and ideas from the sources, which seem to agree with the question's contention. On the other side, try to find material from the sources that contradicts the assertion being put forward. You should end up with one or more relevant points on each side of the argument.

Using the sources. Try to pick out brief quotations from the sources in order to back up the relevant ideas you are putting forward. Careful selection is the key thing here. Make sure you pick out the exact word or phrase that backs up your point. Don't use extensive quotations, as this will reduce the clarity of your argument.

Evaluation of sources. Next, think about the reliability and value of each source, since this will add another important strand to the quality of your argument. Is the source really a piece of propaganda? Is the author in a position to know what he or she is talking about? For example, the disclaimers by Ferdinand and Isabella in Sources B and C that they are not motivated by financial gain sound a little unconvincing and show that the idea of financial/political gains for the Crown is circulating at the time. Likewise, Philip II's claim that he is acting in Aragon from purely religious motives needs to be treated with caution. This idea is backed up by Davies' comments in Source G.

Writing the essay. When the plan is completed, judge which side of the argument seems more convincing to you and put that in the second part of the essay. Start the essay with the less convincing argument and introduce it with some fairly neutral words. For example, you might start by saying:

In some ways these sources seem to bear out the contention in the question. Sources B and C indicate Ferdinand and Isabella's religious concerns in expelling the Jews and attacking the Moors. By contrast Sources D, F and G show later monarchs, Charles V and Philip II, more concerned with political problems.

As you start the second, and presumably longer, part of your answer you might introduce your main argument by saying:

Although, religious motivation in the development of royal policy seems to become less important during this period, this change is largely deceptive. Source A shows that, at the outset of their reign, Ferdinand and Isabella were primarily motivated by the need to enforce justice after the civil wars under Henry IV. Although Pulgar, Queen Isabella's secretary, tends to exaggerate the results of their policy, there is no doubting his sincerity when he talks of their aim being to '[administer] justice to certain criminals' who 'had committed many crimes and evils …'

Two final points. First, the question does not require any direct own knowledge except that you will need your own knowledge of the period to understand and interpret the sources. Second, ensure that you have referred directly to *all* the sources in the course of your answer.

---

2 To what extent and for what reasons should the phrase 'The Golden Age of Spain' be applied to the reign of Philip II rather than to the whole period 1474–1598 (44)

How to answer this question. This question is designed to test your ability to understand, analyse and explain the process and nature of change in a specific historical context over a period of not less than 100 years.

You must be prepared to range widely over the chronology in order to reach a judgement about which period, of the two on offer, better deserves the epithet 'The Golden Age of Spain'. The emphasis in the assessment of answers will be on your ability to analyse a range of points over the whole period under review rather than on the depth of your knowledge.

Plan. You will need to structure your answer carefully by means of a detailed plan. Your problem here is that there is no right answer, so you need to plan carefully and see what emerges. Logically, there are three possible lines of argument here.

- Agree largely with the question – Philip's reign was a Golden Age and the earlier period was not.
- Disagree with the viewpoint in the question – Philip's reign was a Golden Age, but so too was the earlier period.
- Disagree with the question – neither period is worthy of the epithet Golden Age.

You might start by noting down all the factors that you think show that Philip II's reign was a Golden Age. These might include:

- Spain's power compared to its European rivals
- success against the Ottomans
- crushing of the Alpujarras Rising
- royal control over the Church and Inquisition.

Then add to this list of ideas those factors from the period before Philip's reign that might show Spain was not enjoying a Golden Age at that time. This group might include:

- persecution of the *Conversos* and *Moriscos*
- serious persecution by the Inquisition
- Comuneros and Germania Revolts
- the problems inherited by Ferdinand and Isabella.

Next, you need to consider the other side of the argument. Draw up a list of factors showing that Philip's reign was not particularly 'golden' and a list of factors indicating that Spain was enjoying power and prosperity unknown in its recent history, long before Philip's accession.

Finally, you need to assess what you have found and decide which side seems to you more convincing.

Using own knowledge and sources. Unlike Question 1 (see page 282) where you had to examine and evaluate sources, this question is based squarely on your own knowledge of sixteenth-century Spain. However, this does not mean that the sources should now be ignored. They are designed to act as a stimulus for your essay answer, and may provide valuable relevant ideas. In this answer, then, sources can be used as own knowledge!

284   Spain 1474–1700

Appropriate and telling references to contemporary sources and/or historians will improve the quality of your answer and might well convince the examiner that you should be placed at the top end of the mark band he or she awards your essay.

Writing the essay. When you write the essay, you will need to follow four stages.

* First, explain briefly in one paragraph your overall line of argument. You might well include your definition of 'Golden Age', so that the examiner knows the yardstick you are using in your answer.
* Second, in a few paragraphs explain the side of the argument that you find less persuasive and say why you find it unconvincing.
* Third, explain and explore all the points that back up your main answer (for or against the contention in the question).
* Fourth, finish your essay by quickly summarising your overall answer and considering the question more widely. In this particular case you might (if you have studied seventeenth-century Spain) consider the whole Golden Age idea in the context of the supposed decline of Spain after Philip II's reign. You might also like to define your own period, which you consider as Spain's Golden Age, or you might spend time explaining just how 'golden' it was!

QUESTIONS IN THE STYLE OF OCR

The reign of Philip II, 1556–98
You will need to read and note Chapter 3 and Sections 2, 3 and 4 before you attempt to answer this question.

Study Sources A to E, then answer the questions that follow.

Source A
The intervention of the English in Holland and Zeeland, together with their infestation of the Indies and the Ocean, is of such a nature that defensive methods are not enough to cover everything, but forces us to apply the fire in their homeland, and so fiercely that they will have to rush back and retire from elsewhere … They are powerful at sea, and that is their great asset; therefore His Majesty's Armada should not sail under-strength but should be the largest and most powerful one possible. On this assumption His Majesty requires your opinion on whether the New Spain fleet had better be detached from its normal duties this year in order to reinforce the Armada with its full complement of troops, seamen, ships, artillery and the rest. For the objective of this Armada is not only the security of the Indies but also the recovery of the Netherlands.

Adapted from a letter giving reasons for sending an Armada against England, written on 28 February 1587 by Philip II's Secretary Idiáquez to the Duke of Medina Sidonia.

Source B

If the Armada is not as successful as we hoped but yet not entirely defeated, then you may offer England peace on the following terms.

The first is that in England the free use and exercise of our Holy Catholic faith shall be permitted to all Catholics, native and foreign, and that those that are in exile shall be permitted to return. The second is that all the places in my Netherlands which the English hold shall be restored to me; and the third that they [the English] shall recompense me for the injury they have done me, my dominions and my subjects, which will amount to an exceeding great sum. With regard to the free exercise of Catholicism, you may point out to them that since freedom of worship is permitted to the Huguenots of France, there will be no sacrifice of dignity in allowing the same privilege to Catholics in England.

> Adapted from a letter written in April 1588 in which Philip II informs the Duke of Parma of his intentions in sending the Armada.

Source C

The origins of the Enterprise of England can be traced back to the 1530s, when English Catholics first appealed to the Emperor Charles V [King Charles I of Spain] for aid against the schismatic Henry VIII.

Intervention in England thereafter became an important issue in the making of Habsburg policy. There was from this point on both an 'interventionist' party, and a cautious one, who regarded an invasion without evidence of overwhelming popular support as a very risky enterprise. If the direct Spanish experience of England during Philip's short reign [as king of England] gave further weight to the advocates of caution, the king himself felt a personal responsibility towards English Catholics, but only at the end of the 1570s did the balance shift decisively towards intervention.

Underlying this shift was the identification of Elizabeth as his chief enemy. For this there were three main reasons. It was clear after 1577 that the English would not cease meddling in the rebellion of the Netherlands. Drake's circumnavigation voyage of 1577–80 had demonstrated dramatically the vulnerability of the empire in the Indies to piratical raids. The English had also taken up the protection of the Portuguese claimant Don Antonio. What precipitated the final decision was the open English intervention in the Netherlands and the dispatch of Drake to the West Indies in the summer of 1585.

> Adapted from S. Adams, *The Armada Campaign of 1588*, 1988.

Source D

To make sure that France would not intervene [in the Netherlands] again, Philip, at the end of 1584, had recognised the importance of the Guises and the Catholic League by coming to a secret agreement whereby they would support the catholic cause in the Netherlands in return for Spanish subsidies. Then in May 1585 he warned off England by seizing all English ships in Spanish ports in retaliation for English piracies. The move angered English opinion and enabled Elizabeth to advance to a position of open war. In August 1585 by the Treaty of Nonsuch, she agreed to send some 6000 men under the earl of Leicester to help the Dutch. Philip now agreed with his advisers that a direct invasion of England was necessary. A key feature of the plan was to be the proclamation of Mary Queen of Scots as queen.

Adapted from Henry Kamen, *Spain 1469–1714: A Society of Conflict*, 1983.

Source E

[Philip II] had already sounded Farnese in words which showed that the idea of Santa Cruz [to send an Armada against England] had already found a response in his own sentiments: 'We must stop the help which the rebels receive from England, and restore the latter to Catholicism'; if necessary force would have to be considered, but he admitted that 'to launch the expedition in the sole expectation of assistance from the Catholics would be hazardous'. Farnese replied with characteristic realism. In his view little could be expected from the Catholic population in England which was too weak to organise a rising, while 'the English Catholic exiles speak more from a desire to return home than with a sense of reality'.

Adapted from John Lynch, *Spain under the Habsburgs, Volume 1: Empire and Absolutism 1516–1598*, 1981 (2nd edn).

1 Compare the value of Sources A, B and C as explanations of Philip II's reasons for sending the Armada. (15)

How to answer this question. The question is asking you to do more than just pick out from Sources A to C the reasons for Philip's decision to send the Armada against England. In addition, you must evaluate the sources.

- In Source A, we hear of Philip's reasons via his Secretary, Idiáquez. He stresses the importance of the English attacks on the Indies but this may be because he wants to use the fleet designed to protect the Indies as part of the Armada.
- Source B is valuable as it is directly from Philip and shows that he has considered the possibility that the Armada might not conquer England. He aims to grant English Catholics freedom of worship, to expel the English from the Low Countries, and to gain compensation for all the English attacks on Spanish lands and property.
- Source C, with a historian's overview of the reasons for sending the Armada, is valuable but perhaps puts too much emphasis on the long-term reasons. After all, Adams shows, as one would expect, that Philip's advisers were divided on the issue of whether to attack England until the English invaded the Netherlands in 1585 – so the reasons for the attack are more short term than long term.

2 How far do Sources C, D and E show that modern historians agree that the restoration of Catholicism in England was a secondary consideration in Philip's decision to send the Armada in 1588? (30)

How to answer this question. Consider what each source tells you.

- Source C shows that while Philip felt some responsibility towards English Catholics, as he had been King of England, the decision to go to war against England had more to do with the English invasion of the Netherlands.
- Source D indicates that English attacks on the Spanish empire as well as English help for the Dutch rebels were the main reasons for his intervention. However, the source also stresses that the Armada would help to overthrow the Protestant Elizabeth in favour of the Catholic Mary Queen of Scots. This would provide a long-term solution for the problem of English intervention in the Spanish Netherlands.
- Source E has most to say about the restoration of Catholicism in England, though it is still seen as a secondary consideration. Philip realises that it will be difficult since English Catholics seem to be passive and unwilling to organise serious opposition to the Protestant Church of England.

Structure. Be sure to compare the sources in two ways.

- First, pick out the areas where the sources agree with the contention.
- Second, put forward ways in which they vary in emphasis about the restoration of Catholicism.

Use brief quotations from *all* the sources to back up the two sides of the argument.

> 3 How far do Sources C, D and E show that modern historians agree that
> Philip II's Armada was an act of 'self-defence'? (30)

How to answer this question. Here all the sources seem to indicate that Philip was acting in self-defence. They each refer to England's intervention in the Netherlands as the reason for Philip's decision to send the Armada.

Use brief quotations to back up this viewpoint. Then look for the ways in which the sources vary in terms of other reasons for the Spanish attack on England. Source E only mentions the Netherlands, while the other sources give other reasons, again indicating that Philip acted in self-defence. In addition, one might consider whether the restoration of Catholicism in Sources C and D show that Philip was going beyond measures that might be seen as essentially defensive.

> 4 Consider the arguments for and against the claim that Philip II seriously
> mishandled the Revolt of the Netherlands. (45)

How to answer this question. The question specifically instructs you to consider arguments for and against, so you must formulate ideas on both sides in your plan. Having done this, it is important not to fall between two stools and produce an essay that is too well balanced.

In the end, the examiner wants to know whether you think Philip 'seriously mishandled the revolt' or not. So when you come to consider the two sides try to decide which side is more convincing to you and explore the ideas relevant to that side in the second and more extensive part of the essay. For example, on one side you might consider:

- Philip's role in starting the revolt
- his sending in of Alva
- his involvement in France
- his attack on England
- his principled stand against religious toleration.

On the other side you might look at the broader reasons for the revolt in the context of:

- the spread of the European Reformation
- Spanish rule over the Netherlands
- the successes of Parma
- the scale of Spanish problems.

With a question of this nature a good answer might consider the possibility that Philip handled the revolt better at some times than at other times. In other words, does your answer change during the long period of the revolt (1559–1609)? Did Philip mishandle the revolt continually, occasionally or not at all?

> 5 Does Philip II's title of 'The Most Catholic King' provide a convincing
>   explanation for the policies he pursued during his reign?   (45)

How to answer this question. You will need to trawl carefully through your notes and draw up ideas that support both sides of this contention – both yes and no.

There is no right answer, though many would argue that Philip did pursue policies that, in his eyes at least, were designed to consolidate the power and effectiveness of the Catholic faith at a time when it was under attack in so many parts of Europe. However, that struggle was primarily to preserve Catholicism within Spain's empire, not to destroy it elsewhere. So, the reasons for sending the armadas against England might be central to an argument that claimed Philip's primary purpose in foreign policy was to defend the Catholic faith within his domains (that is, the Netherlands) rather than to defeat Protestantism in France and England.

The same line could be taken over his views about Islam. Lepanto and its aftermath showed that Philip wished to defend Spain's Mediterranean interests rather than engage in a titanic crusade against the Infidel. He had learnt well the lessons taught him by his father, that to fight seriously against Islam would jeopardise the Spanish empire. Within Spain, Philip's Catholic views meant an assumption that the Crown was a better protector of the faith than the papacy. Furthermore his support for the Inquisition and crushing of the Alpujarras Revolt also demonstrate his drive for religious uniformity within Spain. Philip was an extremely religious and devout individual. His religious beliefs, conventional enough in themselves, were the mainsprings of his actions.

Naturally, arguments can also be marshalled on the other side. The important thing is to give your essay a real sense of direction by arguing clearly that overall you agree with the question *or* overall you disagree with the question. The most important prerequisite of a good answer will be the clarity of your main arguments, together with the depth of knowledge and range of ideas.

QUESTIONS IN THE STYLE OF AQA

The Netherlands, 1565–1609

You will need to read and note Section 3 and the relevant sections of Chapter 3 before you attempt to answer the following two questions.

These questions are synoptic in nature and you will be rewarded for the range of relevant issues your answer covers.

> 1 'Political conflict was more important than religious issues in causing and sustaining the first revolt of the Netherlands.' To what extent is this a valid summary of the period 1565–73? (20)

How to answer this question. Answers will need to identify issues that fall into each of the two categories and be aware of the overlap between them.

Religious issues might include:

- the spread of Calvinism and other types of heresy in the Low Countries
- the Iconoclastic disturbances 1565–6
- Philip's new bishoprics scheme
- the use of the Inquisition under Alva.

On the political side, you might explore:

- the views of Orange and other members of the aristocracy
- the idea of traditional liberties being infringed
- the Council of Troubles
- heavy taxation
- the unpopularity of Granvelle.

Better assessments will realise that political and religious issues overlapped considerably both in terms of Spain's actions and policies, and also in terms of the reactions of both sides to the escalating conflict and instability.

Assessment. To reach the top band (19/20 marks) you will need to offer a balanced assessment covering the whole period together with an evaluation of evidence that reflects the complexity of the situation.

2 How important was foreign aid in contributing to Dutch success by 1609?

(20 marks)

How to answer this question. You will need to show not only awareness of the foreign aid offered to the Dutch but also an ability to evaluate the significance of that aid in the context of other reasons for Dutch success by 1609.

The best answers might well start with a clear and direct line of argument asserting that foreign aid was (or was not) very important. Clearly the Dutch did receive important help from the French and the English, but it might be argued that the most important aid was the indirect foreign aid the rebels received when Philip II diverted his energies into revenging himself on England and France for their interference.

In addition, Philip was distracted by a number of other issues and these helped to ensure Dutch success. Set against these reasons, you will need to explore reasons not associated with foreign aid (direct or indirect) such as the economic, political and religious strengths of the Dutch provinces, the quality of rebel leadership and the problems facing the Spanish armies.

Assessment. To reach the top band (19/20 marks) you will need to put forward and sustain a relevant and detailed line of argument throughout the essay.

An important feature of such an answer will be the ability to start each paragraph with a relevant idea and to link your paragraphs into a convincing assessment. Once again the better answers, while considering various reasons for success will take a clear and fairly decisive line about the relative importance of foreign aid. This can only be achieved by taking time to think very carefully about the issues as you draw up your plan.

The 'Decline of Spain', 1598–1700

You will need to read and note Chapters 4 and 5 and Section 4 before you answer the following two questions.

These questions are synoptic in nature, so you will be rewarded for the range of relevant ideas and information on offer.

1 To what extent did the power of Spanish rulers within Spain decline during the seventeenth century?

(60)

How to answer this question. It is important to recognise that this question deals with the power of the rulers, *not* with the power of Spain.

Traditionally, it has been easy to claim that the power of the Crown within Spain declined during the seventeenth century. Philip III was lazy and uninterested in the business of government, preferring to make use of dissolute favourites such as Lerma. Philip IV took much persuasion from Olivares before he came to realise his own importance within government and Charles II was mentally retarded. At the same time the power of the monarchy ought to have decreased because this century was, supposedly, a time when Spain as a whole slipped into terminal decline.

On closer inspection, however, it can be argued that despite personal failings, the monarchy as an institution remained strong. Regional difficulties did arise in Portugal and Catalonia, but these were long-term problems that no Spanish ruler had been able to solve – Spain had never been a united country. Furthermore, the Crown took greater control of Granada through the expulsion of the *Moriscos* and the Crown continued to levy heavy taxes, especially on Castile, without causing rebellion. Crown control of the Church remained strong and the economy did not suffer as grievously as some historians used to believe. Linked to this, the Crown remained powerful in Spain because its international reputation did not suffer serious reversals in Europe or the New World. The art of Velázquez might also be used to show that the monarchy remained powerful and aloof during the seventeenth century.

At another level, you will need to consider variations in the power of the monarchy during the century. Many candidates will write about the power of the Crown as though it declined uniformly during the century. But if Charles' reign saw most political instability and faction fighting, by how much had the power of the Crown declined by 1700? In the same way, did the power of the Crown in fact increase in the early part of Philip IV's reign when Olivares proved to be an effective minister prepared to give serious consideration to ideas of reform?

Assessment. Overall, the examiner will be judging the quality and range of the argument that you put forward.

At the top level of response, examiners will expect to see an ability to take a view of the monarchy across the whole century with an awareness of the importance of particular factors. In addition, they will want to see you evaluating directly the weight of different factors. The weight of supporting evidence will vary and the emphasis on this type of question will be range rather than depth. Nonetheless, it is advisable to make your main points, coming at the start of each paragraph, in some depth and detail, to indicate that you do have sufficient depth to sound convincing. Less important arguments can then be dealt with in a more discursive way, once you have got the argument off to a good start.

2 'A great European power.' How valid is this assertion when applied to Spain's international prestige in the period 1621–1700?   (60)

How to answer this question. This question focuses on Spain's international position within Europe rather than on its domestic situation, but the latter may be important in a rounded consideration of the question.

The period under review takes us from the restart of the Dutch wars to the death of Charles II and you will be expected to demonstrate a sound knowledge and understanding of Spanish 'foreign policy' in this period.

In many ways, Spain appeared to be weaker internationally after Rocroi, the Treaty of the Pyrenees and other subsequent treaties with Louis XIV. However, you will need to evaluate carefully the extent of any discernible decline during the period.

Really good answers might make use of material before and after the period in the question, to argue that Spain's international reputation was already tarnished before 1621 and that the loss of Spain's European empire after the War of the Spanish Succession was not foreseen by 1700.

At the same time, you might deepen your argument by looking at the relative strength of other great European powers – France, Austria, England and the Dutch – in the period. All suffered reverses during the Thirty Years War. Despite losing ground to France, perhaps Spain was still more powerful, militarily and economically than the other major nations?

Assessment. Top band answers will range across the period thematically rather than chronologically and adopt, from the beginning, a clear line of argument about the quotation in the question. Notions of the 'Decline of Spain' will be carefully interwoven to produce a clear and wide-ranging answer. Candidates who can review convincingly areas other than the political – that is, economic, military and even cultural – might be worthy of consideration for the top mark band.

BIBLIOGRAPHY

This bibliography lists those books that the author has found particularly helpful, those that have been quoted from and those that he would recommend to any student of the period. The books have been divided into two lists – those used in and relevant to AS level, and those used in and relevant to A2 level.

AS LEVEL

Graham Darby, *Spain in the Seventeenth Century*, Longman Seminar Series (1994)

Bernal Diaz, *The Conquest of New Spain*, Penguin Classics (1963)

J.H. Elliott, *Imperial Spain 1469–1716*, Pelican Books (1970)

Pieter Geyl, *Revolt of the Netherlands 1555–1609*, Ernest Benn (1958)

Henry Kamen, *Spain 1469–1714: A Society of Conflict*, Longman (1983)

Henry Kamen, *Philip II*, Yale University Press (1997)

P. Limm, *The Dutch Revolt*, Longman (1987)

John Lynch, *Spain under the Habsburgs, Volume 1: Empire and Absolutism 1516–1598*, Basil Blackwell (1964; 2nd edn 1981)

John Lynch, *Spain under the Habsburgs, Volume 2: Spain and America 1598–1700*, Basil Blackwell (1981)

S. Newman, *The Power of Spain – Europe 1545–1610*, Cambridge University Press (2000)

Geoffrey Parker, *The Dutch Revolt*, Pelican Books (1979)

Martyn Rady, *From Revolt to Independence, The Netherlands 1550–1650*, Hodder and Stoughton (1990)

R. Trevor Davies, *The Golden Century of Spain 1501–1621*, Macmillan (1937)

R. Trevor Davies, *Spain in Decline 1621–1700*, Macmillan (1957)

Geoffrey Woodward, *Spain in the Reigns of Isabella and Ferdinand, 1474–1516*, Hodder and Stoughton (1997)

Geoffrey Woodward, *Philip II*, Longman (1997)

A.D. Wright, *Catholicism and Spanish Society under the Reigns of Philip II and Philip III*, E. Mellen Press (1992)

A2 LEVEL

M.F. Alvarez, *Charles V. Elected Emperor and Hereditary Ruler*, London (1975)

William C. Atkinson, *A History of Spain and Portugal*, Penguin (1960)

F. Braudel, *The Mediterranean and the Mediterranean World in the Age of Philip II* (two volumes), William Collins (1972)

James Casey, *Early Modern Spain – A Social History*, Routledge (1999)

Graham Darby (ed.), *The Origins and Development of the Dutch Revolt*, Routledge (2001)

J.H. Elliott, 'Self-perception and decline in early seventeenth-century Spain', *Past and Present*, 74 (1977)

J.H. Elliott, *Richelieu and Olivares*, Cambridge University Press (1984)

Fernández-Armesto and Henry Kamen in Raymond Carr (ed.), *Spain – A History*, Oxford University Press (2000)

Edward Grierson, *The Fatal Inheritance, Philip II and the Revolt of the Netherlands*, Gollancz (1969)

Earl J. Hamilton, *American Treasure and the Price Revolution in Spain, 1501–1650*, Harvard University Press (1934)

Jonathan Israel, *The Dutch Republic 1477–1806*, Oxford University Press (1995)

Jonathan Israel, 'The Decline of Spain': a historical myth?, *Past and Present*, 91 (1981)

Henry Kamen, *Spain in the Later Seventeenth Century 1665–1700*, Longman (1980)

Henry Kamen, 'The Decline of Spain' – a historical myth?, *Past and Present*, 81 (1978)

Henry Kamen, *Golden Age of Spain*, Macmillan (1988)

Henry Kamen, *Inquisition and Society in Spain*, Wiedenfeld and Nicolson (1985)

P.K. Liss, *Isabel. The Queen*, Oxford University Press (1992)

Colin Martin and Geoffrey Parker, *The Spanish Armada*, Guild Publishing (1988)

Geoffrey Parker, *The Army of Flanders and the Spanish Road*, Cambridge University Press (1972)

Geoffrey Parker, *Philip II*, Yale University Press (1979)

Geoffrey Parker, *Spain and the Netherlands 1559–1659 – Ten Studies*, Fontana (1979)

Geoffrey Parker, *The Grand Strategy of Philip II*, Yale University Press (1998)

J.H. Parry, *The Spanish Seaborne Empire*, Pelican Books (1973)

R.A. Stradling, *Europe and the Decline of Spain: a Study of the Spanish System 1580–1720*, Allen and Unwin (1981)

C.V. Wedgwood, *William the Silent*, Jonathan Cape (1944)

INDEX

HEINEMANN ADVANCED HISTORY